Adolescents'
W●rlds

NEGOTIATING
FAMILY,
PEERS,
and
SCHOOL

Adolescents' Worlds

NEGOTIATING FAMILY, PEERS, and SCHOOL

Patricia Phelan
Ann Locke Davidson
Hanh Cao Yu

Foreword by George and Louise Spindler

Teachers College
Columbia University
New York and London

For

MILBREY McLAUGHLIN

who provided nurturance, guidance, and unconditional support
throughout this critical period in each of our lives

And for our children

SEAMUS

JONATHAN

CAROLINE

Chapters 4 and 6 are adapted from *Making and Molding Identity in Schools* by
Ann Locke Davidson by permission of the State University of New York Press.
© 1996.

Published by Teachers College Press, 1234 Amsterdam Avenue, New York, NY 10027

Library of Congress Cataloging-in-Publication Data

Phelan, Patricia.
    Adolescents' worlds : negotiating family, peers, and school / Patricia Phelan, Ann
Locke Davidson, Hanh Cao Yu.
        p.   cm.
    Includes bibliographical references and index.
    ISBN 0-8077-3682-1 (cloth).—ISBN 0-8077-3681-3 (pbk.)
        1. Teenagers—United States—Attitudes.   2. Teenagers—United States—Conduct
of life.   3. High school students—United States—Attitudes.   4. High school students—United States—Conduct of life.   I. Davidson, Ann Locke.   II. Yu, Hanh
Cao.   III. Title
HQ796.P469   1997
305.235—dc21   97-37091

ISBN 0-8077-3681-3 (paper)
ISBN 0-8077-3682-1 (cloth)

Printed on acid-free paper
Manufactured in the United States of America

04   03   02   01   00   99   98   97   8   7   6   5   4   3   2   1

CONTENTS

FOREWORD

Adolescents' Worlds: Negotiating Family, Peers, and School is an authoritative contribution to the ethnographic tradition. It focuses on the lives of young people as they struggle with the boundaries and borders between major sectors of their social and personal space. The authors spent hundreds of hours talking to, observing, and following their subjects around—in the true ethnographic tradition. The intimacy of their reporting gives their efforts an authenticity that is not often found—except in good ethnography. The natives' voices are heard as they explain what they encounter in their daily lives as boundaries and borders are negotiated, crossed, avoided, or crashed into. In considering these relationships readers will find ways to reflect on the borders and boundaries that structure their own lives, the lives of students they study, and the lives of students with whom they work.

This book stands as a monument to a sound case-study approach. Case studies can do for the reader what other approaches cannot since they are a direct approach to social reality rather than a translation of that reality into generalizations and theory. Our professional lives have been spent doing case studies, and promoting case studies. The series *Case Studies in Cultural Anthropology*, for which we are editors, includes over 200 titles. In our field work with the Menominee and Blood Indians we did case studies of adaptation to radical sociocultural change. In our studies of schools in the United States and Germany, we did case studies of teachers coping with problems of communities and kids. The doing and writing of case studies has been a major part of our professional career. There has always been a prejudice against case studies in some circles in education and in the social sciences. We are reminded of a comment by a valued senior colleague when we were doing an *Education and Culture* series in the 1970s. We had mentioned that one of the case studies in that series—probably the one on the Hutterites—had sold about 2,000 copies that year. The comment was, "That is surprising. I wouldn't think that a study with such a narrow focus would sell that well." It sold that well because the Hutterites represent highly significant phenomena, such as extraordinary boundary maintenance and an educational system designed to produce homogeneity and cultural commitment that characterize most enclaved religious communities. The richly textured descriptive analysis by Hostetler and Huntington (1996) gave readers a direct understanding of these processes, which could be applied elsewhere. That is what this book by

Phelan, Davidson, and Yu does. It offers richly textured descriptive analyses of seven students representing different contexts and adaptation patterns. The reader acquires insight into phenomena found in every school, in every community. Further, looking at schools through the eyes and experiences of youth allows the reader to analyze and reflect on the processes, practices, and structures of the educational environments we have created for students from very different and important perspectives.

Though no two schools or communities are exactly the same, the insights acquired by reading these cases can be adapted to every school and community in this country. The prejudice against case studies runs deep in the number-crunching and survey segments of education, and for that matter, in parts of anthropology. Not that there is anything wrong with number crunching—we have done our share of it—but case studies tend to be regarded an antithetical to good "science" among many of our statistically oriented colleagues. We have come a long way since the 1970s, but we bet that there will be some criticism of the use of seven case studies of students coping with boundaries and borders to speak for wider social and psychological processes. No matter that the case studies represent highly selected individuals who do represent their group and their typology. No matter that the contextualization of the cases is extensive and rich. No matter that the cases serve to move us to broader generalizations and ways of viewing adolescents' lives and contexts. Single cases tell us nothing except about those single cases, so say the nay-sayers. This book does a great deal to move us beyond such a narrow and circumscribed view and illustrates well the strength and contribution that a case-study approach can make.

We appreciate the book also because it does not fall into the pitfall that many of our colleagues and their books have fallen into—that is, reporting only on minorities, students of diverse cultural backgrounds who have problems in and with school. The authors make the important point that differences between worlds do not always create problems; rather, differences are often made into problems by virtue of the meanings assigned to those differences. Conversely many "Type I," "programmed for success" white students are not only possessed by the need to be successful, but do not develop skills that will enable them to move easily across the divisive worlds of contemporary society. Further, the lives of many students in this category type are not as much fun as adolescent lives should be, and these students tend to lose sight of the intrinsic merit of knowledge in favor of grades and test scores.

In the 1950s we met a fifth-grade girl named Beth Anne who had been picked by the faculty of her school as the "best adjusted" child in the entire school. We had asked them to pick a student who was well adjusted, and we would study her, as we had studied others who were regarded as problems. We did, and we found that her personal adjustment left much to be desired.

She was a perfectionist, worried a lot, was tense, and had an abdominal tic, but her achievement in school and her obviously upper-middle-class social status blinded the teachers to the price she was paying for her achievements.

Our task was to get the teachers and her parents to let up, let her know that she was a worthwhile person just for herself, and that an occasional poor performance was tolerable—was, in fact, to be expected of a learner. In many ways Beth Anne's case is reminiscent of the Type I students described by Phelan, Davidson, and Yu in this volume. Beth Anne taught all of us much (Spindler, 1997). The cases in this book also teach us a great deal about students' lives that we can easily miss when we have no other way to view the world of adolescence but through our teacher, researcher, and adult lenses.

The seven case studies in this book show us how things look from the viewpoint of students (the natives). They also show us that whatever the adjustment of a young person may be, it is a product of forces beyond the individual. The whole system of interactions, the entire process of variables in context, produces categories, groups, boundaries, and borders that adolescents somehow have to handle. The much maligned "Pygmalion" hypothesis is an aspect (teacher expectations of student behavior) but the process is much more complex and much wider. The causes of behavior are never skin-contained. The inside of the person and the outside environment are in constant interaction. They constitute a flowing process that is scarcely describable. Phelan, Davidson, and Yu come as close as anybody to date has come to describing it. Teachers and professors (not necessarily mutually exclusive categories) will find the seven cases that constitute the empirical backbone of *Adolescents' Worlds: Negotiating Family, Peers, and School* an important addition to their classes, particularly in teacher training programs and also in a wide variety of courses treating sociocultural processes in education. Further, psychologists interested in adolescence and in teaching about adolescence will also find that the contextualization of students' lives provides a broadened view of the kinds of problems and issues that adolescents face. Though there is a lot of talk about case studies, there are not many detailed, interpreted case studies available for teaching purposes. This book is an important contribution toward filling that gap.

We need to mention one other matter. We have been engaged recently in the development of something called "cultural therapy." The basic idea is that there are ways to bring submerged aspects of one's culture to a level of consciousness where they can be dealt with objectively. Hidden assumptions by teachers about the ways and whys of student behavior, and vice versa, cause a lot of static in interpersonal relations. If that static is cleared up communication improves, and if communication improves so will teaching and learning. There are many ways of doing cultural therapy. We and our co-authors have developed some (Spindler & Spindler, 1994) but there are many others. Phelan, Davidson, and Yu have done notable cultural therapy both in their interviewing and in the group discussions held with students representing the various typologies of handling cultural borders and boundaries.

This is a book you will want to have on your shelf, that you will use in your teaching and learning, and that you will want others to read.

George and Louise Spindler

REFERENCES

Hostetler, J., & Huntington, G. (1996). *The Hutterites: A case study in cultural anthropology* (rev. ed.). Fort Worth, TX: Harcourt Brace and Company.

Spindler, G. (1997). Beth Anne: A case study of culturally defined adjustment and teacher perceptions. In G. Spindler (Ed.), *Education and cultural process* (3rd ed.; pp. 246–261) Prospect Hts., IL: Waveland Press.

Spindler, G., & Spindler, L. (1994). *Pathways to cultural awareness: Cultural therapy with teachers and students.* Thousand Oaks, CA: Corwin.

ACKNOWLEDGMENTS

This book results from the help, assistance, and support of many people. First and foremost, we are deeply grateful to the 67 students whose voices result in this work. In particular, we owe a special debt to Ryan, Trinh, Patricia, Donna, Sonia, Robert, and Carmelita—the seven youths whose lives we portray. Over a period of three years, these students unhesitantly shared with us their lives, their thoughts, and their views. Their openness and generosity remind us that adolescents not only have a great deal to say but that they very much appreciate being heard. These students welcomed us into their lives, introduced us to their friends, provided us with untold amounts of time, and worked hard at helping us understand their worlds. They taught us much and they enriched our lives.

Teachers and administrators in the schools in which we worked also provided us with a great deal of time and support and graciously allowed us to spend many hours in their classrooms. We found that in almost all cases these adults are tremendously committed individuals who have made it their life's work to provide the best opportunities possible for youth. While their perspectives were often different from the students' with whom they worked, their ideas and views were imperative in order for us to understand educational contexts from multiple perspectives. We are grateful for their help and assistance.

Milbrey McLaughlin, Director, Center for the Context of Secondary School Teaching, and Joan Talbert, Associate Director, made this study possible. They not only invited our initial participation in the center, they also provided encouragement, support, and guidance throughout the tenure of this work. We cannot thank them enough. (The center was established in the fall of 1987, through funding by the Office of Educational Research and Improvement [OERI], U.S. Department of Education [Grant No. G0087C0234], with the goal of advancing knowledge of contextual factors that affect secondary-school teachers and teaching.) Also critical to the development of our work was Don Hill, director of the Professional Development Center of the Stanford School Collaborative, who encouraged us to consider the application of our model to teachers' and students' lives.

George and Louise Spindler, our intellectual forebearers, were a sounding board throughout this project. Many of the ideas presented in this book result from long conversations with George and Louise. We continue to be grateful for their mentoring, their insights, and their unfailingly positive support.

Elinore Brown transcribed over 300 interviews that resulted from this study. This was a monumental task and we are indeed grateful. Julianne Cummer, Project Administrator, Stanford University, assisted us with myriad details throughout this project. We were also assisted in the final preparation of the manuscript by Kristin Kajer-Cline, graduate student, University of Washington, Bothell, and Judy Shuskey, Education Program, University of Washington, Bothell. We very much appreciate the efforts of all of these people.

Finally, we are indebted to our families who have supported us with humor and encouragement during our frequent preoccupation with the doing and writing of this book.

INTRODUCTION: STUDENTS' MULTIPLE WORLDS

I don't think people around me know that I struggle with the transitions I make everyday. The biggest difference for me would be the economic situations in school and at my home. I live in the lower part of Braxton where lower-middle-class families live, but at school the majority of my friends live in Pinebluff [an upper-middle-class community]. When I first came to Wilson [High School], I tried to keep the friends from middle school who lived where I did and at the same time be in advanced classes. It was always difficult for me to have friends in my classes and a different set of friends outside of school. I couldn't really belong to either group. It's really hard for me to move from my home life, where I feel secure, to my school life, where I wonder who will talk to me today.

Sarah, high school junior
(Written Comments)

My mother is a high school teacher, she knows many (if not the majority) of my teachers and counselors. She and my father both graduated from college and have taught me how to learn, keep up on college applications, etc. Because of this, it is almost impossible to separate home from school. We talk about the same subjects, discuss the same issues. There is virtually no transition for me, making life easier. The problem is, my world is often totally school without differences to give it variety and life.

Will, high school junior
(Written Comments)

Sarah and Will speak with clarity and candor about the contexts of their lives and the daily transitions they make. As they so aptly point out, moving among their family, peer, and school worlds can present challenges and obstacles to overcome, or shifts so smooth that opportunities for variety and growth are minimized. The students' comments, made during the course of seven one-hour group investigation sessions in which they and their peers read and discussed abbreviated versions of the case studies presented in this book, illustrate adolescents' orientation toward understanding and reflecting on the situations and circumstances of their lives and the patterns that characterize their own behaviors. We find that adolescents, given the opportunity, have a great deal to say.

This book is about adolescents' worlds and the types of transitions they make as they move from one context to another. It is about borders that young people face, adaptation strategies they use, and bridges that can increase their chances of successfully navigating a variety of settings—particularly the world of school. It is about *all* youths—not only those typically identified as "at-risk"; not only those representative of one cultural, ethnic, gender, or socioeconomic group; and not only those who are considered to be "in trouble" academically. Rather we delineate and describe patterns that crosscut familiar classification schemes in order to provide a generic and holistic view of adolescents' lives and contexts.

Attention to the developmentally defined stage of adolescence is not new. Understanding and describing the characteristics of this particular age have for years captivated the interest of scholars across disciplines. Anthropologists have asked questions about the significance of adolescence and its meaning across cultures, sociologists have highlighted the importance of peer groups and friends, and psychologists have provided insights into underlying developmental and cognitive processes of this particular life phase. Concurrently, educators and educational researchers seek understanding and knowledge that will assist them in designing the types of learning environments and activities most appropriate to middle- and high-school age youth. The interest of scholars emanates to some extent from a broader societal preoccupation with adolescence as a critical period fraught with promise and peril—a time of passage in which biological, emotional, and social factors converge to forecast the future of young adults.

Perhaps because of continued debate over the relative importance of biological, familial, peer, and institutional influences on adolescents' development, research across disciplines has, for the most part, focused on distinct aspects of young peoples' lives. We know, for example, that peer groups can have particular potency and force in pulling young people toward the norms of groups (Clasen & Brown, 1985; Clement & Harding, 1978; Coleman, 1963; Eckert, 1989; Larkin, 1979; Ueda, 1987; Varenne, 1982; Vigil, 1988, 1993). We know, too, that family indices, such as socioeconomic status and parents' educational levels, are important predictors of students' success (Entwisle & Alexander, 1995; Jencks et al., 1972), and that parenting style, family constellation, and a wide range of family circumstances can impact students' engagement in school and classroom settings (Dornbusch, Ritter, Leiderman, Roberts, & Fraleigh, 1987; Featherstone, Cundick, & Jensen, 1992; Furstenberg, 1990; Steinberg, Lamborn, Darling, Mounts, & Dornbusch, 1994; Steinberg, Lamborn, Dornbusch, & Darling, 1992). Further, cultural differences—as embedded in cognitive, communication, motivational, linguistic, interactional, and literacy and writing styles—can be paramount in affecting the types of interactions (positive and/or negative) that occur in school (Clark, 1983; Erickson, 1993; Fordham, 1988; Hoffman, 1988; McDermott, 1987; Spindler, 1987; Spindler & Spindler, 1994; Spindler, Spindler, Trueba, & Williams, 1990; Trueba, 1988a, 1988b). Likewise, historical, social, and economic circumstances that characterize the experience of diverse cultural groups are critical in shaping students' actions and interactions (Deyhle, 1995; Gibson, 1993; Ogbu, 1983, 1993; Suarez-Orozco, 1993; Suarez-Orozco & Suarez-Orozco, 1993, 1995). Finally, we know that dynamic teachers, vigorous schools, and programs targeted to override the negative effects associated with low socioeconomic status, limited motivation, and language and cultural barriers can produce committed, interested, and academically engaged individuals (Abi-Nader, 1990; Cohen, 1986; Davidson, 1996; Edmonds, 1979; Heath, 1982; Johnson & Johnson, 1981, 1989, 1991; Rutter, Maughan, Mortimore, & Ouston, 1979; Sharan, 1980; Sharan & Shachar, 1988; Slavin, l988; Slavin & Madden, 1989; Trueba, 1988b; Trueba, Moll, Diaz, & Diaz, 1982; Vogt, Jordan, & Tharp, 1993; Walberg, 1986). In short, we know a great deal about the manner in which peer groups, families, teachers, and schools independently affect educational outcomes.

However, we know relatively little about how aspects of these worlds combine in the day-to-day lives of adolescents to affect their engagement in educational settings. Further, while it is in these different arenas that young people negotiate and construct their realities, their movements and adaptations from one setting to another are, for the most part, taken for granted. And yet, the process of transitioning from home to school, moving from one classroom to the next, responding to a variety of teachers, adjusting to myriad peers, and coping with changing family configurations requires adjustment and adaptation. While it seems obvious that adolescents must possess competencies and skills for transitions to be successful (especially when contexts are governed by different values and norms), to date there has been relatively little study of this process.[1] It appears that in our culture many adolescents are left to navigate transitions without direct assistance from persons in any of their contexts, most notably the school. Further, young people's success in managing these transitions varies widely. Yet students' ability to move between settings and adapt to varieties of circumstances has tremendous implications for the quality of their lives and their chances of using the educational system as a stepping-stone to further education, productive work experiences, and a meaningful adult life.

In this book we learn from students like Sarah and Will, whose comments open this chapter. Our focus is on the individual as *mediator* and *integrator* of meaning and experience in contrast to single-context approaches that compartmentalize aspects of adolescents' lives—those studies that examine peer group, family, and school variables independently of one another. Although research in these areas has provided a great deal of important information, it is the researcher who determines the focus. Rather, our emphasis is guided by the perspectives of youths and the ways in which they interpret and give meaning to their lives. Specifically, we are concerned with the interrelationships between students' family, peer, and school worlds and particularly how meanings and understandings from students' worlds combine to affect their engagement in classroom and school settings. Further, because young people's circumstances and their success in managing transitions vary widely, we focus on students' perceptions of borders and boundaries between worlds and adaptation strategies they employ as they move from one context to another. Our overall goal is to provide a clearer understanding of features in school and classroom environments that aid or impede students in making successful transitions among their worlds and the world of school—both social and academic.

THE STUDENTS' MULTIPLE WORLDS STUDY

The case studies we present result from research with 55 adolescents in four desegregated high schools in two urban school districts in California. In the fall of 1989, Patricia Phelan, an educational anthropologist, joined the staff of the Center for Research on the Context of Secondary School Teaching (CRC) at Stanford University. Ann Locke Davidson and Hanh Cao Yu, research assistants at the center and doctoral students in Stanford's School of Education at that time, joined the research team. Together we designed the Students' Multiple Worlds Study—a three-year investigation of factors that affect students' engagement in schools and learning. As part of this work, Davidson also carried out an in-depth study concerned with the ways in which students experience race and ethnicity and the implications of these experiences for academic engagement (Davidson, 1996).

Our study emanated out of the broader CRC strategy that assumed that the workplace is socially constructed by the participants in the setting. During 1988, the center instigated a five-year period of research aimed at understanding the way in which varied contextual factors (e.g., professional development opportunities, school organization, unions, district policies, academic departments, and students) affect teachers' decisions, their work setting, and their view of their roles and responsibilities. Student characteristics (motivation and goals, attitudes and abilities, behaviors, language proficiency, family supports) were primary in teachers' descriptions and concerns (McLaughlin, 1993; McLaughlin & Talbert, 1990, 1993). We initiated the "Student as Context Study" to better understand this dimension of teachers' professional lives. From the beginning, our emphasis was on obtaining students' perspectives— specifically, how adolescents view and define what is significant in affecting their school experiences. We operated from the premise that understanding the meanings students give to events, discerning the ways in which they view their circumstances, uncovering their perceptions of people with whom they interact, and clarifying their interpretation of actions and attitudes could help illuminate those aspects of students' behavior that teachers had defined as important, curious, or problematic. In short, operating from the perspective of educational anthropology, we sought to develop a research agenda that would provide teachers and researchers with an "emic" or insider's view of students' lives, concerns, and experiences.

We began the study by focusing on a small number of students in each school. The students varied with respect to gender, ethnicity, socioeconomic status, achievement level, immigrant history, and transportation status (participation in the districts' transportation program). A majority of the students were freshman when the study began, although some older students were included. By including a number of older students we were able to gain temporal triangulation—a term coined by G. D. Spindler and L. Spindler (personal communication, September 18, 1989), who have found that people are frequently able to describe the process of events more cogently after they have occurred.

Over the course of 2 years, we spent literally hundreds of hours with these youths. In addition to conducting four in-depth interviews with each student (ranging from 45 minutes to over 2 hours), we spent more than 80 full days shadowing youth (well over 300 classroom observations), and many hours in hallways, lunchrooms, and on school grounds. We also collected students' cumulative record data (including standardized test scores, grades, teacher comments, attendance and referral records) and demographic information about all students and their families.

Following the first wave of interviews, we selected a subset of 16 youths in order to obtain more in-depth observational and interview data on a small group of students throughout the remaining 1½ year of the study. The 16 case-study youths represented the variety found in the overall sample. Some of the youths were successful, in terms of traditional definitions of school success, while others were not. We began by asking students if we might spend a few hours with them in their school environments. None declined and, in fact, most seemed pleased that we appeared interested enough in their lives to follow them around and actually sit through their classes. As the students became increasingly comfortable, we spent time with them on a regular basis. We found that their descriptions of teachers and classroom events were inherently more understandable when we observed what they described. As we visited on a more regular basis, the students introduced us to their friends and sometimes their families. We spent time in peer groups comprised of recent Mexican and Vietnamese immigrants; second-generation Mexican and Filipino youth; those involved peripherally in gang-related social activities; youth who went through periods of homelessness; youth who were described variously as preppies, surfers, and heavy metals; and youth who participated in weekend horse shows, fashion shows, and teas. In some cases we got to know the friends almost as well as the participants in our study themselves.

With our frequent presence in schools, we also came to know teachers, counselors, and school administrators. These adults proved invaluable in providing us with a variety of perspectives on individual youths' academic performance, classroom interactions, social and peer group behavior, and family background. The mismatch between students' and teachers' perceptions of circumstances and events was particularly illuminating. Sometimes we were stunned at the differences in their views. We also asked these adults about more general issues, such as support and information available to them and the students in their particular schools.

To help verify and extend our findings, we spent time with a second group of students in a fifth California high school during the third year of our study (Phelan & Davidson, 1994). Over a course of seven one-hour sessions, these ethnically diverse youth examined data and critiqued the work we had done. The quotes that begin this chapter resulted from our work with this second group of students. In essence, these youth served as apprentice researchers, examining data, generating hypotheses, and assessing the applicability and relevance of our findings to their lives. Participation and analysis by these youths led us to further develop our initial conceptualization by expanding our descriptions of the range of transition and adaptation patterns that students exhibit (described in more detail in the following section).

Over the course of 3 years, we listened carefully to what students had to say. While we were certainly committed to contributing information of value to the larger educational and research communities, we also became deeply enmeshed in students' lives. Rather than finding it hard to talk with youths, we often experienced difficulty getting away. In almost all cases, students expressed a desire to share their thoughts, discuss their views, and examine their own reality as they rendered descriptions of events, circumstances, and relationships.

Model and Typology

As in other ethnographic work (Spindler & Spindler, 1992), the character of our study and a clarification of students' perspectives evolved as the study progressed. For example, we used themes that emerged from each wave of interviewing to guide the emphasis of the interviews that followed. Likewise, classroom observations and informal conversations led us to explore hunches more systematically as data collection proceeded. In essence, our work can be considered generative, inductive, and constructive as discussed by Goetz and LeCompte (1984).

To begin, our emphasis was on students' descriptions of school factors that affect their engagement with learning—for example, classroom organization, teacher attitudes and behaviors, pedagogy, and overall school climate. However, the use of open-ended interviews allowed students to talk about other features of their lives (i.e., peer and family concerns) relevant to their feelings about school. "I wouldn't let them put me in a higher track because I wanted to be with my friends," reported one student. "At least in my family it's sort of expected that you're going to try to get A's or something close," said another. "Being Mexican means being popular, cutting classes, acting crazy," reported yet another student. Thus, as the study proceeded, students began to reveal an inherently complex picture of their daily lives and to discuss a multitude of factors emanating from their family, peer, and school worlds that they described as affecting their ability to connect with teachers, classrooms, and schools. As a result we developed a model, depicted in Figure 1.1, to describe students' multiple worlds and the relationships among them. The meanings drawn from each of these worlds combine to influence students' actions and interactions.

The concept of culture is central to the development of the Students' Multiple Worlds Model. While culture encompasses those visible aspects and artifacts of a particular group (i.e., food, clothing, housing, implements, and so forth), it also refers to people's values and beliefs, expectations, actions, and interactions, as well as the meanings people construct about what is appropriate, inappropriate, normative, and aberrant. In short, cultural knowledge is what people need to know in order to think, act, and behave appropriately (Spindler, 1982, 1987).

In the Students' Multiple Worlds Study we use the term "world" to mean cultural knowledge and behavior found within the boundaries of students' particular families, peer groups, and schools; we presume that each world contains values and beliefs, expectations, actions, and emotional responses familiar to insiders. We use the terms "social setting," "arena," and "context" to refer to places and events within which individuals act and interact. Students employ cultural knowledge acquired from their family, peer, and school

FIGURE 1.1:   **The Students' Multiple Worlds Model**

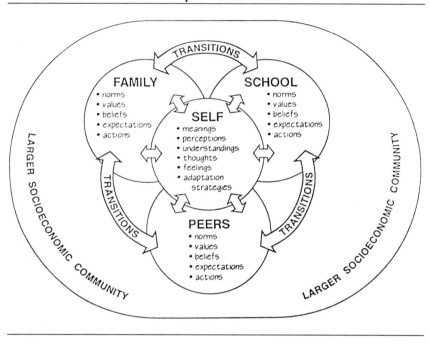

worlds in social settings and contexts. Social settings and contexts may be found within the bounds of any one world (e.g., a student having dinner with family members) or may include actors from various worlds (e.g., students interacting with friends in classrooms or friends in each other's homes). In the latter case, people in the same social setting may or may not share the same cultural knowledge acquired from the constellation of their individual worlds.[2]

While the model we developed emerged inductively from data gathered in the field, we were guided at the same time by the theoretical orientations of educational anthropology—particularly as such theory has been used to interpret the adaptation of diverse students to mainstream American classrooms. Specifically, the Students' Multiple Worlds Model reflects ideas emanating from cultural compatibility theory as well as theoretical perspectives concerned with the creation and maintenance of social borders.

Theoretical Perspectives Informing Our Work

Cultural compatibility theory was developed in an effort to explain differential achievement patterns in the school performance of minority children in the United States. This theoretical framework (as well as most cross-cultural research) assumes that values, beliefs, expectations, and normative ways of behaving are acquired first in children's home environments. However, when children enter school, what is expected and thought to be appropriate can be quite different from what children learned at home—particularly for minority youth in the United States. Further, the patterns that children develop with respect to their learning and motivational styles, communication styles, and literacy and writing styles may not match teachers' views and beliefs about what is suitable for school. Cultural compatibility theorists argue that when schools require children to act in ways that are incongruent with what they have learned at home, misunderstandings, problems, and conflicts can arise. These theorists hypothesize that such problems are related to the fact that differences in cultural knowledge and culturally learned patterns of behavior lead to different and often conflicting expectations and views. This theoretical perspective assumes that systematic and recurrent miscommunication can escalate over time into academic trouble and failure (Erickson, 1993).

Cultural compatibility theorists draw on empirical work that documents important differences between home and school for culturally diverse children. They also point to studies that describe the rich, though different, learning environments that characterize these homes and communities (cf. Cazden & John, 1971; Gallimore, Boggs, & Jordan, 1974; John, 1972; Philips, 1972, 1983). Further, there is a good deal of empirical work that supports the premise that problematic interactions in schools are, in fact, related to cultural differences (cf. Au, 1980; Au & Mason, 1981; Delgado-Gaitan, 1987; Erickson & Mohatt, 1982; Heath, 1982; Moll & Diaz, 1993; Philips, 1983; Vogt, Jordan, & Tharp, 1993).

Like cultural compatibility theorists, we are interested in ascertaining the congruence of the sociocultural components across students' worlds. We believe that the level of congruence can potentially affect students' adaptation to school. However, one criticism of cultural compatibility theory is its assumption that cultural differences between home and school necessarily create difficulties and problems. Such an assumption does not leave room to explain the many instances in which, despite differences in communicative, cognitive, and learning styles, as well as values and beliefs, ethnically diverse children do well. Further, because cultural compatibility theory draws support from studies of specific cultural groups, it tends to assume that the sociocultural components of any one group are the same. Thus, variability within groups is obscured (cf. Bloch & Swadener, 1992; Cazden, 1990; Tabachnick & Bloch, 1995; Trueba, 1988a, b). As Tabachnick and Bloch point out, "there is a great deal of variability within groups and . . . cultural compatibility theory is often used in such a way as to overlook this variability, supporting stereotypes that work to the disadvantage of some groups" (1995, p. 205).

In order to address these weaknesses, our model incorporates concepts that emanate from work concerned with the social organization of cultural differences. In particular, we are influenced by theorists who argue that cultural differences in and of themselves do not preclude successful interaction; rather, people develop vested interests in being different from one another and thus emphasize and highlight divisions (often unwittingly) in response to their relative positions in the social order (McDermott & Gospodinoff, 1979) or in order to maximize their economic and political security (Barth, 1969).

The distinction between social boundaries and social borders emanating from work in this area relates directly to our conceptualization. Specifically, boundaries have been described as behavioral evidence of culturally different standards of appropriateness that are politically neutral (Erickson, 1993). When boundaries exist, no special rights or obligations accrue to individuals or groups of individuals for adapting one set of standards rather than another. In contrast, borders are features of cultural difference that are not politically neutral. Erickson (1993) hypothesizes that boundaries are transformed into borders when the knowledge, skills, and behaviors in one world are more highly valued and rewarded than those in another. Incorporating Erickson's definitions, we find that when boundaries exist (even when sociocultural components of students' worlds are different), movement between worlds can occur with relative ease—that is, social, psychological, and academic costs are minimal. Alternatively, when students encounter borders, movement and adaptation are difficult because knowledge and skills or particular ways of behaving in one world are more highly valued and esteemed than those in another. Although it is possible for students to navigate borders with apparent success, these transitions can incur personal and psychic costs invisible to teachers and others. Moreover, boundaries can become impenetrable borders when the psychosocial and sociocultural consequences of adaptation become too great.

The Students' Multiple Worlds Model assumes that differences in the sociocultural components of students' worlds can function as boundaries. However, because of historical, political, and economic conditions, differences between students' worlds can be transformed into borders that impede students' connection with schools and learning. We find that such differences are not only cultural (as described by Barth, 1969; Erickson, 1993; Erickson & Bekker, 1986; McDermott & Gospidonoff, 1979) but emanate from other sources as well.

Types of Borders That Students Face

The inductive nature of our inquiry allowed us to identify a number of types of borders that students face. As youths talked about their worlds, they also spontaneously related their experiences in navigating their various settings. In so doing, they discussed problems they face, obstacles they encounter, and difficulties they experience. Thus they began to articulate the nature and dimensions of the borders that stand in their way. Sociocultural, socioeconomic, psychosocial, linguistic, gender, heterosexist, and structural borders all impede students' connection with classroom and school contexts. Although we observed the presence of gender borders and heterosexist borders in the schools in which we worked, our focus was on students' descriptions of borders they faced and factors they described as affecting their engagement with school. For the most part, students emphasized psychosocial, sociocultural, socioeconomic, and structural borders. The case studies we present illustrate a variety of ways in which borders are constructed. Further, while the borders we describe are frequently interrelated, each has distinctive properties that are important to understand as educators attempt to identify strategies that will enable students to make transitions successfully.

Sociocultural Borders. When the sociocultural components in one world (family, peer, or school) are viewed as inferior to or not as worthwhile as those in another, borders are created. For example, when the communication, cognitive, interactional, learning, motivational, literacy, or writing styles expected of children in school are considered to be superior to, rather than simply different from, those used at home, sociocultural borders arise. However, like Erickson (1993) and Delgado-Gaitan and Trueba (1991), we believe that cultural differences per se do not necessarily create borders blocking school participation and learning. In fact, cultural differences can be viewed as assets rather than liabilities.

Socioeconomic Borders. Socioeconomic borders are generated when economic circumstances create severe limitations. For example, the economic situation of a family may require a student to work outside the home, thus making school participation (academic, social, and/or extracurricular) difficult or impossible. Or an economically constrained student may be precluded from involvement with peers whose economic circumstances are better. Finally, socioeconomic borders can result from students' community and neighborhood conditions that stand in contrast to their school environment, particularly for students who are transported from other neighborhoods or communities. Although sociocultural and socioeconomic borders combine frequently, this is not always the case. We think the distinction is worthwhile when intervention strategies are considered.

Psychosocial Borders. Psychosocial borders are constructed when children experience anxiety, depression, apprehension, or fear that prevents them from adopting the mindset and emotional and attitudinal orientation required and valorized by schools. Such borders disrupt or hinder students' ability to focus on classroom tasks, participate fully in learning, or establish positive relationships with teachers or peers in school environments. Psychosocial borders can also prevent students' connections with peers or family. While it is possible that psychosocial borders can be secondary to or result from sociocultural, socioeconomic, linguistic, or heterosexist borders, other events in children's lives can also create undue anxiety and stress (e.g., a physically or sexually abusive home situation, parents' divorce, serious illness or death of a family member, etc.). In some cases, psychosocial borders are temporal in nature. In other words, anxiety and stress connected with a particular event or life circumstance can lessen as circumstances change. The problems associated with psychological borders are amplified when school personnel are unable, unwilling, or ill-equipped to uncover sources of anxiety or stress.

Linguistic Borders. Linguistic borders result when communication between students' worlds (i.e., home/school, peer/home) is obstructed, not because of different languages per se, but because one group regards another group's language as unacceptable or inferior. As Delgado-Gaitan and Trueba (1991) state, "The very act of learning English as a second language is a cultural variation, but it does not necessarily create distress for children. A conflict ensues when children, limited in English proficiency, are taught all of their academic curriculum in English in such a way that their native language and culture are invalidated" (p. 28). In our study, we observed that language differences became borders when teachers or students saw language as a problem or acted in ways that devalued languages other than English.

Gender Borders. When the school as an institution, or the people in it, promote roles, aspirations, or estimates of worth to girls that differ from those it offers to boys, gender borders exist. Gender borders can be found in both the substance and the process of the educational experience—in the content of the curriculum (i.e., when the history and accomplishments of one gender group are fully or partially excluded), in pedagogical styles and methods (i.e., when teacher attention and encouragement are more frequently directed toward one gender group), and in attitudes and expectations (i.e., when the sensibilities, problems, and assets of one gender group are viewed differently from those of the other). Gender borders not only undermine self-confidence and block students' perceptions of what is possible for themselves and others, but also discourage or impede the acquisition of skills necessary to pursue specific careers.

Heterosexist Borders. Heterosexist borders exist when individuals find themselves in a world constructed on the belief that heterosexuality is the superior, if not the only, form of legitimate sexual expression. Features of this border include homophobia, ridicule or silencing of gay voices and lives, and the structuring of activities to promote heterosexual behavior only. When lesbian, gay, bisexual, and transgendered youth are ostracized by schoolmates, verbally and physically attacked, condemned for other than blatant heterosexual behaviors, and generally perceived as sick, sinful, and criminal, heterosexist borders exist. Whether at school, at home, or with friends, heterosexist borders negatively impact students' academic, social, and emotional development by creating fear, confusion, and low self-esteem. These borders can also impact students' ability to make successful transitions among their worlds (Eddy, personal communication [May 23, 1996]; Meisner, 1995).

Structural Borders. We define structural borders as features in school environments that prevent, impede, or discourage student learning—whether social or academic. Structural borders emanate largely from differences in expectations for how schools as institutions should operate. These expectations may include notions about what services schools are obligated to provide, how school authorities should behave toward and relate to students and their families, how learning and counseling environments should be organized, and what substance and content should be included in the curriculum. Three types of conditions at either the classroom or the school level give rise to structural borders:

1. *Availability*—In this case, the school environment lacks adequate resources and supports to meet students' needs, for example, inadequate tutoring, no counselors, no links to mental health services, insufficiently equipped libraries and classrooms, inadequate second-language training, and so forth.
2. *Bridges*—Services and opportunities for students exist in the school setting but there are no bridges to connect students with available resources. In other words, students do not have information about programs and opportunities that are available to them or, if they possess such knowledge, no one in the environment assists them in accessing resources that may be potentially beneficial.
3. *Match*—Structures and services are available and visible to students but either do not match students' needs or actually impede their connection with school and classroom settings. Mismatches can occur with respect to pedagogy, teacher attitudes, curriculum, and/or classroom organization, for example, an anti-abortion poster hung on a counselor's office door, tracking, severe and punitive discipline policies (school level), Euro-

centered only curriculum, inattention to varieties of learning styles, teachers' uncaring attitudes and behaviors (classroom level).

Although there is often overlap between these distinctions, we believe that the development and implementation of successful intervention strategies depends on the ability of teachers and others in school environments to recognize and identify not only where and when borders exist (i.e., between peers and schools, school and home), but also the nature of the borders that students encounter.

Students' Transition Patterns

As our study proceeded we found a good deal of variety in students' descriptions of their worlds and in their perceptions of borders. At the same time, we uncovered initially four distinctive patterns as students made transitions from one setting to another (Phelan, Davidson, & Cao, 1991; Phelan, Davidson, & Yu, 1993; Phelan, Yu, & Davidson, 1994). Our involvement with a second group of youths during the third year of the study (whom we enlisted to review and comment on our findings) led us to expand our typology to include the six types we describe below (Phelan & Davidson, 1994). While these six types do not necessarily include all students, they do depict the general patterns of youth in this study.

I. *Congruent Worlds/Smooth Transitions:* These students describe values, beliefs, expectations, and normative ways of behaving as similar across their worlds. Moving from one setting to another is harmonious and uncomplicated. Many but not all of these students are white, middle to upper-middle-class, and high achieving. Some minority students describe little difference across their worlds and find transitions easy. Likewise, academically average students can exhibit patterns that fit this type.

II. *Different Worlds/Border Crossings Managed:* For some students, differences in family, peer, and/or school worlds (with respect to culture, ethnicity, socioeconomic status, and/or religion) require students to adjust and reorient as movement among contexts occurs. Students in this category perceive differences in their worlds but utilize strategies that enable them to manage crossings successfully (in terms of what is valued in each setting). High-achieving minority students frequently exhibit patterns common to this type.

III. *Different Worlds/Border Crossings Difficult:* In this category, like the former, students define their family, peer, and/or school worlds as distinct from one another. They must adjust and reorient as they move across borders and among contexts. However, unlike students who make adjustments in spite of difficulties, these students find transitions difficult. Common to this type are students who adapt in some circumstances but not in others, that is, they may do well in one or two classes and poorly in the rest.

IV. *Different Worlds/Border Crossings Resisted:* In this type, the values, beliefs, and expectations across worlds are so discordant that students perceive borders as insurmountable and actively or passively resist transitions. Low-achieving students (seemingly unable to profit from school and classroom settings) are typical of this type, although high-achieving students who do not connect with peers or family also exhibit Type IV patterns.

V. *Congruent Worlds/Border Crossings Resisted:* While these students describe the sociocultural components of their worlds as congruent, they are unable to successfully accomplish transitions. Typical of this type are students who do exceptionally well on standardized tests but receive low to failing grades. Often these youths' parents have high academic expectations for their children and express concern and consternation over their low achievement. It is not infrequent that teachers, counselors, and parents are frustrated and unable to understand why these students fail. However, teachers' explanations for students' lack of success, motivation, or willingness to put forth effort are found frequently in deficit views of children and families.

VI. *Different Worlds/Smooth Transitions:* These youths describe their worlds as distinct but experience transitions as relatively effortless. They have little difficulty in switching from one cultural mode to another or in blending aspects from each of their worlds. These students describe the people with whom they interact and the circumstances in which they find themselves as supportive and enabling of bicultural and blended transcultural identities. Further, their worlds are ones in which diversity and difference are valued. Some of these youths have international experiences that have allowed them to thrive in a variety of cultural settings. In our study only four youths described patterns that fit this type.

Each of the six types includes the variety of combinations possible with respect to perceived boundaries and borders (i.e., between family and school, peers and family) and each combination is characterized in different ways by different students. However, the patterns we describe are not necessarily stable for individual students over time but rather can be affected by external

FIGURE 1.2:   **The Students' Multiple Worlds Typology**

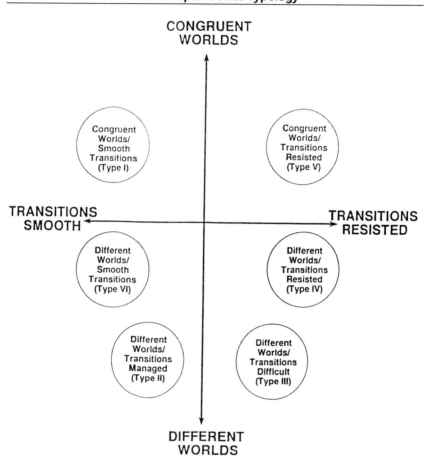

conditions such as classroom or school climate, family circumstances, or changes in peer-group affiliations. Further, while we identify and illustrate only six types, students' patterns can be located on a continuum from congruent worlds to different worlds (vertical axis) and transitions smooth to transitions resisted (horizontal axis). See Figure 1.2.

Both enabling and limiting patterns of behavior are contained in this typology. The cases we present illustrate that some of the more superficially approved styles of adaptation—those perceived by many to be the least problematic—can be as potentially restricting as those where discordant patterns seem to dominate.

Among youths who encounter borders, we have uncovered three distinct adaptation strategies, each of which results in specific emotional costs and benefits. Using one strategy, students attempt to adapt completely, conforming to mainstream patterns of academic and social interaction while at school, and hiding aspects of their home lives that might differentiate them from the majority of their peers. Frequently, these students devalue or disparage aspects of their home worlds, their voices reflecting an internalization of roles and an acceptance of the status quo that some scholars refer to as "internalized oppression" (Delgado-Gaitan & Trueba, 1991; Gaventa, 1980). As Delgado-Gaitan and Trueba state, "Here is where the cultural and social conflicts between home and school can become a nightmare of contrasting demands that confuse or lead to rejection of the home culture or language, and even in some extreme cases to rejection of ones' own self" (1991, p. 31).

A second strategy occurs when students adapt situationally, conforming to mainstream patterns of interaction when they are in the minority, returning to home/community patterns of interaction when with their peers in social settings or at home with their families. These students do not devalue or seek to distance themselves from their different worlds, but rather adapt as a practical matter by switching to the expectations of different settings.

Using a third strategy, some students develop a capacity to blend aspects of their different worlds, often maintaining high levels of academic achievement without hiding or devaluing aspects of their home or community lives that differentiate them from their majority peers. These students both value and criticize aspects of their multiple worlds, drawing elements from each to create an identity that transcends conventional categories. Yet the assertion of this "transcultural" identity (Rosaldo, 1989) can bring with it emotional costs as well as benefits, for in not succumbing to the normative press to "fit in" (in community, peer, and school worlds), these youths open themselves up to criticism from actors in their various worlds who expect adherence to social rules and expectations.

A New Perspective

This work and the cases we present differ from previous research efforts in several respects. First, rather than assuming that minority status, linguistic differences, part-time employment, peers, and/or poverty are primary factors that impact students' lives in school, we have asked students to tell us what is important to them. The perspectives of youth and the ways in which they attach meaning to the circumstances in which they find themselves is not a common focus in the educational literature. For the most part, constructs and concepts thought to be important are identified and defined by adults— namely, researchers and educators. In this study, youths' perspectives are central. Second, by using a qualitative, generative approach and drawing on the theoretical perspectives of educational anthropology, we have developed a model and typology that emerged inductively from data gathered directly from interviews and observations. The Students' Multiple Worlds Model is a primary product of this research. Our conceptualization cuts the pie differently, so to speak—first, by focusing on the congruence of sociocultural aspects of students' worlds, and second, by paying attention to transition and adaptation patterns. Third, unlike most other approaches, which focus attention on stable characteristics of individuals (i.e., gender and ethnicity) or concentrate on language acquisition or achievement level alone, the Students' Multiple Worlds Model is generic. It is neither ethnic-, achievement-, nor gender-specific, but transcends these categories to consider multiple worlds, border crossings, and adaptation for *all* students. The generic nature of the model is particularly useful for understanding diversity within ethnic groups. For example, we have seen that all students—Latino, Vietnamese, Filipino, African-American, and European-American—may perceive borders very differently and utilize various adaptation strategies as they move from one setting to another.

Fourth, as educators continue to search for adequate responses to the problems that youths face, our delineation and emphasis on borders shifts attention from individual and family circumstances to contextual factors that inhibit youths from connecting optimally with school. Rather than viewing individual characteristics as creating risk, we see risk as contained in the borders that students face. Our purpose is to move away from a deficit view of children and families and embrace instead a view of children, youth, and families as "at-promise" (Swadener & Lubeck, 1995).

Finally, we present case studies of youths in an attempt to engage teachers and students in discussions, analysis, and consideration of contexts and experiences that impact adolescents' lives. Our own experience has been that case studies capture teachers' attention and engage them in independent, constructive thinking and analysis about their own classrooms and schools.

Overall, the cases we present recount the vagaries of everyday life, highlight the perspectives of youth, and uncover at least partially the intended, as well as the unintended, consequences of interactions for students, teachers, and other adults in school settings.

OVERVIEW OF THE BOOK

Consonant with our commitment to highlighting the importance and significance of the individual as integrator and mediator of meaning and experiences, we illustrate the Students' Multiple Worlds Model and Typology by presenting case studies of seven adolescents. We use cases specifically to illustrate the variety of circumstances and patterns found among the students with whom we worked. We also use case studies in an effort to enable our readers to "enter students' worlds," to discern their view of the circumstances in which they find themselves, and to explore their thoughts, interpretations, and responses to the contexts of their daily lives—in particular, their family, peer, and school worlds. The cases portray students' efforts and abilities in making transitions among their worlds—the types of borders they face, the ease and difficulty with which they navigate their various settings, the meanings they derive from the contexts in which they find themselves, and the ways in which meanings combine to impact their engagement in schools and learning.

The presentation of case studies of youths is not a form common in the educational literature. While there are increasing examples of case studies of teachers being accumulated and used by innovative teacher educators (Bullough, 1989; Casey, 1993; Cohen, 1991; Shulman & Mesa-Bains, 1993), there has been little written that details the perspectives of students or their interpretation of circumstances and events that impinge on their lives and their ability to connect with educational settings. In general, we find that the educational literature and a good deal of what the media present are characterized by a focus on "end results" and a detached view of the educational process. The abstract reporting of test score results, the rather clinical discussion of "at-risk" youth, the high numbers of students (somewhere out there) who "drop out," the devastation of teenage pregnancies (in someone else's neighborhood), statistics that document suicide as the second leading cause of death of young adults—all are presented frequently in a form that leave us disconnected, emotionally distanced, and, even worse, dispassionate about the lives of those involved.

The seven cases we present, while chosen to illustrate our model and typology, are also an attempt to draw educators (and researchers) closer to the clientele they serve. Our overall purpose is to provide information that will assist teachers, counselors, administrators, and others who work with children and youth to build bridges between their worlds and those of school. As educators attempt to create optimal school environments for increasingly diverse populations, we need to know how students negotiate borders successfully, or alternatively, how they are impeded by borders that prevent their connection, not only with institutional contexts, but with peers who are different from themselves. Finally, we think it is particularly important to understand school features that enable smooth transitions, and serve to transform borders, real or perceived, into manageable boundaries.

We begin with the case study of Ryan Moore (Type I), a European-American middle-class student at Explorer High School. Ryan typifies an adolescent whose worlds are congruent and transitions smooth. At school, teachers' language and communication styles, teachers' conceptions of the necessary strategies for success (such as compliance, hard work, and academic achievement), and pervading upward-mobility norms match the values, beliefs, and behaviors of Ryan's family and friends, making transitions between home, school, and peers unproblematic. Ryan and his friends are in an accelerated academic track and frequently have the same teachers. Teachers not only know Ryan's friends but they also know or at least have some knowledge of his parents, who are actively involved in school affairs. However, Ryan and his friends have little sustained contact with or knowledge about students different from themselves. While Ryan's congruent worlds and smooth transitions imply harmony and ease, they also signal a lack of opportunity to acquire or practice border-crossing strategies—that is, to know or interact meaningfully with others whose worlds are different from his own.

The next two cases portray students whose worlds are different but who manage border crossings successfully (Type II youth). These students illustrate two of the three adaptation strategies described previously. Trinh Le, who arrived in the United States as an infant in the first wave of Vietnamese immigrants, is typical of youths who conform to mainstream patterns of academic and social interaction while at school, hiding aspects of their home lives that might differentiate them from the majority of their peers. Trinh is stereotypically perceived by teachers as a model, well-adjusted, high-achieving Asian youth. Class valedictorian, a straight-A student, quiet and deferential, are characteristics teachers cite to support their views. Part of a diverse, high-achieving group of peers at school, Trinh (like many other adolescents) is preoccupied with "fitting in." But for Trinh this means minimizing cultural background factors that might distinguish her from peers. Trinh's friends and teachers have little or no knowledge of her home life or the pressure she feels from her parents, who make concerted attempts to socialize Trinh to pivotal Vietnamese values. While there is a large Vietnamese student population at Huntington High School, Trinh consciously distances herself from recent immigrant youths and expresses apprehension at being identified as "one of them." Hiding parts of who she is has emotional and educational costs unsuspected by teachers who fail to recognize the sociocultural borders with which she is faced.

A second adaptation strategy is exemplified by Patricia Schmidt, a Latina/European-American girl from a working-class background. Unlike Trinh, who hides parts of who she is, or youths who operate biculturally, Patricia blends the sociocultural aspects of her worlds, projecting an identity that transcends conventional categories. Maintaining an outstanding academic record throughout her school years, Patricia is transported to Maple High from Northside, a low-income community stigmatized by local (primarily majority) students. Her school involvement, academic achievement, and Latina, working-class heritage are visible aspects of her public persona, earning her the nickname "rebel" among her peers. In contrast to the majority of students in this volume, Patricia is assisted by teachers in crossing the socioeconomic and sociocultural borders between home and school. Nevertheless, her assertion of a "transcultural" identity (Rosaldo, 1989) brings emotional costs as well as benefits. In not succumbing to the normative press to "fit in," Patricia is criticized by peers who press her to adhere to more traditional visions of the female role.

Moving to Type III youth, we present the case of Donna Carlyle, a Latina/European-American student who experiences difficulty navigating the socioeconomic and sociocultural borders between home and school and who faces structural borders that impede her from planning her academic future. Donna typifies those youths who do extremely well in some classes and not so well in others. While Donna has maintained a C average at Huntington High School, her grades fluctuate across classes. She thrives academically and socially in classrooms where she perceives the teacher as caring and where the norms and behaviors that characterize her family and peer worlds—group over self, listening and empathizing with others, and mediation skills—are required. In classroom contexts that are teacher-dominated and where her abilities go unnoticed, Donna's attention shifts to peer-group concerns.

Our fifth case is that of Sonia Gonzales (Type IV), a young person for whom sociocultural borders between home and school are insurmountable. Daughter of Mexican immigrants, Sonia describes her feelings of being an outsider at school. Though her family is concerned about her school performance and pushes her to do well, Sonia is failing almost all of her classes and skips school on a regular basis. Adults in her environment know nothing about Sonia's background and make little attempt to understand her behavior. Sonia describes aspects of her environment that contribute to her feelings of marginalization and difference: little meaningful contact with her high school teachers, little support and even direct hostility from her non-Mexican peers, little access to information about colleges and careers. Combined with peer-group norms and behaviors that often conflict with those required for academic success, the borders Sonia perceives become impassable.

Our sixth case, Robert Hirschman, typifies a Type V student—one whose worlds are congruent but who fails miserably to achieve the level of academic success of which his family, peers, and teachers think he is capable. Described as "brilliant," "talented," and "quirky," Robert has defied all attempts by educators and his grandparents (with whom he lives) to persuade him to comply with even the most basic requirements for passing grades. At the same time, Robert's connection with school is evidenced by an excellent attendance record, animated participation in his classes, social involvement with peers, and a high degree of visibility generally in the school environment. Teachers, counselors, and administrators with whom we spoke *all* knew and commented on Robert. However, inability to identify rational reasons for Robert's academic failure have turned teachers' views to "within-child" deficit interpretations for his lack of success.

Carmelita Abello, our last case, illustrates patterns typical of Type VI youth—those whose worlds are different but find transitions smooth. Carmelita, a Filipina-American student at Rancho High School, moves easily between her family, peer, and school worlds. Carmelita's appreciation of and commitment to upholding some of the traditional Filipino values of her family are exemplified as she proudly recounts aspects of Filipino culture and custom in class presentations and talks openly about her family's visits to the Philippines with her culturally diverse friends. For the most part, Carmelita perceives her parents, teachers, and peers as supportive of her immediate and long-term academic goals, appreciative of and interested in her heritage, and enabling of her movements among the various contexts of her life.

CONCLUSION

Students' voices and concerns—their role as mediators of their own experience—must be taken into account as pedagogical strategies, programs, and services are developed and implemented. In this book we present case studies of youths to illuminate important themes that crosscut students' lives—in particular, the importance of the ways in which meanings from family, peer, and school worlds combine to impact students' involvement in educational and learning endeavors. Further, the case studies we include are intended to highlight aspects of classroom and school contexts that students say affect their ability to connect positively with the educational environments in which they find themselves. It is our hope that the case studies will provide a distinctive view of the experiences of youths and will encourage consideration of the complexity of factors that impinge on students' lives. Our own experience of using case studies as a pedagogical tool (described in detail in Chapter 9) has involved teachers, high school students, and graduate students in extended discussions about the contexts of students' lives and the circumstances that might best support and promote their academic, social, and emotional growth.

On the practical side, we anticipate that the framework we have developed will eventually have utility for differentiating methods of counseling and for informing the way in which instructional settings can best be organized to enable students to successfully navigate their worlds. Modulating to individual differences appropriately has always been a major challenge in both counseling and instruction. We expect that this framework, by focusing on students' transition and adaptation patterns and the borders they face, will have greatest utility by helping to make these particular dimensions of individual differences more comprehensible, thus adding to the base of frameworks that are available for selecting counseling and educational strategies.

It is our hope that the framework we have developed will be useful to those disciplines and practices that attempt to better understand the needs of youth and the types of interventions that can positively impact their lives.

NOTES

1. Ruth Benedict's (1938) observation over 50 years ago that American institutions provide inadequate support in helping young people progress from one role to another appears to be relevant today: "adult activity demands traits that are interdicted in children, and that far from redoubling efforts to help children bridge this gap, adults in our culture put all the blame on the child when he fails to manifest spontaneously the new behavior or, overstepping the mark, manifests it with untoward belligerence" (p. 432).

2. Our use of the term "world" corresponds closely to Spradley and McCurdy's definition of "cultural scene." Likewise, the terms "social settings," "arenas," and "contexts" in this study parallel their definition of "social situations" (Spradley & McCurdy, 1972, pp. 25–30).

2

RYAN MOORE

"WOULDN'T MIND IN THE NEIGHBORHOOD TYPE"

[Ryan] Oh, a wonderful young man. . . . Well, you know, he comes from very caring parents. Wonderful leadership skills, very responsible, highly focused.

. . . he was selected for this prestigious Leadership Training Program. So, and before I selected him, I went to different people. Now see, because he's an officer and that type of thing. And I went to different people and I said, "OK, these are the ones [list of possible students], what do you think?" Ryan Moore (unanimously). . . . Self-motivated, self-directed. Very responsible, leadership skills, uh hmm, people like him. You know, and much respected by his teachers also. He's just that kind of a student.

I mean he just stands out. And his parents are very active here in school. Father's the head of the Parent Fund Raising Organization. Mother's in the office. Anyway, so just lovely people. And he reflects that.

These comments about Ryan, made by the vice-principal of guidance at Explorer High School, parallel closely the comments made by *all* of Ryan Moore's freshman and sophomore high school teachers. In fact, as I spoke with one person after another about Ryan over a period of 2 years, I began to feel that there was a prepared script from which people spoke. (In this instance, and throughout the book, "I" refers to the author primarily responsible for data collection for the specific case-study student. While each author interviewed and shadowed specific students, all of the authors reviewed the data, talked about the cases, and identified the major case-study themes.) Ten teachers and three administrators not only said the same things but uttered nearly identical phrases: "an excellent student," "a really nice person," "conscientious," "thoughtful," "considerate," "involved." Further, not one person failed to mention that Ryan's father heads one of the school's parent organizations and that his mother is actively involved in school affairs. "A wonderful family, and he shows it," was a phrase repeated often.

It soon became clear that comments about Ryan go well beyond a mere description of one outstanding student to personify as well the implicit characteristics and attributes valued and esteemed by adults in the Explorer High School setting. Likewise, Ryan's family circumstances are those that teachers believe are the most advantageous for preparing and supporting students' engagement with school and learning. The values, beliefs, and expectations of Ryan's family match almost perfectly those fostered and promoted in the school setting. Further, Ryan and his family are people with whom teachers identify and feel comfortable. For example, Ryan's sophomore science teacher had this to say:

> He seems very nice. He's out for sports and seems to come from a nice family. I don't know his parents personally but they are involved with the Boosters Club and taking him to sports. So seems like a nice family and a nice person. . . . type you would like to have—wouldn't mind in the neighborhood type—he would be ideal.

The description of Ryan by his algebra teacher further illustrates adults' beliefs that Ryan possesses characteristics that will ensure his future success: "He comes from an area where kids are really good. The kids he pals around with are participators—programmed for success in advance. I know his father. I was on a committee with him. . . . I have no doubt he will do fine in life. He'll have three secretaries to take care of him."

Ryan's professional, educationally sophisticated, and involved family represent an American cultural ideal—in many respects, they are the Ozzie and Harriets of the 1990s—personifying the attributes esteemed and aspired to by many in the society. Ryan's teachers believe that his family and peer worlds foster and support his school success. As a consequence, teachers and administrators see no borders, no barriers, no impediments between Ryan's outside worlds and the world of school. Students like Ryan affirm that everything is going well—that teachers are successful in their efforts to provide quality education. Further, Ryan's characteristics are those against which other students are implicitly appraised—"If only *all* students were like Ryan."

But who is Ryan and what is it about him that elicits such positive comments from the adults in his school environment? What does Ryan bring to school that other students lack? In what ways do Ryan's family and peer worlds support and foster his school involvement? How does Ryan feel and do his perceptions about the school mirror those of his teachers? Most important, what has Ryan's experience in the Explorer High School setting taught him?

BLURRED BOUNDARIES

The large urban area of Mostaza has always been Ryan's home. Although his parents met and married on the East Coast, where both were working for a national corporation, his father's family moved to the Mostaza area in the late 1950s. Ryan's father attended a high school not far from Explorer and later went to California Polytechnic University before taking a position as an engineer. Never expecting to leave the East Coast where she was raised, Ryan's mother, also a college graduate, reluctantly agreed to her husband's transfer to California in the early 1970s, 2 years after they married. Now, almost 20 years later, she considers it her home.

Both of Ryan's parents maintain strong ties with their own families, where primary values center around family cohesiveness, professionalism, hard work, and the importance of education. Frequent visits to paternal grandparents in a not too distant city in California and maternal grandparents in the East have been important aspects of Ryan and his sister's childhoods. When I asked Ryan, "What is most important to your family—what do they value most?" he replied: "It would probably be just being together, like being a family. And we're religious and everything but it's not like—I don't know how to say it—like shrines everywhere."

Ryan's mother suspended her career in 1975 when Ryan was born. His sister, Stacey, was born 3 years later. Committed to "being at home with her children," Ryan's mother has only recently resumed part-time employment. As Mrs. Moore explains, the early years with her children were far more important than income from outside work. She recounts spending hours with Ryan and Stacey reading, working on art projects, going to parks and museums, and generally encouraging their interests. For example, at 3 Ryan became fascinated with boats and ships. Over the years, in an effort to foster his curiosity, his parents helped him obtain books and models and taught him the skills needed to gather historical information. As he grew older, family trips were organized to visit shipyards and ports and magazines and journals on boats and ships arrived monthly. Ryan's early interest in ships, promoted and encouraged by his parents, has today become a consuming hobby. According to Ryan's mother, being at home when the children were small allowed her to encourage their interests as well as assure their readiness for school.

Also during these early years, Mrs. Moore took the children with her as she volunteered on a variety of community and church projects. When Ryan began kindergarten in 1980, Mrs. Moore worked in his classroom and, with her husband, actively participated in the school's parent/teacher association. The Moores' efforts match almost perfectly those preschool experiences identified repeatedly by teachers as ideal (and necessary) for school success.

For Ryan, boundaries between home and school were blurred from early on. Preschool activities in his home were little different from those he encountered in kindergarten and elementary school. Further, by working as an aide in Ryan's classroom, his mother paved the way from home to school, thus assuring that his transitions were barely discernible.

"A Delightful Child, An Outstanding Student"

Comments in Ryan's cumulative records for elementary school are not dissimilar to those made by his teachers in high school. A delightful child, an outstanding student, a wonderful family, are mentioned repeatedly.

> (*1st grade*) Good student, great ideas, able to express vocabulary above grade level. Interested in all academic areas. Very responsible. He is a delightful child.
>
> (*2nd grade*) Extremely capable young man who is able to deal in the abstract areas. Ryan is an outstanding student.
>
> (*3rd grade*) Ryan is performing at a high level. He always puts "his best foot forward." Ryan can be counted on to keep up on his studies. He seems to enjoy research projects. He's an outstanding student.
>
> (*4th grade*) [The teacher writes,] "Ryan, you're a wonderful person. Your enthusiasm added much to our class."
>
> (*5th grade*) Ryan is a mature, well-rounded leader. Great to have in class. Students like Ryan make teaching a very rewarding experience.

Besides teachers' laudatory comments, Ryan's elementary school records also document his early academic achievements. With little exception his report cards contain the highest marks possible and his test scores are consistently impressive. On the Comprehensive Test of Basic Skills (CTBS), administered twice in the first grade and every year thereafter, his scores range from the 87th to 98th percentile. While his math scores (66%, 71%, 80%) are lower than language and reading in the second, third, and fourth grades, by fifth grade he achieves at the 95th percentile in math with a total battery score of 98%.

Not surprisingly, by second grade Ryan is identified to participate in the Gifted and Talented Education Program (GATE). The Screening and Nominating Form for this program is telling:

> Extremely capable young man who is able to deal in the abstract areas. Ryan is an outstanding student with a fantastic vocabulary. His expression in reading is outstanding. His reasoning skills have been helped by his travel experiences. Family atmosphere contributes to opening new experiences for him. He is outstanding in all subject areas. Early ver-

balized difficult ideas. He is able to concentrate on things for a long period of time. He looks for problems to solve and is not easily frustrated.

Not only does this form record his academic aptitude, it also illustrates, once again, the congruency between his home and school worlds. Continued testing in the third grade indicates a full-scale IQ of 141 (verbal, 142; nonverbal, 130). Ryan's own evaluation of the GATE program illustrates his orientation toward challenging academic activities and his frustration with projects that he perceives as having minimal educational merit.

> Grade 2:
> (*Which activity was especially valuable to you?*) Photography, because I liked
>   taking pictures and developing them.
> (*Which activity benefited you least?*) Mother's Day card. Because I didn't
>   learn anything.
> Grade 4:
> (*Which activity helped you the most?*) Flight, I had an aviation report.
> (*Which activity helped you the least?*) Art on the Christmas card. I can draw.
> (*What things would you like to do that we have not done?*) Transportation,
>   yesterday and today.

While there is often little in cumulative records to provide insight into students' perceptions of early educational experiences, Ryan notes under *Extra Comments* on the GATE evaluation form, "I get uptight at night trying to do all my homework." He also indicates his concern about dropping behind peers in his regular classroom as a result of participation in the gifted pullout program. Ryan's written comments suggest that as early as 10 he is beginning to feel stress over academic achievement although his teachers continue to portray him as exceptionally well-adjusted and mature. It is not unlikely that Ryan's success with respect to formal standards of academic performance led teachers to overlook any psychic costs that may have resulted from pressure he felt to achieve. Ryan's elementary school teachers appear to be more preoccupied with the fact that "students like Ryan make teaching a rewarding experience."[1]

However, for the most part Ryan remembers his elementary school years as happy—according to him no particularly negative incidents occurred during this time. A motivated learner, many friends, active and involved, are the ways in which he characterizes these early years.

> Well elementary school, that was great. I was enjoying it. And fifth
> grade was great. I got into student council and I got elected president

cause I was a representative the year before and I was the only one that wanted the job. So I was like, I did that. . . . It was pretty much, everybody was everybody's friends. And I liked my teachers.

Ryan's elementary school records, interviews with his parents, and his own retrospective descriptions indicate that many of his academic and social patterns were set early on. For example, Ryan's involvement in student government in the fifth grade proved to be a precursor to his continuing interest and active role in student affairs throughout junior high and high school. Further, his expressed interest in learning and his motivation to succeed (as exemplified in elementary school teachers' descriptions) are characteristics that continue to elicit praise from almost all of the adults with whom he has contact. However, Ryan's comfort and ease in elementary school did little to prepare him for the difficulties he would face in junior high.

DISCOVERING WHO YOU ARE

"Middle school would have to be three years of hell. I hated middle school." Ryan's recollections of middle school are not only vivid, they are unequivocally negative. The smooth transitions between home and school that characterized his entry into kindergarten were not to be repeated. Ryan recounts his own foreboding. "I was very naive. I didn't know what to expect or anything from this junior high thing. It was like a whole new—I was scared. I was like truly mortified. I didn't want to go. . . . And I don't know really why I was so scared. It was just scary. I just dreaded it."

While Ryan's parents were supportive, they were unable to ensure his easy transition to middle school. Ryan's recollections provide a moving account of his attempt to adapt to the middle-school peer culture.

I mean there were some big guys walking around in the hall. And I was—I mean I was used to fifth grade so I didn't understand. And my mom. . . . She didn't understand anything about fashion or anything. And I didn't really realize it either until I started looking around and it was like, [people] not just in every day clothes but people were starting to make looks for themselves. And plus I was really into the army—in the fifth and sixth grades.

And so I went to school and I had army stickers all over my binder so they started calling me GI Joe which didn't bother me at first. But then the GI Joe stuck with me until about halfway through eighth grade and so that was—I was GI Joe—I was just—I can't imagine how I was so stupid. I did weird things. I drew like army pictures. I was still very much like a little kid.

I don't really know what made it tough for me but it was like— socially doors started to close. . . . And so while people were making their new friends for the middle school segment, I was off being a GI Joe, hanging around with the same couple of shy friends.

For the first time, Ryan found himself on the periphery of a world that was unknown. Not surprisingly, his records contains no suggestion of social difficulty and his own recollection is that no adult in his middle school environment was aware of the obstacles he faced or the emotional turmoil he experienced. In fact, all indicators are that his teachers continued to see only those aspects of Ryan that fit their image of the "model," well-adjusted, thriving student.

While Ryan did continue to do well academically, his middle-school experience was not only emotionally painful, it served to harden his outlook toward others and narrow his view of the types of people with whom it is worthwhile to associate. The antipathy he felt for those unwilling to adhere to school norms appears to have risen not only because of differences in academic orientation but also because of Ryan's perception of being socially stigmatized.

Part of the problem was also—at middle school—the only sport they have is basketball. So if you don't play basketball but you get good grades—you're nonathletic and you're a nerd. So I was aceing my classes, literally, very happy. Very happy with myself about that. And here I'm getting flack for being a nerd. . . . In middle school you were cool if you failed your classes and had general disrespect. You know, made fun of everybody else. And seems impossible but I couldn't believe it. I mean I realized it by eighth grade that that was the case. And so—disrespect for just about anything and failing—and if you played basketball, more power to you.

So then in seventh grade it started out and I thought, "Oh cool." I wasn't scared anymore. And I go in and its more of the same, elevated now because people are older. So now you're cool if you've got a record. Like a criminal record. "Oh man, you got arrested for shoplifting, right on." "Yeah. Oh yeah, five D's and an F. Way to go." It was really bad. And there was like—you were either in this big popular clique or you weren't. And there was like a select few. And they thought they were bad. I mean they were so awesome. And so it was really hard to even—I mean I hated seventh grade.

(Was there anything about that group that made you want to be in it?)

Yeah. Just that the—the feeling that you were okay. I was like, if you weren't in there, you weren't okay. There was something wrong with you. You weren't okay.

Ryan's description illustrates his encounter with peer group norms anti-thetical to those of his family and close friends and inconsistent with those promulgated by the school. While Ryan remembers experiencing some self-doubt, it is also clear that he was unwilling to jeopardize his relationship with his parents or his academic status by yielding to peer pressure. In fact, the dissonance he experienced seems to reaffirm his orientation toward achieving academically. In Ryan's case, rejection by "popular" peers and his resultant disdain for many of these students solidified his orientation toward the future and the necessity of deferring rewards.

> (*But you didn't want to be in [with the popular crowd] enough to compromise your own values?*) No, I didn't because I knew that if I did that my parents would be upset. If I started pulling D's. Plus I figured, you know, I've been pulling A's here for a year and a half. It's illogical to throw it away, so just stick with it. There's gotta be something better out there. So I didn't forget about my grades. I kept those up because I could beat the people there. You know what I mean. I could—that was a place where, yeah, I was better. Even if they didn't realize it then. I developed my—it was like a philosophy of "you can come, you can come talk to me while I'm running the country and you're working in Mickey D's for the rest of your life."

Ryan's description of his attention to school work is confirmed by his junior high school records. During sixth and seventh grades his grade point average ranged from 3.83 to 4.0. In *every* class during these three years teachers indicate "excellent conduct and attitude." Ryan's scores on the CTBS in seventh grade are in the 99th percentile in reading and language and the 93rd percentile in math. By eighth grade all of his scores are at the 99th percentile. Also, by eighth grade Ryan involved himself once again in student government—an activity encouraged by teachers but of little interest to the "popular" crowd.

In Ryan's case (and we suspect in many others) it appears that borders between student groups can become cemented during these early adolescent years. Unfortunately, many of the students that Ryan describes as possessing values and orientations different from his own are students of color. Yet teachers and others (according to Ryan) pay little attention to the effect of peer group interactions on students' feelings or the significance of students' developing attitudes and outlooks about others. Particularly significant is the fact that students' fears can lock them into patterns that mitigate against learning to connect with others. Without direct assistance from adults with respect to understanding differences and increasing tolerance, there was nothing in Ryan's middle-school experiences to dissuade him from developing stereotypes about others. Further, it is likely that Ryan internalized tacit messages prevalent in the school environment that his actions and attitudes were of value while those of others were not.

Overall, Ryan's middle-school ordeal served to solidify family and school values—the importance of academic success and achievement, the value of hard work, and the necessity of delaying gratification for future satisfaction. When Ryan encountered students whose values were not the same, it only fortified his resolve to adhere to those he possessed. At the same time, Ryan says that his interaction with peers in middle school also made him more aware of the plight of others and increased his sensitivity toward those who experience rejection. His description highlights his own need for assistance during this time:

> Yeah and like now I won't really make fun of somebody cause I've been there. And like if there is some kid—like the little kids on our street— most of the kids on our street are between six and like third grade and so if there is one of them that is getting a lot of flack from the others I'll take his side because all I would have needed earlier would have been a helping hand and I would have felt a lot better.

In order to cope, Ryan did develop strategies that would serve him well in high school. His description demonstrates his awareness of behaviors he was determined to change:

> Middle school really changed me because otherwise I think I would still be shy. Like, my friend Brendan, I don't hang around with him as much any more because its like we both went into middle school with something written on our forehead, "Step on Me, Push me Aside." Well I don't take it anymore and he still does. And it's just something you have to come to with yourself. And that's what made me not be so easily pushed aside, written off. It kind of made me want to fight more.

According to Ryan, "Nothing could have been as bad as middle school." There is no indication in Ryan's school records that any adults in the school environment were aware of his distress, his conflicting feelings about his peers, his feeling of distaste for a large part of his middle-school experience. In many respects, Ryan's experiences mirror the experiences of students described by Kinney (1993), who examines the daily lives of teenagers labeled unpopular in middle school and their subsequent adjustment in high school.

HIGH SCHOOL: THE COMING TOGETHER
OF FAMILY, PEER, AND SCHOOL WORLDS

Ryan was one of the first students identified by Explorer High School personnel as a possible candidate to participate in our study. Having been at Explorer (a school of 1,200 students) for only 2 months, Ryan was already visible in the school environment. "He will be wonderful for your study," we were told by the vice-principal's administrative assistant.

I first met Ryan in March 1990. As I explained the purpose of our study (to understand his view of the high school experience), I was struck by his interest and attention. His thoughtful, straightforward responses and un-flinching gaze suggested maturity and self-confidence beyond that of the gangling, six-foot tall, 14-year-old adolescent with whom I spoke. During this first interview I learned about Ryan's initial reaction to the Explorer High School and his general orientation toward school and learning. Over the following 16 months as I watched Ryan adapt to the high school environment, observed him in classrooms, talked with him and his friends at lunch, interviewed his parents, and engaged him in extended conversations about teachers and school, a more in-depth picture of Ryan's high school experience emerged.

What became evident is that Ryan purposefully orients toward environments where the sociocultural components of his worlds match—choosing peers with similar goals, responding most positively to teachers whose values and beliefs are in line with his and those of his family, and adapting easily to classes where expectations are clear and other students have similar goals. For the most part, elements of the Explorer High School setting make this relatively easy, since the language and communication style of teachers; conceptions of the necessary strategies for success such as compliance, hard work, and academic achievement; and pervading upward-mobility norms match the values, beliefs, and behaviors of Ryan's family and friends. To an outside observer and to adults in the setting, Ryan's high school experience to date has been exceptionally successful. Further, people's perceptions of Ryan are remarkably similar. Parents, friends, and teachers all report that Ryan is an excellent student, a thoughtful learner, and a "really nice kid, well-liked by everybody." Everyone expects that Ryan will get good grades, will behave in a thoughtful and mature manner, and will no doubt attend an excellent university. Ryan's expectations of himself are not dissimilar. "Everybody wants to get good grades because I mean now, everybody sees their future. And they realize that you can't mess around in school—you can mess around after school but you've got to be serious while you're here."

An important feature binding Ryan's worlds together is that the actors in his life move across boundaries as well. Ryan's parents actively participate in high school affairs—serving on committees and as officers in parent organizations. Ryan's teachers either know his parents or are aware of their school involvement. Ryan describes his parents as very supportive and he likes the fact that they are active (as long as they don't chaperon dances). Likewise, Ryan's friends live in his neighborhood, "hang out" at his house, and interact comfortably with his parents. There is nothing about Ryan's family (culturally or socioeconomically) that sets him apart from his friends or their families. In short, Ryan's high school experience well illuminates congruent worlds and smooth transitions.

School as a Stepping-Stone: Helps and Hindrances

There is no question that Ryan entered Explorer determined to achieve. From the beginning, he understood clearly that high school is a stepping-stone to further education and success. Ryan's comments and those of his teachers and parents indicate that he is a self-motivated and intrinsically interested learner. For example, his second-year Spanish teacher says:

> He is a neat kid and a very strong student. . . . He is an exceptional
> foreign language student because he possesses the qualities required to
> be good—for example, lack of self-consciousness in using the language.
> He looks for meaning in everything and he uses everything. He sees
> a reading assignment as a genuine opportunity to read Spanish unlike
> many students who see it as a chore. He sees an underlying purpose in
> his work and is motivated by that purpose. He is a purposeful learner.
> I often see him leaning forward, straining to understand when I speak
> Spanish. His mom told me that Ryan even talks to his dog in Spanish.
> He is a terrific and exceptional kid.

While interested in learning generally, Ryan has a view of school that is instrumental—he knows that his academic performance and the types and level of his courses are critical to achieving his long-term goals. As a result, even before entering high school (freshman course selection was made during the latter part of eighth grade) he was concerned with the implications of the overall course structure and its affect on his future. For example, Ryan wanted to be sure that the courses he took would maximize his chances for acceptance at a prestigious university. As with most high school freshman, however, Ryan had little choice in the classes he would take. His excellent junior high school grades assured his placement in accelerated English and geometry. Physical education and an experimental freshman history course (Outlook) are required of all entering freshman. With an opportunity to take two electives, Ryan had no trouble choosing Spanish, knowing that a language is necessary for college. However, he was disturbed about his second choice. Knowing that a strong background in science would enhance his high school record, he had hoped to take biology. However, learning from Explorer staff that the University of California system would not count biology as a laboratory science until his sophomore year, Ryan was persuaded to take Integrated Science. The adoption of this course and Outlook [a freshman history course] is the first attempt by Explorer staff to phase out tracking, which has resulted in minority students' being disproportionally clustered in low-track classes. (See Sonia's case for further details.)

According to Ryan, maintaining an A in Integrated Science was no problem since he had covered almost all of the course content in junior high school. Therefore, he found Integrated Science not only dull but frustrating. Further, he was concerned that Outlook, Explorer's experimental freshman history course, had not yet been approved to meet the University of California admittance requirements.

The composition of Ryan's freshman classes also shaped his views. While the efforts of staff to equalize opportunities for all students by detracking appear laudatory, Ryan's description reminds us that without careful attention to the impact of change, such efforts can serve to cement stereotyped views rather than promote appreciation and understanding of others. (See Davidson, 1996, for further discussion of this issue.)

> It's—you're not challenged a lot of times, at least I'm not, in my classes where it's not accelerated. . . . There are people in the class that, you know, sit there—"huhhh how do you do this?" (*So you think that it has to do with the mix in the class rather than the teacher?*) If the teacher—if it's an accelerated class the teacher could teach. If it's a general class the teacher can teach. But when it's a mixed [class] it's basically all general. And so many people are just sitting there twiddling their thumbs most of the time.

Interestingly, Ryan's frustration with the class was directed at other students rather than the teacher. His view is that less able students are responsible for holding him back. "It's kind of drift away. The guy next to me, he doesn't— he's not real bright and 'what's that answer, what's that answer,' and oh well it would be 'how did you know, you were asleep.'"

Ryan's experience exemplifies the fact that detracking alone does not change students' attitudes and, in fact, without attention to changing pedagogical techniques and strategies detracking can have effects that are unintended. It is clear that Ryan attributed the unchallenging curriculum in Integrated Science to the mixed-ability grouping of students. In effect, Ryan's pejorative views about less academically successful students were confirmed.

My observations and Ryan's descriptions of Integrated Science reveal a traditional classroom environment—teacher lecture, silent reading of textbook chapters, and students' individually answering end-of-chapter questions. I observed few attempts by the teacher to involve students with each other, to use cooperative learning strategies, or to highlight or draw on the various strengths of individuals. Further, Ryan explained that on the few occasions when students were asked to work together (answering end-of-chapter questions) he ended up doing not only his own work but that of less-motivated students as well. Ryan's feelings of exploitation are similar to those of other high-achieving students who are asked to work in mixed-ability groups without *any* instruction in group-participation skills. The tension and frustration these students feel is exacerbated when teachers do not communicate effectively to students the rationale behind heterogeneous grouping. For example, as I observed in Ryan's accelerated English class, an administrator gave students the following explanation for plans to detrack English the following year. "Every class in English will be mixed next year. There will not be any accelerated classes. They're putting you in these classes to help the other students along."

This kind of comment not only gave Ryan and other students inaccurate and incomplete information, it also increased his resentment of working in mixed-ability groups. His frustration stemmed, to some extent, from his perception of being "held back," and fear that his long-term goals would be threatened. Further, Ryan is explicit in his desire for classes that are challenging and his perception that mixed-ability classes preclude this possibility.

> What I'm worried about is social studies, because I don't think they're going to have accelerated [next year]. . . . And I don't know maybe it may be at my level if it's general, but I just hope it is. I hope I'm still challenged. If I'm not challenged, I have nothing to do, the class becomes—I can get a lax attitude in that class and then it seems to carry over where . . . I do more in all the classes where when one class is like boring—you punch out the homework—brainless—like a machine and then you almost end up doing that in all your classes just because you're in that mind set.

Lack of communication with parents as to the rationale for detracking also serves to reinforce negative views. Ryan's mother is troubled by what she perceives as circumstances that are less than optimal for ensuring his success.

They want to have one social studies class rather than advanced placement or honors. He [Ryan] is put into a situation where he is frustrated cause these kids aren't as serious about their studies as he is. So it creates a dislike because these kids are anchors. They're tearing him down, they're pulling him away from what he is trying to achieve. That's resentment. And resentment leads to anger.

"Pulling him away from what he is trying to achieve" appears to be the main concern for Ryan and his parents as they evaluate classroom organization and course content. Their perceptions of barriers to Ryan's maximally utilizing high school as a stepping-stone to future opportunities are important in their appraisal of his school experience.

Differentiating Classroom Environments: A Student's View

Although Ryan likes some teachers better than others, his academic performance is unaffected by his preferences—he does well across subjects. For the most part, his long-term goals and aspirations allow him to overlook, ignore, or rationalize classroom circumstances that are not, in his view, optimal. Working toward future aspirations takes precedence over any immediate discomfort he may feel because of a particular class or teacher. At the same time, his overall excellent performance also serves to dissuade teachers and administrators from considering conditions and circumstances that are not optimal.

However, Ryan is explicit about teachers' behaviors that impede his learning. For example, he described his freshman Spanish teacher as very moody, often taking out her bad humor on the students. Nevertheless, his desire to learn Spanish and his feeling that the teacher's personality, though aggravating, did not interfere with his ability to master the subject matter allowed him to overlook characteristics he did not like. Interestingly, he described his second-year Spanish teacher in almost exactly opposite terms. Although he says she is a "very nice person" he is frustrated that her pedagogical style inhibits his mastery of the language.

I don't like the way she teaches it because it was a lot [at the end]. Like my first year of Spanish, we had homework every night. You could expect it. We had our vocabulary test once a week, and we had a unit test once every four weeks. A unit a week. You learned it. . . . The teacher I had this year had been to Spain and Mexico and all these places and she had so many great things to tell you about. So we did all of these cultural readings where we got half vocabulary and half culture out of it. . . . Second year it seems like we need the tenses. We started learning the past tense in first [-year Spanish]. And we were like

drilled on it every day. And it was until you got it. It was more rigorous.
Where this was kinda hang loose.

Ryan responds positively to teachers he can understand, who play by the
rules, and who he feels appreciate him. Ryan's orientation toward circumstances that allow him to maintain control over his academic performance
(i.e., accessible materials, clear instructions, and well-organized assignments)
is exemplified by his description of Mr. Ingalls's biology class.

> It's a good class and there's nothing left to question . . . our assignments
> are there, and it's clear, so we know what we have to do and we get a
> calendar every month and it's nothing like, "Well, I'll assign this and
> I don't know when it's due." You get a calendar. I can look and I know
> when all my tests are in December. . . . There's nothing that's left
> to question.

Further, Ryan describes Mr. Ingalls as always available to help—an important quality in that Ryan's anxiety increases when he is unsure if assistance
will be available should he need it.

> Well anytime you want help, he just said, "If you want help, come in
> at lunch . . . I'll be in here." And during class, if you don't understand
> something, he just walks around during the whole class. . . . And then
> his treatment of students. It's almost like he's a student sometimes,
> because he'll be lecturing or something he makes jokes and he'll just—
> it's not the kind of class where you just sit there and take notes. There's
> not really any time to just be idle and that's good because you end up
> being more productive.

While Ryan responds particularly positively to Ingalls, even in classes
with less than stimulating pedagogy he is basically unconcerned as long as his
long-term goals are unaffected. However, receiving an A in a class does not
necessarily reduce his anxiety about subject matter comprehension. For example, although he received straight A's in his geometry class, he worried
about whether the teacher was covering the material thoroughly. At one point
he was so concerned that he contemplated repeating the class in summer
school.

> Well I think in the case of geometry the teacher is not real put to-
> gether. He kind of runs circles around himself whenever he tries
> to talk about something, just seems kind of unorganized. (*That makes
> it hard on students?*) Yeah, real hard. Cause like you try and learn some-

thing and I'm worried. I am going to take it in summer school this year. Anyway I might, because I want to make sure I know it. Cause I don't want to be behind next year.

Ryan's statement illustrates both his desire to master subject matter knowledge and his increasing concern about the impact on his ability to do well the following year.

While Ryan certainly discriminates between classes and teachers, overall he describes his high school experiences as pretty much the same with respect to teaching methods, homework requirements, and teacher expectations. Further, he says that expectations in high school are merely an extension of what he experienced in middle school—complete homework, pay attention, and get good grades. According to Ryan, "There were no big surprises."

> Overall it's the same. . . . Basically you just do your work and you listen and you take notes and everything. . . . Yeah, it's basically—it's all the same. The [same] basic rules—so it makes it easier. (*So you don't go from one class to another where the expectations are totally different?*) Yeah, and they all basically expect the best. That's the basic thing. You either do your best or—I won't say fail, but be happy with what you get when you think about the fact that you didn't do your best.

During his freshman year, Ryan adjusted quickly to school expectations. For the most part, Ryan's teachers expressed values and beliefs similar to his and those of his family. Although disgruntled with having to repeat course content he had previously covered (general science), irritated with a teacher who displaced her bad humor on students (Spanish), and worried about the disorganization of material presented (geometry), he was able to overlook his grievances as long as he perceived his goals (i.e., maintaining an excellent academic record and mastering subject matter content) as unthwarted.

However, Ryan's descriptions of social studies (his freshman year) and world history (his sophomore year) demonstrate how problems can arise when values, beliefs, and expectations do not match. Ryan's actions and responses also illustrate the types of coping strategies he adopts.

When Sociocultural Components Do Not Match

As his freshman year progressed, Ryan became increasingly disturbed with the experimental history course he was required to take. Ryan described his teacher, Mr. Kula, as inconsistent in his expectations, erratic in his behavior, and generally inconsiderate of students' needs. Further, he expressed dismay at the equivocal presentation of material and the mercurial personality of Mr. Kula. "He just basically has an attitude where he tries to scare us I think to get us to work. . . . I don't know if he likes us or not, it's hard to say because sometimes he'll be like really mean and just like snarling in a lecture, then he'll try and like total like mad . . . then he tries to lighten it up but—he sends mixed signals a lot of times."

While basically positive about course content, Ryan was most disturbed by the sequencing of materials, unclear expectations, and the teacher's attitude. "The substance was good but the time. . . . We'd spend two days on something that you should spend like a half a period on or something. The one that was really bad he was trying to teach us how to write a paragraph and a good essay. Well it was the opposite of what they taught us in English though." Despite his concerns, Ryan was nevertheless thoughtful about the curriculum (knowing the class was experimental) and expressed the view that the class had potential to be good. At the end of the year Ryan and a friend attempted to provide feedback to the social studies department and the administration. According to Ryan they purposively did not comment negatively on the teacher's personality but focused instead on things that could be changed.

> Well we had this whole, like case prepared. We had the course outline, that was highlighted good and bad. And we had a sheet for each of them. . . . And then they didn't even—we didn't even have time really to go into it—let out what we wanted to say. It was like both of us got outside, we stopped, we said, "I wasn't able to say anything I wanted to say."

This experience is a vivid illustration of the silencing of student voices. As far as Ryan is concerned, his efforts to talk seriously and thoughtfully were discounted and the lesson learned from his point of view is that students have little ability to affect change. Ryan's comments reveal the contemptuous feelings with which he was left.

> Well, they always say . . . if you have a problem, talk to them. That's the biggest—that's—you come and talk to them and they're like—and they're still right though. You might have a problem, but of course they're right, they're right from the start and they end up right in the end. Even if you're right, they're right—they say we'll talk and we can work it out. Well sure we can work it out if you're right. That's like there's only one way to work it out. It ends up that they're right and whatever your problem was—it gets discredited through [being made] trivial.

Even more disturbing, Ryan learned toward the end of his freshman year that he had been assigned to Kula's sophomore World History class. However, he soon became resigned and even suggested that maybe it wouldn't be too bad because "at least I know how he operates."

Interviews with Ryan during his sophomore year reveal an even more detailed picture of teacher characteristics that are troublesome. While other students also expressed frustration with Kula, Ryan's response appears to be exacerbated by the fact that rules and expectations in the class are antithetical to those with which Ryan is familiar (in other classes and in his home). For example, according to Ryan, Kula's expectations are frequently unclear, lectures are not relevant to material covered in exams, and it is difficult to complete work because of an insufficient number of textbooks. As a result, Ryan is left feeling frustrated and concerned about his history grade.

Further, Kula's expressed ideological and political positions are often at odds with those of Ryan and his family. Ryan's vision of his future, the opportunities promised for "doing his best," and his belief in his ability to control his life are threatened by the things Kula says.

> He will take a bird walk on a current issue, and he'll preach to us his standpoint. . . . Like he'll be telling like, "well the world is going to fall apart," basically is what he always says and, "your generation is going to be the first generation that's going to have less than your parents." And it's like, "you're supposed to be motivating us?" You know, everybody is like . . . you know, we're going to fail in life. Because that's all he talks about.
>
> I assume he's democrat from what he tells us in class about how we've had two conservative presidents, and all this stuff, and I just can't believe that this is supposed to be world cultures class when he's telling us all this stuff. . . . Yes, one-sided. I mean completely one-sided about the economy and if I want to do that I'll watch a debate on TV or something, or I'll read.

Ryan's description illustrates his increasing disdain of a teacher who "preaches" and who he feels is attempting to coerce him to a particular point of view. According to Ryan, Kula not only fails to elicit students' opinions, he blatantly extols his own positions on controversial issues:

> It's much worse this year because of the war in the Middle East. He is completely antiwar and we get his ideas shoved down our throat every day. He never asks what we think. The way I deal with it is to come in, sit down, stretch my feet out in front of me and try to relax. I get my mind to be somewhere else. Otherwise I get too mad and you have to

maintain a fine line between asking a question or making a comment and disagreeing with him because it would probably affect my grade. When he says something completely outrageous and I know for sure that there is another viewpoint that is also legitimate I will have a coughing fit. I just keep coughing—pretending like I am trying hard to stop—until he gets off his bandwagon.

While Ryan's in-class strategy is one of resistance (similar to that described by Alpert, 1991), he is ambivalent about approaching the administration as a result of his previous experience. In consultation with his parents he decides that silence and compliance are safer strategies than criticism and complaints.

> Yeah, my dad—well I always tell him stuff about it [history] and he says, "Well if it gets to the point where you can't do well in the class because of it then let me know." But until I really—I'm getting an A in the class . . . [they'll say] "well you're getting an A what's wrong with him."

In effect, Ryan's parents encouraged his compliance for the sake of his future. However, Ryan's initial shock at receiving a B for a final grade quickly turned to anger. Now perceiving the situation as jeopardizing his academic record, his response is action—rather than compliance and accommodation. In Kula's class the rules with which he is familiar (work hard, put in the time, don't blatantly disrupt class, study the material assigned) do not assure the results he expects.

> The history final—it was, I'm going to go register a complaint. . . . So it wasn't even from our book. And so 2/3 of it was nonrelated to what we had studied. And everybody after the final goes, "That was not what we studied." . . . The problem was, I got my grades and I was— I've never been so angry in my life
>
> So as soon as Mr. Acevedo [principal] comes back I'm going to go in and see what I can do because I really don't want the next people in classes—the next generation—to have to take his class again. And I tried to do that with the ninth-grade social studies but I pretty much got flushed. . . .
>
> Before I still got an A in the class. Now I didn't get an A. (*Now it's beginning to affect you?*) Yeah. When I got my A last year it's like "Yeah, that's cool. At least I got my A." Now I didn't get my A and it's there, the B grade, forever and that makes me mad.

Ryan's comments and complaints about Kula are similar to those of other students in our study. (All three of us interviewed Kula's students and observed his classes.) However, Ryan's response is unique. While many students complain, their behavior frequently takes a more passive form—not completing work, tuning out, sleeping in class, grumbling to each other, and accepting low grades without comment. Ryan's status as an excellent student and a responsible person, his already established positive connection with the principal, his own sense of efficacy and his long-term academic aspirations, motivate him to confront directly the structural borders he encountered. (In this class structural borders consisted of pedagogy that does not match students' needs, no bridges to connect students with the curriculum content, and a lack of textbooks to enable completion of work. Further, the teacher's attitude is perceived negatively by students.) Registering a complaint and expressing his views are strategies that allow Ryan to resist in a way that will not jeopardize his status. Below Ryan comments on his own response.

(*A lot of students wouldn't do that* [*talk to the principal*]. *What makes it different for you?*) Well, if I get mad enough I'll do just about anything. If it's really affecting me I'll say, "I've got to change this," just because I figure, why sit around when you can change it. And if I'm mad enough I'll do it right away. Otherwise, I don't know, it's always been, kinda, within me—it's also like my parents from the beginning, you know, "If you want something, go out and change it." It's just been like, if I wanted to make something work, I just did it.

Ryan's statement illustrates his sense of power and control and his belief that he can be efficacious in affecting his circumstances. His developing close relationship with the principal, positive feedback from almost all adults in his school environment, and the support of his parents provide a base from which he feels increasingly confident in asserting his own position.

Pressures and Stress

Teachers and administrators' perceptions that Ryan's adjustment to high school is exceptionally smooth mitigates against their "keeping an eye open" for problems that might exist or difficulties that could develop. "Oh, he's a great kid, he'll be fine," is a comment that illustrates adults' general view. While there is no question that Ryan finds transitions between home and school for the most part harmonious and uncomplicated, his descriptions also portray a school experience that is not as smooth as teachers believe. Like a number of other Type I students in our study (Phelan, Yu, & Davidson, 1994), Ryan talks frequently about feeling tremendous pressure and stress to achieve academically—that is, to maintain high grades. While he acknowledges that his own ambitions contribute to his anxiety about doing well in school, he also talks specifically about factors in the school environment that exacerbate his concerns. For example, from his perspective, teachers often overemphasize academic achievement—that is, the importance of getting get good grades and doing well on tests. Teachers' constant reminders that students' futures are at stake and their prospects dependent on their high school performance are perceived by Ryan as a thinly disguised threat about his future life chances. And for a student like Ryan, such threats are taken seriously. Over the period of 2 years, I watched as Ryan's intrinsic motivation, curiosity, and interest in learning began to take second place to his concern about grades and his increasing anxiety about how well he was doing.

> I like writing except that writing is fun until you have to do it for a grade. Like I'll think of schemes or something for my ships—like a history—and I'll write it down. It's fun to write but I always worry that I'm going to get a bad grade when I do it for school. So it seems like for school you have to write the way your teacher wants you to write.

Discussions with Ryan suggest that he spends a great deal of energy trying to comply with what he perceives teachers want in order to assure his academic success. His comments are reminiscent of the suggestions by some researchers that the use of extrinsic rewards in education settings (i.e., grades) can foster compliant behavior (Eisner, 1985) despite the fact that many teachers we interviewed said their goal is to promote student initiative. When I questioned Ryan further, he revealed an even more in-depth picture of what occurs.

> (*It's not as if the teachers are saying it's really great to learn?*) No, it's get your grades for college. . . . It bothers me because it makes messing up even harder to take. Because you think more and more, "Gee, now it's not just my grades, it's my future." . . . As a result I typically don't really relax too much.
> Yeah, [the pressure is] really incredible because I knew college was tough to get into, but as soon as you're a freshman, a naive little freshman walks in, and [from teachers] it's your grades, it's your future, don't mess up! And then, from then on it's just pressure. I don't think anybody would admit it if you asked them, because I don't think they realize what they're doing. I think they want to instill a value to get grades and for you to realize that it affects your future, but it's almost overkill because you get so scared.

While Ryan's statements apply to the school environment generally, his elaborated description reveals that stress and pressure result as well from specific classroom conditions.

> Well, it [the pressure] has to do with the teacher and the curriculum because social studies is all pressure because his tests are few and far between and worth everything . . . whereas in biology he tells us everything we're going to do and we have the book at home. We have everything we need and it's within our power to study it. So if it's put in your hands there's not that much pressure because you know you're affecting what's going to happen. It's your choice. . . . Yeah, the pressure comes when you're not in control.

For Ryan, teachers' emphasis on grades and test scores produced results that were not necessarily those intended, that is, a good deal of pressure and stress, an orientation to suppress his own curiosity and interests in order to comply with teachers' demands, and an increasingly disdainful view of a system that rewards "learning to play the game."

Ryan believes that none of his teachers are aware of how he feels. (Our interviews with teachers and administrators suggest that his perceptions are correct.) Further, he concludes that even if they did know they would probably do nothing to modify their requirements or change their orientation. Teachers are so pleased to have a student like Ryan—conscientious, hardworking, articulate, committed—that they do not consider that he might not experience the world as they perceive it. Ryan feels their lack of empathy. Further, none suspect that their admonitions to excel might actually inhibit Ryan's own motivation and interest in academic pursuits. While congruent worlds and smooth transitions suggest harmony and ease, Ryan's comments and experiences remind us that even those youth perceived as exceptionally well adjusted may indeed experience psychosocial costs that are not always visible.

PEERS: "EVERYBODY SEES THEIR FUTURE"

While Ryan's experience with peers in middle school was painful and problematic, in high school the situation changed. At Explorer, with a larger and more diverse student population than that in junior high, Ryan is able to find peers whose values, beliefs, behaviors, and orientation toward school are the same as his own.

(*So it sounds like you sought out the kids who have the same values you do?*)
Yeah, it works better that way because they all—the people that don't
really get good grades in our group, they want to get good grades
and they're always working. It's not like they're just here because the
state says they have to be.

In fact, when Ryan's peers deviated from known and accepted ways of behaving, not only are eyebrows raised but friends reaffirm with each other what
is acceptable.

(*So you don't have to explain or become ridiculed for doing homework and that
sort of thing?*) No. No, like I remember one of our friends, he was trading baseball cards the day before finals, and it got around—"he was trading baseball cards!" And everybody else was going to people's houses
to study and then here's this guy sitting out on his front lawn with a
couple of other guys trading baseball cards and it was like, "You know
what I saw him doing?" [with shock] "No way!"

Ryan and his friends are well aware that studying hard and earning high
grades are directly related to future opportunities. In many respects, these
youths are representative of the metropolitan, upper-middle-class orientation
described by Spindler, Spindler, Trueba, and Williams (1990):

> The metropolitan orientation is future oriented. Most of the time
> people within this context are planning for the future, thinking about
> the future, and worrying about the future, for themselves, for their
> children. . . . The future orientation is linked very closely to the career
> orientation. One starts planning for a career as a very young person—
> usually somewhere in the high school years but often before then. . . .
> Planning, connected with career development, and entailing advanced
> education and special experience, is a special earmark of the metropoli-
> tan upper-middle class orientation. (p. 109)

Ryan's descriptions of his peers suggest that they too have internalized
parent and teacher messages that academic achievement (as measured by
grades and test scores) is tied directly to future opportunities. "Everybody
[speaking of his friends] wants to get good grades because, I mean now, everybody sees their future. And they realize that you can't mess around in school.
You can mess around after school but you've got to be serious while you're
here."

For the most part, Ryan's school friends move easily between his family
and school worlds. Most of his friends live in his neighborhood, "hang out"

at his house, and interact comfortably with his parents. Further, at school Ryan and his friends are in an accelerated academic track and frequently have the same teachers. Teachers know Ryan's friends and are aware of the types of activities in which these "model" students are engaged.

Rarely however, do Ryan and his friends intermingle with students in other peer groups. As Ryan describes earlier, like-minded peers "find each other" and stick together. Our interviews with students across peer groups at Explorer and our many hours of observations verify students' descriptions of borders between student groups as rigid and impenetrable. Rarely did we see students talk to peers in other groups during lunch or while passing between classes—it seemed as if each group had its own designated space bounded by invisible walls. Ryan's response when asked if students in different groups associate with each other illuminates his view of differences and illustrates border-maintaining measures.

> If they speak Spanish and don't speak English, or they speak Vietnamese but hardly any English they tend to hang together. But if they speak English well, they'll hang around with other people, except for the Hispanics—they tend to hang around in gangs.
>
> Not formal gangs, just—they're kind of like a group that goes around and you see and you realize, "okay, they're here, I want to be there. When they're there, I want to be here." . . . It seems like they don't want to be bused here. So they're going to make our lives miserable here and bring with them the way they hang downtown.
>
> . . . It's because they think, well we had to get bused down here because somebody spoke up and now we don't want to be here so let's let them know that we don't want to be here.

Ryan's comments suggest erroneous assumptions and fear of students different from himself. There is nothing in the school environment to persuade him otherwise—to assist him in examining or questioning his views or in developing strategies to cross borders and develop links with culturally diverse peers. There is no assistance from adults to help Ryan know, understand, or interact with youths who are culturally or socioeconomically different or who hold different world views. In fact, there are a number of structural features that mitigate against such connections being made (i.e., tracking, inaccurate information about reasons for detracking, teacher-dominated classrooms, a primarily Eurocentric curriculum, etc.).

By the end of his sophomore year Ryan talks little about students in other groups as his own circle of friends—those whose values and goals are similar to his own—became increasingly consolidated. Ryan's one Latino friend, whom he met participating in track, came to the United States a year previously and quickly learned English. According to Ryan, Fernando, unlike many Mexican students, has a will to fit in.

> I had this one friend who came from Mexico about a year and a half ago and he's so good in English. In that case we were close because we ran track. We were close because there was no communication barrier. Yes, he ran hurdles with me, that's where I got to know him, and then we got close because we both were new at it.
>
> And the fact that he spoke English made it easier and then I practiced my Spanish on him. In fact, he's got a will to fit in. Its like the classic people coming to America, the classic thing you read about. It's the same kind of will which I don't see it in these people who come across in a bus, or a boxcar, or in the back of a truck. I think they're here for our welfare sometimes. He [Fernando] wants to succeed, he wants to grow and get better and fit in and become a better person, so it's so easy because he shares the same [ideas]. He wants to succeed and go farther and not just take it easy, then it's great.

Ryan's comments about Fernando reveal his "melting pot" ideology. To Ryan, "fitting in" means Fernando must cross the border into Ryan's world. While Ryan clearly likes Fernando and considers him a friend, he has little knowledge or appreciation of Fernando's worlds or struggle.[2]

For example, Ryan is unaware that Fernando's mother crossed the Mexican/U.S. border as an illegal immigrant following the death of her husband in the Mexico City earthquake. Since that time his mother has labored to survive economically working in Basin (a community 6 hours south), leaving Fernando with another struggling immigrant family of six in a two-bedroom apartment in a Latino barrio of Mostaza. Money for rent and food are always on Fernando's mind. While Ryan is correct in believing that Fernando is motivated to learn English and do well in school, he is incorrect in believing that he wants to "melt in" and give up his Mexican heritage and ties. In fact, Fernando's decision to run for junior class vice-president was prompted by his desire to obtain political representation and secure a voice for ESL students at Explorer. Ryan's satisfaction that Fernando won the election resulted not only because Fernando was a friend but also because Ryan needed Fernando's support to achieve future goals. Ryan is explicit about the role he feels Fernando can play in helping him connect with other ESL students.

> It's gonna be great. [Fernando as vice-president and Ryan as treasurer.] What happened was, three people ran for VP, two of them were kind of from the same group of people, so they split the votes and he got the

rest. And plus there is a large majority of ESL people—you know, students who don't vote typically so they voted for Fernando.

(*So you feel good about that?*) Yeah. And also I see it as another way because I plan on running for ASB [Associated Student Body] President this year and so if all of the Spanish speakers are involved coming to our meetings, I'll be more visible to them . . . so they'll vote for me I think when I run.

Ryan's friendship with Fernando appears to require that Fernando cross into Ryan's world. It is Fernando who has learned English—it is Fernando who has made the effort to understand and adapt to Ryan's school and peer worlds. As we have seen, Ryan on the other hand has little knowledge of Fernando's past, his present struggles, or his future challenges.

By the end of his sophomore year Ryan is increasingly involved with extracurricular activities at school, aligning himself almost completely with peers, like himself, whose social worlds revolve around school-connected events. Participation on the school track and soccer teams, involvement in school plays, planning and organizing dances, and carrying out other major responsibilities as a sophomore class officer are activities that increasingly connect him with like-minded peers. There is no question that Ryan's peer and school worlds are almost completely intermingled. Popular, respected, busy, and involved characterize Ryan's experiences with his friends.

FINAL THOUGHTS

There is no question that the sociocultural components of Ryan's worlds (values, beliefs, and expectations) are very much the same. While Ryan does not necessarily talk about the same things with his family as he does with his friends or engage in the same activities or endeavors, similarities outweigh differences with respect to assumptions about what is important, correct, meaningful, and worthwhile. Further, Ryan has little difficulty navigating the various contexts of his life—transitions are smooth and in many cases unnoticeable. The actors in Ryan's life (in particular, his family and peers) cross boundaries as well—in some cases paving the way, in other cases modeling successful transitions, and in still other cases assuring him companionship and support as he navigates the contexts of his life.

Overall Ryan is an excellent student and does well across subjects. At the same time he is discriminating about his teachers and has a good deal to say about curriculum, pedagogy, and classroom and school climate features that impact his ability to profit academically. Ryan's comments and experiences remind us that even students who appear successful (with respect to academic achievement) have a great deal to say about the specific circumstances that impact their learning.

While Ryan's transitions among his worlds are relatively smooth, this does not mean that everything is easy. In fact, Ryan describes feeling a good deal of pressure and stress, particularly with respect to teachers' unrelenting admonitions about the importance of academic achievement. From Ryan's perspective no one in his school environment is oriented toward understanding or assisting him in dealing with the pressure and stress he feels over academic achievement. Further, Ryan's primary adaptation strategy exemplifies the fact that "learning to play the game" can become a more important goal for some students than "learning to learn."

Ryan's relationship with his peers is particularly revealing. While it is understandable that he has chosen friends whose values and goals are the same as his own, what is especially critical is the fact that he has had no assistance in learning about students who are different from himself. In fact, school structures and policies appear to have exacerbated his stereotypes and cemented his views that others are less deserving. In effect, Ryan's congruent worlds appear to have limited his ability to practice or acquire border-crossing strategies—skills that are crucial in an increasingly culturally diverse society.

NOTES

1. Teachers' comments about Ryan in many ways mirror the case study of Beth Anne presented by Spindler (1987). Beth Anne and her family, like Ryan and his family, epitomize the image of what is desirable in American middle-class culture—success and achievement, the value of hard work, the validity of gratification delayed for future satisfaction, the importance of respectability, and so forth. The case study of Beth Anne illustrates how a teacher's background and culture can bias relationships with children—even "successful" middle-class children. It also illuminates the pressures and stress that such children face.

2. Fernando was a close friend of another student in our study and thus we had an opportunity to know and speak with him on occasion.

3

TRINH LE

I don't really consider myself really Vietnamese because I don't speak it, and I was raised here so it's different. . . . I don't really know anything about being Vietnamese. I don't know why—the culture and everything—I don't really feel I am very much Vietnamese.

Trinh Le appears amid a throng of tenth-grade adolescents shuffling into accelerated English at Huntington High School. Dressed in an oversized faded green T-shirt, sneakers, and blue jeans, she blends easily into the crowd. While her left hand balances an armload of textbooks against her body, her right hand pushes the black strap of a backpack over her rounded shoulder. I notice her watchful eyes behind black-rimmed spectacles, darting from one classmate to another. Trinh turns from my gaze, quietly slipping into her assigned seat near the front of the classroom.

A buzz descends on the classroom and numerous students ask questions in an attempt to discover my identity. Trinh remains silent. Half an hour elapses; the noise level rises to a loud pitch as the teacher hands back homework assignments. Students move to and fro, chatting with their neighbors and the teacher. Trinh, who remains stationary, finally turns around to give me a brief, acknowledging glance. This is the only sign of recognition she offers during the remainder of the period.

A soft-spoken Vietnamese refugee, Trinh Le typifies the stereotypical, high-achieving Asian student. Her outstanding scholastic record reinforces the general belief that Vietnamese students perform well in school. In elementary school, for example, Trinh earned "excellent" marks across all core subjects and in the eighth grade, she scored in the 99th, 98th, and the 93rd percentiles in math, language, and reading respectively, on the Comprehensive Tests of Basic Skills (CTBS). She earned a perfect 4.0 grade point average throughout middle school and the first 2 years of high school. Now, at the end of her sophomore year, Trinh ranks first academically in a class of 628 students. It is not surprising that her teachers describe her using superlatives such as "super," "delightful," "excellent conduct and attitude," "preparation shows a high degree of responsibility." These comments indicate that Trinh has been perceived consistently as a "model" Asian youth.

At a glance, it appears that Trinh crosses the sociocultural borders between her school and family worlds with ease. Trinh's fluent English skills, academic success, school involvement, and stable friendships give the impression that she has acquired the skills necessary to transcend cultural differences and adapt to her American school environment. And in many ways, she has. Not only does Trinh excel in math and science (areas in which Southeast-Asian students have consistently done well), but she is equally successful in English, social studies, and French. In addition, her interaction and regular contact with a variety of friends display her ability to adapt socially. In the classroom, during lunch time, and in between classes, I observed Trinh mingling and talking with European-American, Chinese, and Filipina peers from her high-track, college-preparatory classes.

Trinh's peers and teachers confirm my observations that she is adept at fitting in. One of Trinh's European-American classmates exemplifies this view as she compares Trinh with less acculturated Vietnamese students: "I don't think of [Trinh] as being like the [Vietnamese] people at the skating rink who speak Vietnamese. They wouldn't speak English . . . so I view them differently even though they are [of] the same race. I think there's two kinds [of Vietnamese]—those who speak English and are more American, and then the kind who keep pretty much to their heritage." Similarly, adults at Huntington, such as Trinh's chemistry teacher, think of her as well-acculturated to mainstream school culture:

> She's more bubbly and vocal than the typical Asian kid. Because she's the youngest, I would guess, she's more assimilated than [her two older sisters]. More gregarious. She's socially outgoing, and she seems to have a lot of friends. . . . Her friends are the group that I would characterize as not *quite* totally assimilated, but comfortable with themselves. They are not worried about being white, or about being labeled f.o.b. [fresh off the boat]. . . . Her friends are a mix.

Not only do these comments illuminate Trinh's persona, they also provide insight into her public presentation of self.

There are possible costs associated with Trinh's adaptation patterns, however. Outward indicators of academic success and social adaptation necessarily imply that her transitions from home to school are as smooth as they appear. Over time, as I gained Trinh's trust, a much more complex picture emerged. I found that Trinh does not see herself as either Vietnamese or American. She is caught between her family's hopes and expectations that she retain her heritage and culture and her intense desire to be accepted by her peers. These two conditions require that Trinh not only cope with bridging two disparate worlds, but that she do so at a time when the burdens of adolescent development are at its greatest.

In Trinh's case, the dual burdens of acculturation and adolescence are exemplified by her description of the marginality she feels: "I don't really think I'm American or Vietnamese. Some American people have the same values as I do, and it isn't like they're 'American,' and I don't really consider myself [Vietnamese]—just because you're Vietnamese doesn't mean you have certain values."[1]

While such feelings are not in themselves necessarily negative, they create intense pressure for Trinh to conform, and in so doing, she feels compelled to keep her school and family worlds apart. There are important characteristics of her ethnic self that Trinh attempts to conceal while at school and with her friends. Because adolescence is a time when peer acceptance becomes an overriding preoccupation, Trinh fears being seen as different. For example, Trinh describes her discomfort and feelings of isolation in classes where she is the only Vietnamese student: "I'm most conscious of being Vietnamese when I'm alone . . . in [my high-level] classes, there are mostly Americans[2] [who] I don't really know or I don't like. . . . The thing with being Vietnamese—when I'm alone, I'm more nervous over little things, more than other people." When not with peers with whom she has established a bond, Trinh is intensely aware of aspects of her background that differentiate her from her American-born peers.

To cope with the sociocultural borders between home and school, Trinh has developed strategies that serve to distract attention from herself, thus allowing her to blend in more easily. For example, in many instances Trinh submerges those aspects of her culture and nationality that she perceives as hindering her acceptance at school and among peers. Trinh feels compelled to conceal aspects of her ethnic self and, in some cases, reject those aspects. One wonders why, and what strategies she uses to cross the borders between home and school, and finally what the costs are of the adaptation strategies she has adopted.

TRINH'S PRIVATE WORLD

Trinh Le was born in 1975, 2 months before the end of the Vietnam War. With the fall of Saigon, Trinh's family fled. Her father, a pilot in the South Vietnamese Air Force, flew his family (wife and three daughters) out of the country in a small aircraft. In May 1975 the Le family arrived in the United States along with hundreds of thousands of other first-wave Vietnamese refugees who sought political asylum. Trinh was 3 months old.

Trinh's family, like other educated, professional families, was forced to relinquish all their possessions, as well as their language and culture—risking everything, including their lives, to escape political persecution. Once in the United States, after some employment retraining, both of Trinh's parents achieved economic self-sufficiency working as engineers in Mostaza's burgeoning high-technology industry. Relocating the family only three times within the United States (a low figure compared with other refugee families), Trinh's parents began to rebuild a secure and stable life. Since 1976, the Le family has lived in a predominantly European-American, affluent, upper-middle-class neighborhood close to Trinh's high school.

Trinh's family appears to have made a smooth transition to the United States. Her memories center on her parents' rapid attainment of economic self-sufficiency, the general stability of her family life, and her parents' emphasis on the importance of education, unlike many more recently arrived Vietnamese youth who speak of the hardship and the feelings of alienation their families experienced during resettlement.

While Trinh's parents tried to acquire the knowledge and competencies necessary to survive and prosper in a new society, they were equally committed to maintaining fundamental aspects of their heritage. According to Trinh, the values, beliefs, and expectations of her family reflect the basic elements of the Vietnamese value system as described by Huynh (1989)—allegiance to the family, striving for a "good name," love of learning, and respect for other people. Throughout her interviews, Trinh describes her parents' emphasis on education, their reminders to her of the importance of respecting adults (parents and teachers especially), their stress on age- and gender-appropriate behavior, and their attempts to preserve her natal culture. To understand Trinh's private world, it is essential to understand the basis of her family values, the ways in which she has been socialized, and her responses to these influencing forces.

Education Above All Else

Probably [what I value most about the Vietnamese culture] is appreciating things, not taking anything for granted, being serious, and working hard—all of this comes from all the training my parents gave me and my Vietnamese background. I think [American kids] take things for granted a lot, but some of them don't. It sounds like their parents don't really care about their kids. [If they did], then they'd make sure that their children know the [proper] values.

Education is commonly viewed as a necessary prerequisite to status, power, wealth, and the acquisition of amenities indicative of a high standard of living in the American culture. Vietnamese immigrant parents are aware of the links between education and economic attainment; nonetheless, for many, scholarship and academic achievement go beyond material rewards. In Vietnamese society, education is associated with an intrinsically higher purpose and, consequently, the learned individual is admired and esteemed by community members, regardless of material status or wealth.

Vietnamese parents also believe that they bear primary responsibility for their children's behavior, which can bring either honor and fame or dishonor and disgrace to the family. Thus, children who do well in academic endeavors bring a great deal of respect and honor to their family by virtue of collective family responsibility. In short, Vietnamese parents believe that educational attainment will not only increase their children's chances of economic and professional success, but it will also instill them with the character necessary to commit to lifelong learning—a strength believed necessary for coping with adversity and dramatic changes in their economic and political surroundings. Trinh's family reflects these cultural beliefs. For example, when asked about his expectations for his children, Trinh's father emphasized the ethic of hard work and the importance of the learning process, as well as its end results. According to Trinh, her parents consistently remind her that effort is fundamentally more important than innate ability (a view different from that found in American school culture). Her family's expectations are transmitted explicitly in family discussions that frequently center on Trinh's plans for the future and her postsecondary educational goals.

Trinh's parents further their goals for high-quality education by making strategic choices that they believe will best benefit their children: "My parents think that Huntington is okay. My sister went to a private school for about a year, but then they stopped . . . my mom got laid off. So [my sister] went to Huntington. I think if they had the money they'd wish that we went to a private school."

Trinh's parents communicate the importance of education in a variety of ways; however, they seldom cross the schoolhouse border to participate in "traditional" parent activities in school. "My parents don't really get involved with teacher/parents activities like PTA or whatever. But, they know that I do my homework, and they're not really involved. I guess they trust me to do well." Her father echoes this trust in Trinh: "I just ask Trinh to study hard. She doesn't ask me or my wife for help any homework or assignment from school. She understands it, but, I used to help her to study a little bit of English when she was very, very young. Now, she can teach me. She studies hard at school and at home. She's a good daughter."

Like many Vietnamese parents, however, the Les closely monitor their children's schoolwork, and when necessary acquire supplemental instruction outside the public school system. For example, when Trinh was young her parents were her first English teachers. When the local high school did not offer advanced-level courses, they sent Trinh's sister to a nearby state college to take classes.

While the Le family's emphasis on school achievement is similar to that of many highly motivated European-American middle-class parents, it is important to note that the cultural values that underlie the push for achievement are actually quite different. Vietnamese refugees and immigrants (like Jewish immigrants in years past) are well aware that educational attainment is the most viable means of regaining the stability and status they left behind. Trinh's academic performance to date suggests that she has internalized her parents' messages about the importance of academic achievement. It is uncertain, however, if she has fully embraced the fundamental Vietnamese values underlying the importance of education.

Observing Norms of Deference

Because of the strong norms of respect, Trinh's father expresses the difficulty he faces in reconciling differences between the Vietnamese and American cultures: "When I see children who are the same age as my children, they show no respect at all. I feel that they are very impolite. . . . The children do not respect the parents here as they do in Vietnam. Many things are different." Trinh's identity is forged in an environment where respect for family and parents come first. Below she describes her explicit awareness of her parents' expectations and the consequences should they not be upheld.

> In the family world, my parents expect us to know all the rules they laid out and know the consequences for breaking them. They expect us to help with all the chores in the house. . . . They expect our rooms to be clean, get good grades, be happy about everything they tell us to do, and never talk back. If we were to break these rule or expectations, they would probably lecture us about what we did wrong and yell [at us].

Trinh's home world is characterized by clearly defined rules and explicitly delineated norms of acceptable behavior appropriate for a young Asian woman: "My parents are very strict. I can't go out a lot."

Trinh's parents further expect that she will extend her respect for adults to her teachers. Trinh's parents model their respect for American school authority by refraining from interfering with what they consider to be the rights and responsibilities of the school (as customary in Vietnam). In fact, in Vietnam, parents usually do not have any contact with the school administrators or the teachers unless there are problems related to their children's education (Thuy, 1976).

Struggling with Gender-Role Expectations

Perhaps the greatest area of conflict in the Le family arises as Trinh attempts to be a "normal" teenager. As Trinh struggles to form her identity as a young Vietnamese-American woman, she receives conflicting messages from her family, peer, and school worlds. In Vietnamese society, young women are encouraged to exhibit behaviors that personify virtue, modesty, and purity.[3] Because Trinh's parents are aware of the greater freedom granted to American youth, they too are caught between wanting her to adapt smoothly and their discomfort at the relinquishment of their traditional values vis-à-vis appropriate behavior for female adolescents. Trinh's father is uncomfortable with the gap between Western and Eastern cultural and behavior standards. "U.S. girls are more aggressive, and to me the girls in Vietnam [act] much better."

In their efforts to transmit fundamental cultural values, Trinh's parents restrict their daughters' activities. Trinh's parents instill important aspects of Vietnamese culture in the expectations they voice and the rules they establish for their children—for example, they cannot accept rides from friends; attend unchaperoned teenage activities, even those sponsored by the school; participate in "overnights" though parents are nearby; or date. Trinh's parents grew up in a country where courting and dating are discouraged and, as a consequence, rarely practiced by the majority of young adults. In fact, American-style dating does not exist among Vietnamese high school students nor are the terms "boyfriend" and "girlfriend" found in the Vietnamese lexicon (Thuy, 1976). Trinh is intensely aware of her lack of freedom: "They don't like me to go to the amusement park with friends, because it's you know it's so crowded, and people get lost, and they think I'm going to get kidnapped. All your friends do stuff together, and I always say I can't do this, I can't do that."

From Trinh's perspective, her parents' protectiveness prevents her from participation in activities that will allow her to "fit in." She claims, "They would spy on us, eavesdrop to see what my sister was talking about. That made me mad. They think that we have to be open to them, and they can do that because they're parents." While her parents strive to minimize outside influences, their actions cause Trinh to be resentful. Trinh wishes "my parents would give me more freedom, but . . . it's sad in a way, because you miss all the fun things, and then your friends do them and you feel kind of left out."

Maintaining the Cultural and Language Heritage

> I wish my parents would understand me more. . . . I think that they are
> narrow-minded. They think I should have the same values as they do,
> and be the same kind of person that they are or they want me to be.

Although Trinh's parents very much want Trinh to adapt smoothly to the
American culture, they are determined, like many Vietnamese refugees, to
maintain the cultural and historical continuity and stability of the Vietnamese
people. Aware of the complexity of accomplishing both goals, Trinh's father
talks about taking the best from both worlds: "I explain the mixed culture. I
said in the Vietnamese culture, some things are very good, some things are
not good, and we follow the good things. . . . In the United States, the same
thing."

Trinh's parents are very much aware of the connection between language,
values, and sociocultural identity (e.g., language as an entry into culture
as well as a marker of cultural membership) (Hakuta, 1986). At home
Trinh's parents encourage her to speak Vietnamese, and they have also attempted
to persuade their daughters to take formal Vietnamese-language lessons.
Trinh describes their efforts: "Before we had to do the laundry and vacuum,
but now we don't do that anymore cause they made a deal with us that
we had to do Vietnamese lessons. They want us to learn because of our
grandparents—because they have no idea what we're talking about. And then
so we do that every weekend, for an hour on Saturday and an hour on Sunday."

Trinh's reaction to her parents' effort at language maintenance was at
best, resistant, "My mom got tired . . . cause we wouldn't really do it, you
know." Likewise, her father expressed resignation as he watched his children
lose the Vietnamese-language skills acquired when they were young. "We had
to work," he says, "and I just have a few hours—busy, we never talk to each
other, so they forget, you know, and I have to accept that." Interestingly,
Trinh's uncertainty about her cultural identity appears to be tied closely to
her view of herself as a non-Vietnamese speaker: "I don't really consider myself
Vietnamese because I don't speak it."

Another example of her parents' efforts to preserve her cultural ties is
their stated preference that her friends be Vietnamese. From their perspective,
Vietnamese youth are more likely to hold values and beliefs and practice
behaviors in line with what they consider to be appropriate. Trinh states:

> They have this thing about my having my friends be Vietnamese . . .
> and when my friends call, they would ask, are they Vietnamese? Or if
> I went out with friends, they would ask if they are Vietnamese. Cause
> they always want me to play with Vietnamese friends. . . . They're

specific about people who I should go out with. I think it's kind of stupid that they think that.

Although Trinh's parents are clearly attempting to rear and educate her according to Vietnamese customs, from her perspective, they are asking her to conform unconditionally to a set of conventional behaviors that she does not thoroughly comprehend or accept. It appears as if she may lack a full understanding and appreciation of the motives behind their concerns. As she crosses the sociocultural borders between her traditional home world and the worlds of peers and schools, her varying roles become even more complex.

"WITH FRIENDS, I CAN BE MYSELF"

The friend world is probably either the most important or second most important next to the family world. It often times shares the school world. . . . Friends are important because I can talk and share things that I wouldn't normally with my family. I can tell them things and they would see both sides of the story unlike when I tell my parents, and they usually just talk of their point of view. Friends seem to see things more clearly because they can relate to it more; whereas the parents see things how it was when they were that certain age. . . . [With friends] I can be myself without worrying of their high expectations of me. I can act silly without having them stare at me and think I'm childish like in the family world.

Each day, Trinh leaves her traditional Vietnamese family setting to join an ethnically diverse group of high-achieving friends. As Trinh makes clear in the quote above, being with close friends away from home allows her to relax, have fun, act silly, and express her individualism.

While Huntington has a sizable Vietnamese student population, none of Trinh's close friends are of Vietnamese descent.[4] This is not particularly surprising since there are few Vietnamese students in her advanced-track classes (a sizable percentage of the Vietnamese students at Huntington are recent immigrants and thus assigned to ESL classes). However, my conversations with Trinh indicate that she purposefully maintains distance from fellow immigrant youth for fear of being identified as "one of them." As I became more familiar with Trinh's peer world, I became increasingly interested in what drew Trinh to her friends as well as her reasons for distancing herself from her fellow immigrant peers.

"My Friends Understand Me"

Over the course of two years, Trinh's group of friends changed and evolved, shifting from a large, ethnically mixed high-achieving group of young women to a smaller group of primarily Asian-American youth. According to Trinh, she consistently sought out friends who shared values similar to her own—among other things, values about the importance of education. "I think [my friends] know school is important to me. And they expect me to study and get good grades. . . . They don't like put me down or anything, cause they say that school is important too."

Trinh and her friends have an unspoken pact of acceptable behavior: "Be honest, be yourself, don't put people down, don't look down on people, don't act conceited and snobby, and don't be a different person with different people." However, between her freshman and her sophomore years in high school, a number of friends in Trinh's initial peer group became increasingly involved in behaviors that she did not condone and that were in direct opposition to those she had learned at home.

> I see some of my friends changing, so I don't really hang around with them anymore. I see some of my friends not really counting on school any more. They care about other things that are not really good . . . like guys. I don't consider them bad but . . . they are getting into parties and alcohol. . . . We used to be good friends, and I wasn't good friends with them, but I liked hanging around them. And now, I can't really relate to them anymore or talk to them. That's kind of sad.

The importance that Trinh places on academic achievement and "proper" behavior is revealed in her readiness to dissolve friendships with those whose actions threaten the more deeply ingrained values she brings from home.

Trinh's two closest friends (a Chinese American and a Filipina/Chinese American) also come from families with strict rules (though not as strict as those in her family) and can thus understand, to some extent, why Trinh cannot participate in social events:

> They know that [my parents] are strict. At least I tell them that. And I guess they understand that because most of my good friends, they're Asians too. And we make fun of it because Asian parents are strict. . . . [However,] I think my parents are a little stricter than all my friends' [parents] because my friends go out more than I do, and my mom and dad, they think that I should stay home.

Although Trinh feels comfort with her Asian friends, some fundamental differences remain. These differences arise from Trinh's unique Vietnamese upbringing and her immigration experience. For example, as Trinh states above, even though her friends are Asian, most are not subject to the same degree of rigid academic and sociocultural expectations that she faces. Most of Trinh's friends are third- or fourth-generation immigrant Americans and thus their parents are removed from the emotional pain, deprivation, and cultural shock of leaving a homeland and resettlement problems in a new homeland. Finally, Trinh, unlike her friends, is reminded daily of her immigrant status by the influx of Vietnamese immigrant youth to Huntington High School.

Concealment of Identity Through Disassociation

> I don't ever share my Vietnamese side with my friends. It's not like I speak Vietnamese here; I can't—not really. We don't really talk about our backgrounds or anything. We just talk about people in the school—like teachers and friends. . . . My friends don't interact with my parents. They don't come over. My parents are weird. They're scary, that's what my friends say.

Observations and interviews with Trinh suggest that she identifies in many respects with the "advantaged majority." Trinh appears to feel that in order to fit in and maintain friendships with her Americanized or European-American peers she must conceal aspects of her ethnic self. She does so by avoiding and disassociating herself from recently arrived Vietnamese immigrant youth. Further, she hides her ethnic self by keeping her family separated from peers and school. For example, she does not invite friends to her home nor does she involve her parents in the details of school social life. When possible she conceals the identity of friends from her parents and talks little about her parents with her friends. Although she is comfortable discussing school-related issues with peers—such as homework, strategies for dealing with teachers, extracurricular activities, shopping, and boys—Trinh reserves more personal, family, and culture-related topics for other times and settings. For example, she is likely to talk about both friends and family with her sisters. In contrast to Type I students like Ryan Moore, Trinh spends a great deal of energy keeping the "actors" in her worlds apart. According to Trinh, "I don't bring my parents to open house or have them meet my friends or teachers. . . . If they knew my friends are Vietnamese, they might speak Vietnamese together, or they might embarrass us and ask a lot of questions."

Trinh's orientation to conceal her ethnic self and disassociate herself from other Vietnamese students appears to result, to some extent, from her

perceptions of how others view her ethnicity. For example, another student
in our study in Trinh's peer group made the following comment while talking
about the cultural diversity of Huntington High School: "[Students like
Trinh] are more like Americans because they've deviated away from being
Vietnamese, so I view them differently. I like to think I'm not prejudiced, but
I am. I think if they make an effort to learn the language, then I don't really
view them as being a different race." Trinh's comments suggest that the
European-American peers in her group either forget or overlook the fact that
she is Vietnamese when they blatantly ridicule Asians generally or Vietnam-
ese specifically in her presence.

> Sometimes I see people being prejudiced and racist, (not to me)—and
> it kind of bothers me. It's everywhere . . . they make fun of Asians.
> (*They?*) People, like Caucasians, but I don't mean all Caucasians. They
> make fun of how Asians speak because they have an accent. [The Ameri-
> can students] were talking about some Vietnamese people who just
> came here. They don't really like the Vietnamese because they can't
> relate—adapt to the new culture. I was just thinking that it's hard for
> them [the newcomers] to do it because everything's new. They can't
> learn a new language just like that. . . . [The American kids] don't
> exactly stereotype them, but most of them don't know what it's like to
> be in a foreign country. I was mad [when I heard them talking]. But I
> didn't really say anything. I mean it is kind of true. It depends on how
> long they've been here. Some of them—I understand that they don't
> want to learn English. They seem to just hang around with Vietnamese,
> and they just talk Vietnamese. They don't want to adapt or anything.

Trinh distances herself from recently arrived Vietnamese students at Huntington High School. At the same time, she also appears to feel caught in the
middle. On the one hand, disparaging remarks about Vietnamese youth
heighten Trinh's discomfort and her feelings of marginalization. On the other
hand, while expressing sensitivity to immigrant peers, Trinh remains quiet
and even questions the empathy she feels for these youth. Such incidents undoubtedly raise questions for Trinh about how her friends "really" view her
and what role she should play as a member of a minority group among majority peers. Trinh describes how it feels to be alone (the only Vietnamese American) among majority peers: "I think that because I'm Vietnamese I work
harder. I notice the little things more than other people—like all the popular
people. In class, I know everyone's names. The thing is, being Vietnamese,
. . . I feel I'm more alone. And then when you're alone you're more nervous
[about] little things than other people."

Trinh's comments speak directly to the sense of isolation and pressure
she feels to conform and blend into the crowd. Trinh observes, "I see some

people, it's hard on [the Vietnamese students] when people make fun of them." Trinh continues, "Some of my friends are real bigots—they're insensitive about things. And they'll make fun of people who don't really [fit in], they just want to have fun. They say how stupid they are. It's kind of mean, but . . ."

In searching for peer acceptance, Trinh fears that others transfer stereotypic attributes of recently arrived Vietnamese immigrants to her. Her concerns are heightened by the knowledge that her parents possess many of the "weird" behaviors that her friends criticize in recent immigrants. Trinh's interactions with the primarily European-American students in her classes and her general exposure to the "ideal" American family portrayed in the media accentuate the differences she feels.

> We are not a close family as many of my friends' families are. We don't talk about how the day went or go to family movies and places. I don't think I even talk to them unless necessary, and I don't eat with them because we are all so busy in our own worlds. . . . I don't feel that we have a family world as everyone else. We are close, but not in a regular sense—a sort of distant, close relationship.

Trinh's reflections accentuate cultural differences between her family and her peers and undermine the images she has of her family. For instance, Trinh compares, "I don't know if you know Valerie. Her family's really close. They do all this stuff together. And I would talk about my parents, and she'd say 'They're so mean. . . . Your family's weird.' I'd get mad." Valerie's comments make her less inclined to talk about her family and cautious about bringing up family-related matters with other youth. Such discussions possibly increase Trinh's hesitation about introducing her parents to her friends.

Even though Trinh is able to relax and share things with her friends that she is unable to share with her family, she is also acutely aware of her Vietnamese background. Even with her two best friends she is careful about the information she reveals. With European-American peers her caution increases and her comments suggest that she is fearful of the pejorative view that others might express. These interactions with friends help to transform the differences between her family and peer and school worlds into borders. She adapts by attempting to blend in with the majority crowd, quietly submerging her cultural and linguistic heritage.

MAKING A DIFFERENCE: CLASSROOM ARRANGEMENTS

> In the school world, which shares the friend world, you are expected to be adult like and responsible. . . . They [my teachers] expect me to act responsibly and do my work the best I can. I don't think they think of

me as a goof-off or totally smart either. They probably think I will always try to do my best at school and be responsible for things . . . I know that my teachers want to prepare us for the "real world" and we should act more like adults, but I sometimes feel that they want us to grow up too fast and give us a lot of pressures. They sometimes make me feel as if I'm already an adult.

Freshman English Teacher: Trinh is one of those who I would call a typical high achieving *Chinese* girl. She always has practically the highest number of points in the class. Extremely well organized, always stays on top of things, smart. Her language skills are good. The only thing that will hold her back is that she never participates at all in class. She is very, very shy about ever raising—she never raises her hand. [emphasis added]

The majority of Trinh's teachers describe her as a stereotypical Asian youth—hard working, controlled, compliant, and quiet. My observations of Trinh reveal that she exhibits many of these behaviors. For example, she consistently shows respect for teachers by working hard, never being disruptive, listening attentively, and seldom speaking up in class. Trinh comes to class motivated and serious about her learning. Her outstanding academic work and model behavior require no extra effort or energy on the part of her teachers to motivate her to learn. However, teachers expect Trinh to assume a passive role, thus missing opportunities to encourage her to express her individuality or to assist her in developing a variety of social and communication skills.

Trinh's actions and behaviors are, in fact, quite different across classroom contexts. Classroom organization and pedagogy affected both Trinh's interactions with peers and her presentation of self. The importance that Trinh herself placed on classroom structure was revealed during our interviews when she rated chemistry her favorite class despite the fact that she dislikes the teacher, and English her least favorite class despite the fact that she identified this teacher as her favorite. I became very interested in how the structure of classrooms mediate and impact the values that Trinh brings with her from home; how values from Trinh's family and peer worlds combine to affect her actions, feelings, motivation, and comfort level in different classroom contexts; and finally, how classroom organization and structure affected Trinh's academic and social growth.

In-depth observations of three of Trinh's classes provided information relevant to these questions. I describe Trinh's math class below, which is typical of classes that relegate Trinh to the role of a stereotypical, quiet Asian youth. In contrast, the structure and organization of Trinh's chemistry class allow her adolescent self to surface. Finally, English exemplifies a class that pushes Trinh to grow both academically and socially.

"He Doesn't Even Know My Name"

> *Trinh's Algebra 3–4:* The classroom is long and narrow. Desks and chairs are arranged closely in five neat, straight rows. Every seat is filled except for three in the back. I sit in the last row squinting at the chalkboard as Mr. Rose methodically explains the solution to one homework problem after another. A few students raise questions as he proceeds. As I look around about one-third of the class appears to not be paying much attention. A number of quiet conversations break out in different corners of the room as Mr. Rose lectures on. Trinh, who sits in the third row from the front, has her head down and I can see that she is quietly and diligently doing her math homework. She does not look up at Mr. Rose nor does she interact with her neighbors.
>
> Mr. Rose pauses, walks to his desk, picks up a chart and calls Trinh to the chalkboard to provide the answers to a question that a classmate raises. This request is seconded by a loud chorus of "Yeah! Do that one!"
>
> Trinh responds to this request quickly and efficiently. She rises from her seat, noiselessly walks to the board, and neatly writes the correct steps and procedures in large lettering. Returning to her seat, she resumes working on her homework assignment until the bell rings. She does not talk to anyone throughout the entire period. (Fieldnotes)

In Algebra 3–4, Trinh has little opportunity to challenge the stereotypes of Asians. Like the majority of her classes during the first two years of high school, Trinh's math class is traditionally structured, and students conform to strict standards of behavior. While the teacher lectures and demonstrates algebraic and trigonometric models and functions on the chalkboard, students are expected to remain fixed and quiet in their seats, either paying direct attention to the teacher or doing their work. I noted that Trinh often pays close attention as Mr. Rose explains a new math method (e.g., determining the signs of trigonometric functions), then appears to tune him out as she immerses herself in completing the next day's assignment. In Algebra 3–4 Trinh has almost no contact with those around her. In fact, all interactions are kept to a minimum (there are preassigned seating arrangements), and students are discouraged from working together or helping each other. The classroom environment and the pedagogical methods of the teacher serve to reinforce the values Trinh brought with her from home. While Trinh does not particularly like this class, she is *not* uncomfortable, anxious, or concerned and, in fact, she expresses knowledge and familiarity with the class routine and arrangement.

In particular, two aspects of the class put Trinh at ease. First, the teacher's demand for students' complete attention and his expectation that they will be quiet and orderly are consonant with Trinh's parents' conception of a well-ordered and disciplined classroom. While these are expectations with which Trinh is familiar in school generally, she is also able to transfer what she has learned at home—the proper way to show respect—merely by keeping quiet and doing her work. Second, unlike classes such as English or Social Studies, where students are evaluated in part on their oral presentations and participation in this class, Trinh can demonstrate her academic ability in nonverbal ways (i.e., quizzes and tests). Verbal participation in Algebra 3–4 class is limited and fact-based, and Trinh is rarely called on to participate in class—a comfortable and familiar condition for Trinh. While this highly structured classroom arrangement fits Trinh's parents' expectations of school and makes Trinh feel comfortable, the educational implications for Trinh are questionable.

Among other things, Mr. Rose's traditional methods of teaching and discipline do not allow him to get to know Trinh. According to Trinh, "Mr. Rose—he doesn't even know my name. When he called on me, didn't you see him when he went over [to his desk]—he was looking up the seating chart." Trinh is indignant that Mr. Rose did not know her name 7 weeks after the class has begun. Her feelings about the importance of a personal connection with her teachers are further illustrated as she describes a former math teacher with whom she felt particularly comfortable: "When I have a good teacher, I like [the subject] a lot more. I really liked math a lot last year, because I had Mr. Tishman. He was really nice. Mr. Tishman makes you feel comfortable and is friendly, which I think is important for a teacher to be. I can talk to him about almost anything and can joke around with him, unlike my other teachers."

Trinh's descriptions show the power a teacher can have in shaping students' attitudes toward subject matter. During her sophomore year, Trinh's positive attitudes toward math had changed. "The teacher can really make me not like a subject." Trinh explains, "Like in math, Mr. Rose doesn't expect anything from anybody. He would say 'And why wouldn't you know this answer?'"

Although Mr. Rose has clear rules regarding classroom behavior, he apparently fails to transmit high expectations about academic performance. From Trinh's perspective, Mr. Rose not only fails to establish a connection with her on a personal basis, he also creates the impression that he does not hold high academic standards—a large contrast with Trinh's experiences at home.

Mr. Rose's classroom arrangement does not permit Trinh to get to know or develop friendships with her peers. Interestingly, Mr. Rose's class has the highest number of Vietnamese students in all of Trinh's classes. Most of these are recently arrived immigrants—the same students about whom Trinh expresses so much ambivalence. Unfortunately, the curtailment of interaction among students negates any opportunity that Trinh might have to get to know or make contact with other Vietnamese-born students.

Overall Mr. Rose's pedagogical style is one with which Trinh is familiar—and one that certainly does not pose a threat. Trinh absorbs the academic content and takes charge of her own learning. This classroom structure permits her to appear respectful and responsible as her parents would wish, but the way in which the class is structured prohibits any meaningful interaction between teacher and students or students with each other. Further, Mr. Rose extinguishes rather than ignites Trinh's interest in the subject matter, and he does nothing to create circumstances that assist Trinh in connecting with her peers.

"If I Didn't Have My Friends, I Probably Wouldn't Like This Class at All"

Chemistry: As I pull up a chair to Trinh's lab table, Carla is busy completing her chemistry homework and comparing her answers with those of her lab mates. I sense that the atmosphere is different than Trinh's other classes. Here she appears to be more relaxed as she chats and jokes with Ann, Carla, and Huy. This is a side of Trinh that I have never seen before in class.

Mr. Lu announces the day's assignment and returns results on yesterday's test. Carla, Trinh, and Huy all receive 36 out of 44. Carla complains that Mr. Lu won't tell her other grades. Trinh responds, "What a dork!" and giggles. Given Trinh's usual respectful demeanor, this seems out of character.

Trinh and Ann begin to gather the chemicals, flasks, beakers, and tongs necessary for their experiment. Ann seems to be the leader, calling out directions from the instruction sheet while Trinh performs the experiment. Trinh breaks a glass test tube, incurring a loud chorus of "Oouuu! You're gonna get it!" from her classmates. Again she giggles. With 10 minutes left in the class period the teacher prepares to show some slides. Trinh shouts across the classroom to one of her friends, "What are you doing after school." Mr. Lu ignores all the bantering and continues to show the next slide. (Fieldnotes)

In Trinh's chemistry class, students are arranged in groups of four, sitting at a laboratory table (facing each other). Doing worksheets, listening to the teacher lecture, and performing laboratory experiments as a group are typical class activities. Unlike Mr. Rose's algebra classroom, Mr. Lu's classroom is structured so that students have a great deal more freedom to move about, talk to each other, and seek Mr. Lu's assistance. In contrast to Trinh's silent behavior in math, I witnessed a flurry of activities and exchanges between Trinh and her classmates on academic as well as nonacademic matters from beginning to end of class sessions.

In this class, Trinh takes on a confident, active, and busy role in the group learning activities. Trinh and Ann (a Chinese-American lab mate) usually assume the responsibility for assembling, conducting, and dismantling the laboratory experiments as Carla (a Latina) and Huy (a Vietnamese) take a less active role. Interestingly, Huy is one of a few Vietnamese youth with whom I observe Trinh interacting in her school and classroom settings. Huy, like Trinh, is a high achieving, shy, "Americanized" Vietnamese refugee who has been in the United States since 1980.

Mr. Lu tolerates a considerable amount of gregarious social interaction as students work together on their lab experiments. Even though Mr. Lu tolerates chitchat and talk beyond that of chemistry subject matter, he is aware that Trinh and her three lab mates are motivated to learn and to accomplish the tasks required of them.

How does the structure of the classroom mediate and impact the values that Trinh brings from her home and peer worlds? Although ever conscious of her family values of respect for authority and learning, in chemistry Trinh has much greater latitude to express herself and interact freely with her friends. Trinh is careful not to overstep the bounds of proper conduct, but in this class her lively sense of humor and personality emerge under her close friends' amicable teasing, support, and acceptance of her. Far from the controlled and quiet person she is in all of her other classes, here Trinh displays a rare side of herself. She crosses social boundaries with fluidity and ease. Here she relaxes, enjoys herself, and at the same time feel academically competent. According to Trinh, chemistry is her favorite class because "My friends are in there, and it's kind of a fun class, because you don't do work all the time. It's more like you move around. It's fun because of the experiments."

According to Trinh, another salient characteristic of chemistry is that the class is structured in such a manner that it does not place her under public scrutiny, that is, there are no formal speaking requirements. Further, while the teacher occasionally asks her to answer a factual question, she is not called on to state her views or in any way reveal herself. Trinh points out, "Mr. Lu doesn't really discuss a lot, he just lectures, and then we do labs."

While Trinh values the social opportunities the class arrangement affords her, she is, at the same time, openly critical of the learning experience. According to Trinh, Mr. Lu does not meet her standards of a good teacher, thus lessening her respect for him. "Mr. Lu, he's a fun teacher, but he doesn't want to teach. . . . He knows [the material] but he doesn't feel like giving it to us. Sometimes he lectures and sometimes he doesn't. But the way he lectures is hard to understand. You get really confused about the chapter."

Mr. Lu's unpredictability is also an issue for Trinh, who says, "I don't really know what he thinks. It's hard to read him. Because sometimes he would joke, and sometimes he would be really serious, and you don't know what to expect. He doesn't talk to me at all." Also, according to Trinh, Mr. Lu is not consistent in evaluating students and "plays favorites."

Doing well in chemistry, a subject she particularly likes, is important to Trinh since she plans to pursue a career in medicine, which requires a solid grounding in science. Nevertheless, Trinh expresses frustration at Mr. Lu's inability to further her understanding of this complex subject matter: "I get confused a lot in that class. . . . And the way [Mr. Lu] talks. It makes me more confused. Then, I'd have to ask my friends . . . and it makes more sense sometimes." Trinh welcomes the opportunity to work with others. (In four out of five classes, Trinh says that she will go to friends before going to the teacher or others for help.) From her perspective, the friendships that she has established in chemistry are critical in terms of her feeling secure in being able to get the assistance she needs in understanding course content: "It helps a lot [to get help from friends] because Ann usually knows the answers . . . she took a lot of science. I think science is her favorite subject, and I think she's really good in it."

In sum, Trinh enjoys this class tremendously but not for the reasons we might suspect. The teacher does not conduct the class in a manner that commands her respect, or that she feels gives her a particularly good foundation in chemistry. Rather than feeling particularly connected to the teacher or extremely competent in mastering subject matter content, Trinh is free to shed some of her inhibitions—that is, she interacts freely with friends, develops friendships with those she normally would not have (Carla and Huy), and displays a rare playful adolescent side of herself—because of the way the class is structured.

Optimal Mismatch

Accelerated English: Chairs arranged in five rows. Trinh sits in third seat from the front in second row. Some students are seated—others standing, talking, mingling as they wait for class to begin.

Teacher: "Ladies and gentlemen. Take out one-half sheet of paper and number from one to ten." Students continue to talk as they prepare for questions. "This is in-class exam #5. Number one." Complete quiet as teacher reads ten short-answer questions on assigned reading in *To Kill A Mockingbird.* "Turn papers over, pass forward." Students imme-

diately begin to talk to one another about answers. Teacher collects
papers and passes them to a different row as he interacts informally
with students. Talking about questions continues. Papers corrected as
teacher elicits answers from students. (15 minutes)

Teacher: "Next, take out vocabulary books. We're on page 23."
Teacher calls on student. "Just give the answers so we can move on."
Students correct papers. "For tomorrow take care of synonyms and
antonyms, please." (10 minutes)

Teacher: "Please move your chairs for discussion." The 29 students
chat quietly as they move their chairs into a large circle. *Teacher:* "We
are on chapter 11, which is a story within a story. Could someone sum-
marize?" Teacher proceeds to act as facilitator asking primarily open-
ended, higher-order questions. A discussion ensues with students talking to each other as well as answering the teacher. Trinh does not spontaneously volunteer to talk. Mr. Sugimoto specifically calls on Trinh
and a couple of other students who are quiet. "What are your thoughts
about . . . ?" (Fieldnotes)

Trinh's accelerated English class is unique in that Mr. Sugimoto structures
his class in a creative and unconventional manner. Mr. Sugimoto develops
meaningful relationships with his students and pushes Trinh to grow both
academically and socially. From Trinh's perspective, Mr. Sugimoto uses a diverse and dynamic set of teaching techniques to which she and other students respond.

Mr. Sugimoto, he doesn't do one thing every day. He does different
things in one day so someone won't get bored. Actually, we're reading
Othello now, we'll do that, then we'll have a project to do, all these different things that we do. He'll sometimes give examples of achievement
tests, and that is really helpful. And grammar, the difference between
subjects, when to use them, and . . . he helps us get ready for the SATs
and the PSATs. We sometimes practice analogies and vocabulary. He
knows that people get bored.

Trinh recognizes and appreciates the variety and stimulation of Mr. Sugimoto's class. He not only teaches grammar, vocabulary, and literature, he also
engages students in meaningful discussions and cooperative group work. Further, he requires students to develop individual presentations and to do a great
deal of writing on academic and personal topics. Trinh and several students
in our study also identified Mr. Sugimoto as a rich resource for college information.

Trinh expresses admiration and respect for Mr. Sugimoto and describes him as a caring, understanding, and resourceful teacher: "The teacher's good, really nice. I mean he actually cares because he helps you to get ready for college. He's not really strict, and if you answer something wrong he wouldn't make fun of you. He'd just say no and go on with it."

One of Mr. Sugimoto's explicit goals is to establish a safe environment in which students can take risks and grow. At the same time, he makes it very clear that his academic expectations are high. Trinh as well as other students talk a lot about the stringent academic requirements in Mr. Sugimoto's classes and the fact that his classes are hard. At the same time, Mr. Sugimoto is perceived as fair and impartial (unlike Mr. Lu). As Trinh says, "He doesn't—you can't really tell if he favors anybody or not. Cause he asks mostly the same for each student."

While Trinh responds positively to Mr. Sugimoto (she identifies him as her favorite teacher) and speaks appreciatively about his efforts to assist her academically, she is often uncomfortable and reluctant to participate in his class. In fact, she is explicit about the reasons she dislikes having to express her views verbally and in writing. "I always wonder what people think about me. And, this weird stuff, my [English] essays, and stories and ideas, and stuff. It's not really, it's pressure on me . . . that's why I don't [write] personal type stories." In a sense, Mr. Sugimoto's activities and assignments require her to reveal herself in a more intimate and personal way than she would like. Being required to participate verbally makes Trinh visible—exactly what she tries to avoid. As she says, "I just don't feel comfortable in that class [English] . . . I don't know . . . it depends, if my friends were there, then I probably would."

While many of Trinh's teachers speak of her shyness and reluctance to speak in class, most consider these characteristics typical of Asians. Aside from Mr. Sugimoto, none of Trinh's teachers go beyond stereotypic views to try to understand Trinh's unique situation or consider the types of opportunities that will enable her to develop new communication skills. Mr. Sugimoto comments on Trinh's protective attitude:

> That one I know. . . . She could be pretty quiet if she chose, but I think she comes out of her shell more. . . . When she gets in group situations she will not [speak up]. . . . She's very thoughtful, pensive. But I feel that she really chooses her words very, very deliberately. And I don't know if . . . she's just trying to be protective. Her mind is rapidly working, and she's worried about whether the words are exactly what she wants.

Rather than allowing Trinh to remain comfortably withdrawn, Mr. Sugimoto makes specific attempts to involve her actively in classroom discussions. His comments suggest that he purposefully pushes her to share herself in a context in which she feels safe but challenged. Not surprisingly, Mr. Sugimoto's methods are not those with which Trinh is the most comfortable.

> When we discuss a book he makes us go in a circle—which seems big to me—and that's the way we have discussions. And when he asks questions, he usually picks some of us rather than having us volunteer. I just don't feel comfortable in that class. . . . Most people can volunteer, but I don't like to. If I had my friends there, then I probably would, but I don't really know all the people in the class. Whenever he asks me questions, and he picks on me, I have no idea what to say . . . I'd rather volunteer than be put on the spot.

Trinh describes her *actual* participation in Mr. Sugimoto's class as "never." She further admits that she tries to elude the spotlight no matter how prepared she feels, "I kind of know what the answer is but I just don't really know how to say it, and I don't know if it's right. He tries to make me feel comfortable, but it doesn't really help."

Despite Trinh's discomfort, in Mr. Sugimoto's class she is forced to practice skills and behaviors that she has not previously developed. In a sense, Mr. Sugimoto is instrumental in helping Trinh cross social and cultural borders and in empowering her to connect with ethnically diverse classmates in a different way. While Mr. Sugimoto creates discomfort, he also earns Trinh's highest respect. Trinh's participation in this class also helps her to begin to develop a different conception of herself. By the end of her sophomore year, she is able to articulate some of the areas (promoted by Mr. Sugimoto) in which she has grown: "I think this year, I'm kind of better at it [public speaking] than last year. Last year, I would just get up there and read it out loud or memorize it and not know what I'm saying. But this year, I'm kind of ad libbing. But I'm still nervous . . . I guess my personality has changed . . . I think I'm more open now than before."

Like Ryan Moore and Carmelita Abello, Trinh consistently performs well across her classes. However, the teacher, the environment, and the composition of peers influence greatly her level of comfort and her motivation to learn. While Trinh's views help us to understand the context of school and classrooms from her perspective, the analysis also reminds us that what students perceive to be the most "comfortable" may not always be the most positive with respect to learning. In order to understand and appreciate Trinh's unique circumstances it has been essential to explore fully her rather baffling report that Mr. Sugimoto is her favorite teacher but English is her least favorite class.

FINAL THOUGHTS

Although Trinh demonstrates high scholastic ability and model behavior, the costs associated with her attempts to "fit in" and hide who she is may well be great. A number of other authors also speak to the dangers and myths of "model minority" stereotypes (Chun, 1995; Lee, 1996; Suzuki, 1995). When Trinh attempts to overcome feelings of isolation by "fitting in," there is a danger that she may feel it necessary to devalue aspects of her home and community cultures, in addition to emotional costs and danger to individual identity. In distancing herself from her family, Trinh cuts herself off from an important source of emotional support. She is clear that she finds it difficult to seek comfort and solace from her parents, who fail to understand her "new" world.

There are also school and classroom consequences. Many of Trinh's teachers are puzzled by the Asian model of parent involvement and rarely understand the cultural beliefs behind Trinh's parents' practices of limited involvement at her school. They continue to assume that active parent involvement (as defined by European-American middle-class standards) in the school *setting* is essential to student success. There are weaknesses in this assumption. Trinh and many other Asian students are academically successful despite their parents' minimal contact with the school. (Trinh's parents do not belong to school parent organizations, visit the school, or call her teachers.) Traditional parent-involvement strategies frequently fail to take into account significant language and cultural barriers that block refugee parents from being involved. Vietnamese parents, however, are very interested in what occurs in American schools. For example, they very much appreciate it when schools make Vietnamese-speaking liaisons available to assist them in becoming more involved in ways that are consistent with their cultural orientation.

At the classroom level, Trinh's limited participation restricts the exchange of ideas. Within the broader school context, an important opportunity is lost when students like Trinh feel uncomfortable connecting with less assimilated Vietnamese students in their school environments. In many respects, Trinh has the skills and abilities to model border-crossing strategies and to assist others in transitions between contexts but her strengths go untapped. Instead, Trinh's energies are directed toward protecting herself in an environment that fails to value and promote the unique and important aspects of her heritage.

NOTES

1. Trinh's experience is similar to that described by Rumbaut and Ima (1988), who found that refugee youth of the 1.5 generation (Vietnamese-born children of

adult refugees) face a double crisis: adolescence and the task of managing the transition from childhood to adulthood, and acculturation and the task of managing the transition from one culture to another. Unlike older refugee youth who arrive post-puberty (after the age of 15, with a largely formed Vietnamese identity and orientation), younger Vietnamese youths' struggle with adolescence is intertwined with a search for ways of balancing home and host cultures.

2. Like many other immigrant minority youth, Trinh uses the term "American" to refer to European ("white") Americans.

3. Old Vietnamese customs suggest that a "good woman" must possess four feminine virtues: traditional home economics arts and skills (housework, cooking, needlework); feminine deportment and appearance; gentle and careful speech; and good and virtuous conduct (Thuy, 1976).

4. Huntington High School is the designated center for Vietnamese newcomers in Mostaza District. In order to consolidate resources, the district channels recently arrived Vietnamese youth to Huntington and recent Latino immigrant youth to Esperanza High School. Huntington's student population is 40% European American; 19% Vietnamese; 27% Latino.

4

PATRICIA SCHMIDT

ON BEING A "REBEL"

I just want to get an education, cause I want to go—I want to break the
line between, you know, like Northside and the whole—it's like two different kinds of communities. Like I just want to go over that line and
show people that not all people where I live are as low. They [people
where I live] have low life standards and it's not true. . . . I've got as
much intelligence as anybody else.

Every weekday morning, Patricia Schmidt—daughter of a Mexican immigrant mother and an American-born father of Eastern-European an-
cestry—boards a school bus in Northside to ride 45 minutes to Maple High
School.[1] At home, Patricia speaks both Spanish and English and spends the
majority of her time with her boyfriend, a Mexican immigrant. Her community is comprised primarily of African-American and Latino residents, the
majority of them poor or working-class. Maple is located in a primarily European-American, middle- and upper-middle-class attendance zone. According
to Patricia, the "line" that separates her Northside and Maple communities is
not simply geographic. Rather, from her perspective, a false Northside personality is promoted by Maple and Northside residents alike, as the cultural
and economic differences between Northside and Maple communities are
translated into a set of negative expectations about what it means to be from
her section of town:

Kids that come from Maple I guess [are] sort of in their own world,
because they know the people that are up here and they hang around
with them. I guess I believe that, you know, the kids up here [in Maple]
have a stereotype of the kids that like get bused in. You know, they're
from Northside, there's gangs, there's violence. You know, they always
do this. . . . Down there they don't really—nobody notices you. (*You
mean Northside?*) [nods and continues] Cause they don't want to be
expecting too much. They just know you're there, it's not going to

impress them. . . . They don't give you credit for who you are. You're just there, cause like really if an older person sees you walking down the street, they go "Oh another low life."

Thus, Patricia as well as her fellow Northside peers must grapple with difficult socioeconomic and sociocultural borders as they navigate their courses at Maple High. Patricia is one of a small number of students who stand out in their ability to make the necessary transitions. Patricia maintained a 3.83 grade point average (GPA) in challenging courses, including advanced English, geometry, and computer science, during her sophomore year. In all, during the fall of her sophomore year, 13.5% of Maple's Latinos had GPAs between 3.0 and 4.0.

For Patricia, educational achievement is a means not only to attain personal goals, but also to challenge social stereotypes. In her personal effort to dispel notions about the borders she perceives between her home and school communities, Patricia adopts an unconventional strategy. In both self-presentation and voice, Patricia resists hiding either the "schoolgirl" high-achieving aspects of her character from her working-class peers, or the working-class, Latina aspects of her heritage from her European-American middle-class peers. On her bright yellow notebook, for example, Patricia plays with words from two cultures to proclaim her romantic attachment: Patricia con Roberto, Patricia and Robert, Patrice y Roberto. In her advanced English classroom, she moves without inhibition between English and Spanish while speaking with her Latino classmates. In Spanish, she talks and jokes with friends from her neighborhood yet also returns to her seat, despite their protests, to continue her seatwork. In her active fund-raising efforts for the school (she was the top fund raiser during her freshman year) and her participation on the school's swim team, Patricia also publicizes her allegiance to Maple High.

Patricia's defiance of "typical" standards of behavior have earned her a reputation among peers and teachers alike. Friends from Northside call her "the rebel" while Patricia's teachers describe her independence and readiness to forcefully challenge the ideas and assumptions of her peers. Patricia herself asserts that she is adamantly opposed to conforming to others' expectations:

(*Do you ever feel like you kind of have to change the way you act around certain friends? . . . Do you have to put on one face for some people, and another for other people?*) No, I really don't think I have more than one face. I, you know, they're all—I really think of it as if they don't like me for who I am, I ain't gonna' change for 'em. It's just me. And maybe in time I might evolve in to something else, but, until that time I ain't just gonna snap my fingers and say "Hey, starting acting like this cause that's how, the way they want to see you."

As discussed in Chapter 1, one strategy for crossing social borders is to play different roles in different settings. However, Patricia rejects this strategy: "I don't, personally I wouldn't want to be something that I'm not. I wouldn't, you know, try to play the role. Unless it's in a play."

Patricia's nickname indicates that she has succeeded in asserting an independent identity that her peers find hard to pin down. Yet, as Patricia asserts her "rebel" identity, she distances herself from affiliation with a social group during the prime of her adolescence, a time in American society where, according to some scholars, fitting in is of supreme importance (Chandler, 1978). Who is Patricia Schmidt and what makes it necessary for her to distance herself from peers as she asserts her rebel identity? And what has enabled her to navigate the significant borders between her community and school?

Where Is Patricia Coming From?

Northside has always been Patricia's home. Her mother, who grew up in Veracruz, Mexico, emigrated to the United States when she was 26 years old. Divorced three times and the mother of six children, Patricia's mother earned her GED at an American city college. While working as a waitress in a local cafe to support her family, she met Patricia's father, who had joined the navy immediately after graduating from a high school in Montana, and returned to a local city college for vocational training after his marriage. Currently, he works as a machine distributor, while Patricia's mother stays at home and has not been employed during the marriage. Patricia and her younger brother are the last of her mother's eight children.

The play of Mexican and American cultures is a central feature of Patricia's home life. Multilingual conversations are not uncommon, as Patricia's brothers and father understand Spanish but are uncomfortable speaking the language, while Patricia's mother understands English but prefers to speak Spanish. (Patricia speaks Spanish with her mother, English with her father and brothers.) Patricia's mother has retained strong ties to her large extended family, and Patricia has fond memories of spending almost every weekend in Mexico with aunts and cousins during her elementary and middle school years:

The country, I don't [know], it seems peaceful, more peaceful. Even though, you know, it seems more dirty. I don't know, it's just a peaceful environment to be in. Cause when you drive there you can see all the grass and the ocean and everything. I don't know, I like it down there. . . . Family down there was closer. You know, they had more fun together. Activities and stuff . . . everybody chipped in. With the housework and everything.

Patricia's interest in the Mexican aspects of her heritage and her desire to maintain and improve her Spanish-language skills developed during this period. Explaining why Spanish is her favorite course, Patricia referred to her early childhood experiences:

> I've got a real interest in Spanish because I want to learn about it and its culture. . . . It's because when I was growing up my mom and various others—well she spoke about her hometown, Veracruz, since I was little and I've been wanting to go there. So that got me interested a lot in Mexico and then a lot of my Mexican relatives, they still live in Mexico, and we used to go over there a lot and we stopped.
>
> Then no more Mexico and then so it was like I've had this interest for a long time. It's just, I never wanted to speak—well [when I went to Mexico] I wanted to speak Spanish but I was embarrassed I would say something wrong. So since I was little I knew how to speak it and everything but I just didn't want to.

Patricia views Spanish as a means to develop the Latina aspects of her transcultural identity, as a means to improve her Spanish-language skills and thereby gain the confidence necessary to display the linguistic aspects of her heritage when she crosses the Mexican border.

Aspects of home life, says Patricia, also reflect her mother's Mexican upbringing and values. In particular, Patricia's mother expects her children to place the family before self-interest (two of Patricia's older siblings give her mother half of their paychecks to help support the family) and asks Patricia, rather than her brothers, to stay home to help her with the housework and babysit her niece. On the other hand, independence and self-reliance are supported by Patricia's American-born father. According to Patricia, these differences are reflected in her parents' conveying varied cultural expectations for proper female adolescent behavior:

> My mom, she sort of got mad at my dad because he lets me do what I want. And she—my mom—told him "A Mexican dad would never do this." And my dad did not like it for anything! He said "This isn't a Mexican family, remember? You didn't marry a Mexican, you married me." He goes "I want to raise people the way I want to. And I want to—I trust my daughter." So, that's like the main thing that ever hap-

pened with my parents. . . . Maybe it might be true but he didn't like it for nothing!

Trying to satisfy her mother's demands while at the same time developing her independence has been difficult for Patricia during her first two years of high school.

> I don't want to stay home! You know, I'm at that age where I want to go out. But, I clean around the house and I help her with the house and everything. And I feel like, you know, I help her with the house and everything, and I should have that privilege to go out since I already helped. . . . She likes to stay at home just sitting there. Just sitting there! Not doing nothing.
>
> But, I don't know, maybe it's one of those Spanish traditions, where the girl stays in. And I just, that's what I think most of it is, that she grew up in a family that girls stay home, guys go do whatever you want to do. But I don't know, it just gets me frustrated, because you know, it's the United States. You have certain—you know, it's not like that. You know, equal, equality! And I'm just frustrated, God!

While it is clear that Patricia values many aspects of her Mexican heritage, she critiques and resists traditions that limit her movement and status.[2] She asserts a contemporary U.S. vision of the female role.

Socioeconomic pressure is a second defining feature of Patricia's home life. During Patricia's freshman year, her father worked two jobs in order to raise the family income. At times, the tension associated with making ends meet erupts into family conflict:

> You know, me and my mom never got along. Never. We still don't get along. It's calmed down, it's just when I get mad at her I just go in my room. . . . But, she has gone down to a point where she can't control it and then she tries to hit me or my little brother. My brother still runs, he'll still run. He'll just try to get away from her. I won't run away from her, you know. She wants to hit me let her hit me, cause she's going to get hit back. . . . (*What gets your mom angry enough to hit you or your brother?*) It's just the family. We've always had family problems. Cause it's a big family, a very big family, my dad married my mom when she already had six children and since then, I don't know. And then economic problems, money problems and stuff. They used to be always like [fighting], before [the] water [bill] used to be over $100 a month and the phone bill was high too, everything was high.

Patricia's desire to achieve as well as her varied stints at part-time jobs partially reflect her desire to escape the stress and constraints she associates with economic uncertainties.

While Patricia is at times critical of her parents, she consistently and positively describes their efforts to assist her with her transitions between home and school worlds. During her elementary years, Patricia recalls her father and mother quizzing her on spelling and vocabulary and praising her academic achievements. Patricia's father still readily contacts the school if she runs into difficulties or if he feels that she has been treated unfairly: "My dad, he calls—he called Miss Haight [Patricia's counselor] . . . about the grades. He wasn't satisfied either, he thought I deserved more and then they discussed it." Because neither of Patricia's parents has an advanced education, they have become increasingly unable to assist her with her advanced schoolwork: "They don't really help me in my studies. Cause I'm really—in my studies I'm independent. I've become very independent, unless I really, really need the help." However, within her family, Patricia can look to her half-brother Martin, who graduated from Maple and attends a local state university, for support. Through her ninth-grade year, Martin helped Patricia with math, while she helped type his essays for college in exchange. In addition, it continues to remain clear to Patricia that her parents expect much from her:

> They expect a little bit more out of me than the rest, my brothers and sisters, they always really did. And sometimes I just get frustrated. Like when they saw the C's and they started yelling at me and I got mad, because I was trying and well I knew I could do better but I was putting my effort into it. And I was really mad, because I remember when my brothers and sisters got C's on their report cards they didn't really mind. "That's good, at least you didn't get an F." And they told me "What's wrong with these C's, why aren't they A's?"

As Patricia notes above, she and Martin stand out in the family for their academic achievements. Of Patricia's half-sisters, the oldest lives in Mexico and operates a store, the second dropped out of college during her first year to marry someone in the military, and the third has borne three children and lives on public assistance. Patricia has never met her oldest half-brother, but believes he went to college. A second half-brother works in Adobe Viejo and is estranged from the family.

A perusal of Patricia's early school record provides insight into her parents' high expectations. Through elementary school, teachers cite Patricia's excellent attitude and academic ability: "She readily accepts responsibility for completing daily assignments and is eager to help others," comments her first-grade teacher. "What an excellent young lady to have in class! I expect great things to continue to happen to Patricia," adds her third-grade instructor. Patricia's CTBS scores also reflect steady educational progress. On entering kindergarten, she tested at the 45th percentile in language and the 72nd percentile in mathematics. By the end of her sixth-grade year, these scores had increased to the 88th percentile in math, the 72nd percentile in language, and the 64th percentile in reading. In the third grade Patricia was identified to participate in GATE (Gifted and Talented Education). In middle school, Patricia maintained a 3.53 GPA and received 16 excellent, 3 good, and 4 satisfactory marks in citizenship over a two-year period. Her California Test of Basic Skills (CTBS) scores in seventh grade again reflect improvement: Patricia scored in the 99th percentile in mathematics, the 95th percentile in language, and the 77th percentile in reading.

For Patricia, the ability to cope with socioeconomic hardship and sociocultural differences began at an early age, as she began to work out her relation to her mother's and father's different cultural expectations. Borders between her home and school also became apparent early on, as she saw that her high academic achievement differentiated her from her older siblings, and she realized that her economically strained home life was vastly different from that pictured in the typical elementary school primer. Borders have become more apparent over time, as Patricia has realized that her parents can no longer aid her with her schoolwork, nor help her with the college application process. However, she also is aware of their support and their hopes as she works to succeed academically.

Peer Relationships: Learning Social Categories

> Sometimes they'll call me nerd. Ha-ha. I don't mind. Like it doesn't
> bother me for nothing. And then they said "Future vice-principal of
> a corporation, beauty and brains all in one." It made me happy. . . .
> I don't really have that many friends. Oh, I got friends that like hi, bye,
> like that, but not so many that I really could get close to. I don't
> trust people.

From all outward appearances, Patricia is popular and highly social. For example, as I spent time with her during the school day, Patricia chatted and joked with classmates during passing periods and classes. Students called greetings as we moved through the hallways, walked us to classes, and approached Patricia during the lunch hour. Confirming what I had observed, Patricia's Spanish teacher commented: "I've talked to Patricia some about who she hangs out with, and she describes herself as a loner. But, she's not antisocial. She talks with people in the class and she gets along with all the students. I'd describe her as very independent." Yet, despite outward indications of popularity, over two years of high school, Patricia has come to believe that it is necessary to maintain emotional distance. Patricia views herself as a loner who protects her inner thoughts and feelings from all but her boyfriend.

In listening to Patricia over two years' time, it became increasingly apparent that her reticence to form close emotional bonds with either Northside or Maple peers stemmed largely from her belief that peers reify rather than challenge the borders that lie between Northside and Maple communities. Patricia's perspective emanates from her experiences with school peers over her first two years of high school.

For example, Patricia explained that significant breaks with Northside peers first occurred when she refused to conform to their visions of proper female behavior. At the beginning of ninth grade, Patricia was deeply embedded in a Northside peer group, spending most of her time at school with one member in particular—her popular, academically low-achieving boyfriend. Patricia spent many school days during this period either at the mall or at her boyfriend's house (often cleaning for his sick mother). While she maintained a 3.0 GPA during the first semester of ninth grade, during that same marking period three teachers gave Patricia an unsatisfactory or needs-improvement citizenship grade. Four out of six teachers noted her excessive absences and truancies. (Patricia's absences in these classes ranged from 16 in advanced world history to 24 in algebra during this period.) Midway through ninth grade, Patricia ended her relationship with her boyfriend. Patricia's decision stemmed from the fact that he tended toward fits of jealousy, which he expressed in physical violence, and also from the fact that he pushed Patricia toward a more traditional female role. In particular, he discouraged her academic achievement, involvement in extracurricular activities, and desire to go to college:

> He didn't want me going to college for nothing. And I had my mind set on it. And like the swim team—I was on the swim team and my ex-boyfriend didn't want me to go on it. And he's like "If you get on it you're going to break up with me." I said "Fine!" Cause it's, he must have some, he must not trust me or he just—I don't know. . . . And then I guess in a way, cause I think about it now, and it's like he's jealous that I did well in school this year. Cause I didn't even really try and I still did well . . . and then I got on the swim team and, I don't know, we just quit.

From Patricia's perspective, while involved in this relationship, she was transformed into someone far removed from her "normal" self: "It's just—when I broke up with him I looked back and at times I just realized that wasn't me, it was some other person I changed into." Reflecting on this relationship, Patri-

cia concluded that this boyfriend and his friends also exerted a negative influence on her schoolwork. Her conclusion strongly influenced her decision
to establish independence from school peers in order to focus on her education: "I don't spend much time around my friends, because after Javier, it's
not, it's been different. . . . I don't communicate as much as I used to . . . and
I get better grades in school, than before, cause too many people were my
friends."

At the same time Patricia was involved with male peers as a ninth grader,
she had also established close relationships with female peers from her Northside community. Up to the end of ninth grade, Patricia spoke enthusiastically
about two best friends, both younger girls who attended the middle school
neighboring Maple during Patricia's freshman year: "I can tell [them] all my
problems about my family and friends and other people in the school." According to Patricia, these friends also understood her pro-school orientation.
Again, however, breaks with these peers occurred as Patricia revealed increasing ambition and independence. In this instance, Patricia began working long
hours in order to earn money and thereby establish some independence from
her parents' support. This decision limited the amount of time she could
spend with her friends. Further, the uncle of one of these friends employed
Patricia. When Patricia accepted the job he offered, she knowingly took a
position that this friend wanted: "If I knew at the time that she needed the
job I wouldn't have, but her, she already had two other jobs, and another uncle,
so, I figured that she had more money coming in. So, I needed the job to get
me the things that I wanted to get."

In asserting her ambition over her peers' wishes, Patricia angered her
best friends. When they began to gossip about Patricia's breach of social eti-
quette to others in the neighborhood, Patricia says she responded by building
an emotional barrier between herself and others: "I don't trust people. I can't,
cause I did it before and I got stabbed in the back, you know, they just turn
around and just go against me. And it's like I learned from it, what for?"

While Patricia has removed herself from emotional involvement from
her peers, she continues to experience pressure to conform, most notably
from male peers less academically successful than she is:

> (*I wanted to know if you ever got a hard time for being a woman who is so suc-
> cessful—from any of your friends.*) Ohhhh. A hard time? I heard, let's see,
> I guess they were playing around, but in a way, it was like, it's like ironic
> I guess you would say. Because they used to tell me "Oh, look at Miss
> Executive, getting all these high grades." But, you know, they were actu-
> ally trying [to say], you know, Miss Smarty Pants. I, I really don't care. I
> don't really care if, you know, they say it. I, hey, at least they know, at
> least I'm doing something about my life, you know. Like yesterday, I

saw some friends with some report cards I couldn't *believe*. I could not, you know. D's, F's, straight down the line.

I guess people—this is what I noticed yesterday. People don't really expect me to be smart. You know, they don't see me as a smart person. . . . They don't see me as someone, that, you know, that would get good grades. And they told me that, and I was *laughing*. I go "Not all blondes are bimbos, you know. My roots are brown." . . . And, I guess when they find out, it's like all of a sudden, they start calling me "school girl." And then they forget about it, and then when report [card] time comes again, schoolgirl comes back.

Patricia maintains many aspects of her home/neighborhood ways of interaction and peers frequently "forget" about her high academic achievement. But when reminded, peers suggest that she is taking on behaviors and characteristics of another social class by calling her "Miss Executive." Further, such interactions illustrate that Patricia also faces gender borders in her daily transitions between Maple High and Northside, for it appears that male peers disparage the pro-academic aspects of her persona.

Patricia also feels that peers from the neighborhood immediately surrounding Maple are equally given to promoting a false Northside personality: "Kids that come from Maple I guess [are] sort of in their own world, because they know the people that are up here and they hang around with them. I guess I believe that, you know, the kids up here have a stereotype of the kids like get bused in. You know, they're from Northside, they're gangs, they're violence." Patricia is highly critical of local youths' views on gangs, describing them as ignorant and unjust. When I asked Patricia how she felt about the mixture of students in her classes, for example, she replied:[3]

Well, the only problem I can see in the advanced classes [is] that there's a majority of . . . I don't know if I should use that word. (*White kids?*) White kids. And sometimes we have—like first semester we used to have class discussions with our student teacher. . . . And they used to like sort of put, you know, the other races down. And it used to, you know, sometimes I wanted to blow my top. . . . It was just, I'd be like whoa, God, I'd get so mad at them, you know. . . .

One time we had a class discussion, it was about *Lord of the Flies*. But [the student teacher asked] "Well, what if the schools was like *Lord of the Flies*? No adults around, no nothing. Who do you think would take over the school?" And they [the European-American students in the class] go "The gangs. They would be out there terrorizing" and all this. I was like, boy, I wanted to blow my top! Because I don't think—

you don't see no vandalism around this school. And if it is, it's not a lot. It's a little bit here. If they wanted to vandalize the school, they wouldn't wait until all the adults weren't in the way. . . . They just want to be with their friends. But they don't do any harm to nobody. (*Right. Did you say anything?*) I don't remember, but I don't think I did. I was just—I couldn't because I knew if I started I wasn't going to [stop], I wasn't. It just got me mad. I just held it in.

Given her perception of these attitudes, Patricia finds little reason to invest effort in cultivating friendships with peers from the local neighborhood. Moreover, while she does not hide her heritage in advanced classrooms, she expresses hopelessness about arguing forcefully for her community in a place where she is outnumbered: "I don't really like it but I guess you can't really change someone's thoughts unless they want to change their thoughts and stuff. It bothers me but I can't really do anything about it."

While Patricia perceives herself as isolated at school, she does find a significant source of support in her current boyfriend, Roberto, whom she began dating toward the end of her freshman year just prior to his graduation from Maple High. What stands out particularly in Patricia's descriptions of Roberto is his willingness to reexamine conventional female roles, and his support for the multiethnic self Patricia seeks to assert:

He pushes me to do my best. He pushes me, you know . . . he'll like, he tells me not to let my studies go and he pushes me in school and he pushes me to work on my body and how I want it to be. He helps me. Like we go running and stuff together, and when I have homework, in Spanish, he helps me a lot with my Spanish, also when I have problems. . . . So you know we push each other to strive for our best, cause he's got high goals that he wants to achieve also. And so do I.

Patricia's descriptions of Roberto center on the tremendous support he offers and the comfort she gains from their relationship.

Early in high school, Patricia came to believe that peers can exert a strong, potentially redefining effect on the self one portrays. Her defensive stance toward her peers appears to have grown out of this discovery. In order to create a "rebel" identity that blends linguistic and behavioral aspects of her Northside culture with pro-school behavior, Patricia perceives it necessary to limit contact with school peers and expend little energy on these relationships.

Building Bridges Across Social Borders: Enabling Features
of Patricia's School World

In many ways, the situation at Maple resembles that at other high schools
described in this volume. For example, once viewed as one of the "big
schools," "one of the best in the 1960s," Maple is now defined by its faculty
as a school with "problems." Declining enrollment and drops in indicators
of academic achievement, coming in conjunction with demographic change,
form the basis for teachers' and administrators' perceptions. In the late 1950s,
Maple served primarily European-American, upper-middle-class students,
most of them college bound. However, many of the area's wealthiest families
moved south to newly constructed neighborhoods and a newly constructed
high school. In 1980, Maple's total population was almost 2,000, with European Americans comprising 71.8% of the student body. In 1990–1991,
Maple's enrollment was just 950, less than half that of 1982. Youth of color,
the majority of them (47%) Latino, made up 60% of the population. Almost
40% were transported from Northside to attend. Of these, 23% were limited-
English-proficient (LEP) students and 29% qualified for free lunch. By 1986,
Maple ranked 15th of 20 district schools with regard to parents' educational
background.

Maple's history provides a frame of reference for many of its adults, who
compare and contrast the Maple that was with the Maple that exists today:

> *Teacher:* The teachers here are used to teaching white, middle-class stu-
> dents. It is really hard for a lot of them to adjust. An underlying attitude
> on the part of many teachers is that the minority kids are the problem.
> (122–135)
>   *Vice-principal:* We have a school with declining enrollment, a
> school to the south that took the best, and we are not a magnet. Maple
> is considered a left-over school.

During interviews with 35 teachers, administrators, and staff (conducted by
CRC staff in 1988–1989), 13 characterized their students as lazy and/or unmotivated, 11 characterized their students as lacking basic academic skills,
and 10 characterized their students as lacking parental support. In six cases,
negative characteristics were linked explicitly to a Latino or minority background, with teachers asserting generalizations such as "the Hispanic kids
can't read dialect or decode," "what we have bused in is not the same thing
intellectually," and "the parents of these kids don't support us. It's all too far
away."

In reaction to this discourse, a small but significant number of school
personnel have banded together to resist the dominant definitions that per-

meate their school environment. Based on their belief that Northside students face borders that are structural as well as socioeconomic, these faculty and counselors have organized a variety of efforts designed to address structural, socioeconomic, and sociocultural borders that impede the ability of Northside youths to connect with school. While Patricia's independent spirit and supportive family have undoubtedly played a part in her steady educational progress, it is also clear that Patricia has benefited from the efforts of adults at Maple to transform the structural borders between her home and school communities into navigable boundaries.

Like other Maple students, for example, Patricia meets regularly with an academic counselor and has talked with her school's active career center technician. She also benefits from Maple's participation in the Statewide Opportunity and Access Program (SOAP), an effort designed to inform ninth and tenth graders about the classes they need to enter the University of California system. (The program also assists 11th-grade students with college admissions tests, financial aid, and college applications.) On entering Maple, Patricia enrolled in Algebra 1, first-year Spanish, advanced English, advanced world history, and Personal Effort for Progress (PEP), an academic enrichment program that operates as a regularly scheduled class. By her junior year, she was enrolled in advanced chemistry, advanced U.S. history, trigonometry/analysis, advanced American literature, Spanish for the professions, and PEP. When asked how she went about deciding what classes she would take, Patricia answered:

> There's college counselors [SOAP personnel] that sort of come every once in awhile, and they plan out this thing. And, I see what classes they planned out for me in order to get to college and that's what I'm going for, you know, college entrance. To get all my credits for college entrance.
>
> Mrs. Haight (Patricia's counselor) helps too. If I—sometimes I have questions about my classes. Cause like this year I wanted to take Math 7–8 instead of Math 5–6? Cause I heard 7–8 was like the advanced class of 5–6. And she said "No it isn't. They're two different things."

Because of her meetings with her counselor and SOAP personnel, Patricia chose to take biology during the summer after her sophomore year so that she could enroll in advanced chemistry as a junior and physics her senior year: "I try to take classes that I know that I might use with my future career, like science and math. Cause I want to be a doctor. And that's why I need—that's why I want to take my physics by senior [year]. Try to get as many science classes in as possible."

The most significant of Maple's efforts to address borders, however, is

PEP. The program targets low-income youths and youths of color who come from middle school as mid-level academic achievers, students like Sonia Gonzales (see Chapter 6) who earned B's and C's in middle school.[4] As of the 1990–1991 school year, 98 students—88 of them youths of color—were enrolled at Maple, making up over 10% of the student body. PEP's goal is to empower traditionally underrepresented students to attend the University of California system. Thus far, it has been successful. Between 1980 and 1988, for example, 99% of the 220 students graduating from PEP enrolled in postsecondary education; of these, 89% enrolled in four-year colleges or universities. Patricia has been enrolled in PEP since entering Maple in ninth grade.

Stan Berger, a European-American middle-aged male, is in charge of Maple's PEP students. As a teacher who began teaching in a large, inner-city, primarily African-American school district, Berger came to believe early in his career that the social borders between groups can be bridged, but that institutional barriers can make this process difficult:

> I taught in Bay City and that was my first taste of Black students and Black culture. And at first it was uncomfortable, but then I became more attuned with the kids and they're just kids. They're wonderful students but the system itself—Bay City really did have some major problems. . . . I became dissatisfied and disenfranchised with the whole system. But I love the kids.

Coming to Maple, Berger was given the chance to work in a program that enables him to address many of the institutional barriers low-income youths of color can face. As director of the PEP program, Berger has the explicit mission to empower his students to challenge social borders: "I tell people around here who think Black and Hispanic students aren't going to achieve to walk into my room, and you see stereotypes dying all around you."

Accordingly, program requirements and classroom atmosphere communicate the expectation that all PEP participants will engage in challenging academic work. All students are required to enroll in at least one advanced course; over the course of the year Berger holds regular conferences with students, discussing their academic triumphs and difficulties. With regard to essays completed as part of the PEP curriculum, students earning less than a C redo their work, revising with the aid of tutors until the paper is deemed worthy of an A or a B. Classroom decor conveys the idea that this is all part of preparation for eventual college attendance. College counseling is also a central aspect of the curriculum. According to Patricia, these and other factors combine to make program norms and expectations explicit: (*What about PEP, what do they expect of you?*) They expect you to go to college! Definitely! They expect you to get good grades cause they're there. You know, if there's something, an assignment you don't understand, they're there to help you, so they expect you to get good grades." Referring specifically to the behavior of her teacher, Patricia laughed: "Mr. Berger, he pressures everybody into getting good grades. That's just—I guess that's his job." Amplifying its message, PEP employs a curriculum that both supports students' academic development and communicates the significant intellectual role played by people of color in America. Over a period of 4 years, students work their way through an increasingly difficult writing curriculum. Developed by the program director in collaboration with two of Maple's advanced English teachers, the curriculum centers on ten common writing techniques: autobiography, short story, description, explanation, compare/contrast, cause and effect, problem solving, evaluation, analysis, and persuasion. To demonstrate each technique, students are provided with "model passages"—many by writers of color. A brief biographical sketch follows each model passage. For example, as they prepared to write an essay incorporating themes of cause and effect, Patricia and her classmates analyzed the following model passage from "Letter from a Birmingham Jail," by Martin Luther King, Jr.:

> Segregation distorts the soul and damages the personality. It gives the segregator a false sense of superiority and the segregated a false sense of inferiority. To use the words of Martin Buber, the great Jewish philosopher, segregation substitutes an "I-it" relationship for the "I-thou" relationship, and ends up relegating persons to the status of things. So segregation is not only politically, economically and sociologically unsound, but it is morally wrong and sinful.

Each model passage is followed by an analysis of how the author uses a particular grammatical or stylistic technique to make his or her point and a description of the author:

> *Control:* Note King's use of the coordinating conjunction "and" and "but" in the underlined sentence above. The word "and" is used to connect the series of adverbs "politically," "economically" and "sociologically." The word "but" is used to connect the clauses "So segregation is not only politically, economically and sociologically unsound" and "it is morally wrong and sinful." In your writing, use at least one coordinating conjunction to link words, phrases, clauses, or sentences.
>   *A Closer Look:* Martin Luther King, Jr. (1929–1968), winner of the 1964 Nobel Peace Prize, was an African-American Baptist minister who led the civil rights movement in the United States. His nonviolent approach to his quest for racial harmony contrasts with his powerful literary voice. Other works by Martin Luther King, Jr., include: *Why*

Can't We Wait, The Trumpet of Conscience, Where Do We Go From Here: Chaos and Community.

Because sophisticated technical skills are linked explicitly to specific authors and diverse models of excellence are employed, the curriculum communicates the idea that excellence is manifested in a variety of ways by authors of all ethnic and racial backgrounds.

PEP also makes use of older students and graduates, who not only demonstrate the effects of the program to younger students but also model border-crossing capabilities. Collaboration is a program norm, and because students are not grouped by grade level, seniors and juniors not only work alongside Patricia and her peers, but occasionally help them with work during designated tutorial periods. Providing more extensive academic support, recent graduates of the program, many of them youths of color attending state colleges in the area, are employed as tutors in the classroom. Two such program graduates work in the classroom each period, assisting individuals or groups of individuals with work. Classmates are also encouraged to work together; students sit four to a table and pair up when working on similar assignments.

PEP's academic impact on an individual level is revealed both in the numbers of students it prepares for college and its effect on grade point averages. (Districtwide, PEP students earning GPAs of 2.0 or above increased from 74% prior to enrollment to 81% after enrollment.) Patricia feels that she has benefitted especially from the fact that PEP provides her with valuable information relevant to managing the crossings between her home and school worlds. For example:

> (*Did you get much information from Mr. Berger about college or has PEP been helpful with that?*) Yes, they help you a lot with that because they have these college videos, videos about different colleges, and you get to see the campuses, instead of going all the way out in la-la land. It's right there on tape. So you get to see the campuses and you get to hear about the programs and stuff, and Mr. Berger discusses colleges also with us. He always pushes everybody to go to Berkeley, I don't know for what reason. But he always does. And he just—he wants everybody in PEP to go to college, that we study real hard for college.

At the beginning of her freshman year, Patricia was particularly grateful that PEP was there to help her with the academic problems she encountered:

> PEP, it helps with all your problems, both in school and without—out of school. You can talk to them about everything. . . . It improves your

grades a lot because they help you understand better what you're learning and stuff when you've got problems, and they help you with like say
if you have a problem with the essays. They'll help you get a topic if
you can't think of one or they'll proofread it until they think it's good
enough. So it does help you a lot because it helps you understand better
and it helps you improve your grades and everything.

Consistent with the descriptions above, Patricia's knowledge of the system
has increased noticeably since she entered high school. For example, despite
her excellent academic record, Patricia said in the middle of ninth grade that
she planned to go to a trade school and learn a skill that would enable her to
pay her way through a four-year college. However, by the end of her sophomore year, Patricia had realized that scholarships are a possibility. With this,
she set her sights on applying directly to four-year state and private universities on graduation:

> Every once in awhile they [my parents] ask me—my dad asks me about
> college. "Which one do you want to go to?" and that. And you know, I
> told him either UC Adobe Viejo or Adobe Viejo State. And he was like
> "How do you expect to get there?" And I go "Good grades, scholar-
> ships, grants if I can. Financial aid."

Patricia's access to such information has been important not only because it
has expanded her vision and increased her sense of efficacy, but also because
it increases her ability to direct and manage her future. With information
from PEP, Patricia gains increased independence for she understands the
workings of the system. Perhaps most indicative of PEP's ability to develop
students' border-crossing skills, by the end of her sophomore year Patricia
had come to the point where she felt that she could cope academically on her
own without the assistance of PEP tutors. As she put it, "Sometimes I think
I don't even need PEP. But I guess without it I really wouldn't know where to
go—about college and exams and all that. That's about the only thing."
    It is also important to note that PEP surrounds Patricia with other
Northside youth who are striving to achieve academically. As such, PEP may
make Patricia's journey through high school less lonely. While Patricia keeps
her emotional distance from these peers, on the day I accompanied her to her
classes, she worked with PEP youth in her advanced English class, walked
with PEP youth to classes, and chatted with PEP youth during lunch. When
Patricia went to English, for example, she was not isolated but rather one of
13 youths of color out of a class of 33 students. Of those in advanced English,
I recognized four from Patricia's particular PEP period. Patricia's conversations in English ranged from the academic to the social, as she and her friends

moved between Spanish and English. Thus, manifestations of social difference were quite visible in the classroom.

It was also important to Patricia that as she moved through her school
day, she found opportunity to develop the Latina aspects of her identity and
encountered a Latino teacher who challenged the border that separates the
Northside and Maple communities. In second-year Spanish—Patricia's favorite course—she not only learned grammar and vocabulary, but also participated in a creative project designed to help students broaden their understanding of Central and South American geographies and cultures. Patricia
waxed enthusiastic about this aspect of the class as well as about her teacher,
Tomás Casteneda. Casteneda, a middle-aged Mexican-American male who
has taught at Maple for six years, also teaches bilingual pre-algebra, bilingual
physical science, and Spanish for Spanish speakers. In addition, he teaches
English as a Second Language to Latino adults in Patricia's Northside community. From Patricia's perspective, Casteneda displays his ability to blend a
pro-Latino/professional identity proudly. She values this aspect of his personality: "He's got this real Mexican look, he likes nice things. He dresses real
nice for a teacher—and expensive. (laughs) Like he brings his wool shirts to
the class so we can look at some things he buys for some price and oh my
God—costs more than my whole wardrobe."

Casteneda demonstrates that one can blur the socioeconomic border between communities, as he shows that economic and professional success do
not necessarily imply renunciation of community roots. Patricia also appreciates the fact that Casteneda encourages her to develop her bicultural skills
and recognizes her scholastic efforts: "He knows that I strive to do my best
in everything, he figured that out. He wanted to put me in Spanish 7–8. I can't
do that, it's too hard . . . I'm in 3–4 [now], and he wanted to put me in 7–8."

While Patricia attends classes where teachers provide the educational
conditions necessary for her empowerment, she coped with less pleasant
classroom environments during her sophomore year. Her geometry teacher,
for example, was infamous for the large number of students he sent from his
classroom on referrals. Moreover, Patricia found his explanations confusing:

> Ohh . . . I *dread* that class. . . . I didn't do well. At the end, I got a B. But
> it wasn't what I was hoping for . . . it was a hard class, because he didn't
> really explain the material. It was like, he taught college also at the same
> time that he teaches high school. So it's sort of like, he brought those
> techniques to high school. And he'd move around really quick, and you
> couldn't follow him. And it was just really difficult.

Teachers like this present a challenge to students who seek to cross structural
borders. Here, however, is where Patricia's school experience differs im-

portantly from that of youths who have little access to outside academic assistance. Patricia can manage a classroom like geometry by going to her PEP tutors or fellow PEP classmates. While her teacher creates a border in the classroom, Patricia can find ways and means around it with the aid of others who do not expect her to conform to mainstream standards of behavior.

REFLECTION AND CAVEAT

Patricia crafts a public "rebel" identity that blends behaviors and speech patterns characteristic of her working-class barrio and middle-class school communities. Aspects of her multiple worlds are visible as she crosses the border between her home and school worlds; even as Northside peers see Patricia's school girl behaviors, youths from the Maple neighborhood see manifestations of Patricia's Northside identity. Based on her experiences with Mexican family and friends, European-American father and teachers, Patricia prefers not to switch personas: "I value all of the different things equally, it's not one more than the other. I can't see myself picking one thing out." Yet, as she asserts her rebel persona, Patricia grapples with disempowering stereotypes and encounters verbal criticism. All around her, people appear to struggle to make sense of this young woman who fails to fit into Maple's dominant social categories.

I have argued that aspects of Patricia's rebel identity are enabled by aspects of her school environment, and particularly her experiences in PEP. As Patricia's PEP teacher insists that his pupils enroll in advanced courses and provides his students with access to cultural capital, he narrows the knowledge gap that may exist between students with identical grades and test scores. At the same time, because PEP's policies impact the character of academic differentiation at Maple and because PEP helps adolescents develop mutually supportive peer networks, it also supports Patricia's ability to assert the Northside aspects of her identity in mainstream cultural contexts. Given Patricia's perceptions of her peer world, it is probably important that she finds support and encouragement for aspects of her rebel self in this environment.

At the same time, even as efforts like PEP challenge dominant categorical meanings, it is important to note that they provide a rationale for ignoring other parts of the environment, distracting attention from salient issues. For example, while Maple employs some Latino and African-American faculty, in general students transported from Northside encounter adults who differ from them in terms of class and cultural background. By the end of her sophomore year, for example, Patricia had had just two teachers of color out of a total of 12. The potential importance of diverse adult role models for youths like Patricia can be seen in her descriptions of her Spanish course.

Further, with PEP being a separate program, and with PEP enrollees adapting readily to the academic and behavioral demands of their teachers in mainstream classrooms, it becomes easier for teachers to ignore their curricular and pedagogical practices. For example, data on Maple's suspensions and grades indicate that teachers experience relatively more difficulty negotiating for the attention of African Americans and Latinos. (Students from both groups are more likely to be suspended than their European-American and Asian-American peers; Latino and African-American youths are also disproportionately represented among those earning D's and F's, particularly during their ninth- and tenth-grade years.) Yet, as one teacher states, some faculty at Maple resist frank discussions of strategies to address these gaps, feeling youths from these groups have already received ample attention: "Let me tell you what happened in a meeting I was in last week. You know the district has made a commitment to empowering the African American male and the Latina female. And they were sitting there talking about this, and a guy sitting behind me said 'God, haven't we given them enough?! What more do they want?'" Thus, even as PEP enables students to cross socioeconomic and sociocultural borders, it may work to discourage examination of more basic features of the school, including academic tracking, classroom pedagogy, and curriculum.

Finally, with PEP functioning as a separate enrichment program, it may perpetuate the notion that Northsiders suffer from deficits even as it generates discourse about possibilities and capabilities. Because one must be special to belong (low-income or minority), PEP enrollees are defined as different. In some cases, as the program director notes, this works to generate anger about the special attention received by individuals from this group: "I sometimes have to fend off people who believe the program might be an extravagant expense. Not so much here in the school but when I go out and people find out what I do and then find out its focused on minorities." In others, it provides a reason for European American students to question the validity of the Northside presence in their classrooms: "It's supposedly (quote) 'advanced English' class, but the students in there, are not supposed to be—should not be in advanced English class. You know, I mean they're just dumb. They're straight stupid students. . . . Most of the class isn't even—it's a very Hispanic class. And the people are not qualified to be in that classroom. It's not because they're Hispanic, it's just that they shouldn't be in there."

Nonetheless, PEP does support its enrollees in their efforts to cross borders. Because of PEP, Patricia navigates a context where meanings are challenged by a significant number of students. It is in this sense that Patricia's school experience differs from that of individuals like Sonia Gonzales and Trinh Le. Patricia finds space and opportunity for her resistance to become part of a greater collective statement about the capabilities of adolescents from her community. She is left better able to publicize an identity that goes against the mainstream.

NOTES

1. An earlier version of this chapter appeared in Davidson (1996).

2. According to Mirande and Enriquez (1979), the strong division in male and female roles found frequently in traditional Latino families emanates from Aztec society, which was characterized by the concept of "dual spheres." While Aztec women were active in all aspects of society, their participation was often governed by expectations drawing on their domestic attributes and skills. With the arrival of Spanish conquistadores, women's roles were further circumscribed to that of housekeeper, wife, and mother.

3. As at the other high schools in our study, Latino and African-American youths are underrepresented in Maple's advanced classrooms.

4. Patricia's outstanding academic record is not typical of program enrollees; her parents asked that she be enrolled in PEP due to her older brother's success in the program.

5

DONNA CARLYLE

JUGGLING DEMANDS IN TWO SOCIOCULTURAL WORLDS

To us . . . well, there's a couple of our people [that matter]—your family, your parents, and your brothers and sisters. You know they [my friends] think like that . . . if you probably ask anybody about what their most valuable things are [those] would be people probably.

"Let's walk fast. I don't want to be late!" Donna urges me to move quickly and picks up her pace. We round the corner, nearing Donna's locker. "Donna!" Donna's best friend Anita is screaming, jumping, beckoning from across the hall. "What?" Donna yells, hesitating and slowing. "Come're!" Donna stops, working her way through the crowd. Clutching Anita's arm and leaning against the locker, Donna chats, smiles, and banters with the many males and females who surround her.

Two minutes later, Donna and I are running. Bursting through the doors of the main school building, we move outside. The one-minute bell rings. Donna sees Mr. Barston, who looks at his watch. We run faster, making our way to Donna's second-period math class, held in an outlying building approximately 100 yards away. We are late.

Almost 50 minutes later, the bell rings for dismissal. Donna and I move outside. After carefully placing her books on the desk in her English classroom, just two doors down, Donna takes me back to the main building. Donna approaches her friends, hugging Anita and Angel. Angel turns around, showing off his new hair style. Carlos approaches me, smiles and extends his hand: "Hey, are you a homie too?"

The one-minute bell rings. Donna and I turn around. Running again, we make our way back to the outlying buildings. Breathless, we slide into our seats as the bell rings. This scene will repeat itself twice more that day. "I have so many tardies, Ann!" Donna later laments, concerned about the prospect of after-school detention.

During the 8 days I spent with Donna at school, I went with her to 20 classes. She was late to eight and we ran, arriving just at the bell, to four others. Students who fall into these patterns are often described as irresponsible or disrespectful. Yet Donna is not viewed in this way by her teachers. Rather, their descriptions suggest that once inside the classroom door, Donna works hard to adapt to the demands of her school environment. Donna is viewed as "responsible," "mature," and a "good influence" on her classmates:

> *Language arts teacher, 9th grade:* I love Donna, Donna is a lady. You know what I mean? She's very sensitive, down to earth, mature, responsible, I would hire her if I had a job opening in a minute. She is considerate of others, she is friendly, she is helpful, she is just a teacher's dream for a student.
>
> *Language arts teacher, 10th grade:* She will try. She will work her butt off. And not only that, she is a good influence among her classmates as well . . . she listens, she pays attention, she even *discourages* some interruption from her classmates.

Consistent with her teachers' descriptions, Donna's classroom behavior does not indicate any desire to resist or disrespect; in general, Donna listens and works quietly while in class. "The way I was raised by my mom, you know, I don't smart talk the teacher," Donna explains. Donna's grades offer further evidence of her desire to adapt to the demands of her high school; though her grades may fluctuate, she has maintained a C average through her freshman and sophomore years. In sum, some factor other than lack of care for schooling and its demands seems critical to understanding Donna.

We came to view Donna's running as one indication of her focussed, active efforts to meet the demands of two distinct social worlds. Her first world, comprised of her highly social peer group and family, is rooted in norms and values emanating from Mexican culture. Here, "everyone values everyone" and behaviors and activities are organized to encourage interdependence and to promote group solidarity. Her second world, located in the halls and classrooms of Huntington High School, is characterized by the norms and values typical of northern American middle-class culture. Here, independence and individual achievement are valued, and behaviors and activities are organized to promote competition and encourage displays of individual competence. For Donna, the differences between her worlds as well as her family's difficult economic circumstances make transitions difficult, creating both sociocultural and socioeconomic borders. Donna's attention to school is often diverted by the conflicts she faces and the difficult choices she must make.

Background

> If I do graduate, do graduate from high school I'll probably be one
> of the first ones in my family. College is the first one for sure and high
> school—most of them dropped out. . . . [My mom] she says graduate
> [from high school] and get a good job and you can have your own car
> and stuff. She wants me to have things she never had.

Donna is the oldest of four children in a single-parent family headed by
her mother. Cousins, grandmother, aunts, and uncles live near Donna and are
regular fixtures in her day-to-day life. As indicated in the quote that opens
this section, Donna is very much aware of her family's educational history and
her mother's desire that she graduate from high school. In order to provide a
better sense of how Donna combines meanings from each of her worlds in an
effort to navigate school settings, I briefly describe her history as well as the
types of support she receives relevant to her efforts to graduate from high
school.

While Donna's family has stable ties to her home town of Mostaza, for
Donna and her mother, Carmen, the past 16 years have been characterized
by uncertainty and stress. Carmen was raised in a Catholic household that
she portrays as impoverished, highly "traditional," and troubled by alcohol
dependency. Carmen describes her parents warning her repeatedly about the
perils of intimate behavior and associating it with dire consequences—Carmen's
mother, for example, told Carmen that kissing would cause pregnancy.
However, Carmen nevertheless began to experiment and at 15 became pregnant
by a European-American boy who lived in her neighborhood, a Latino
barrio. When the families involved discovered the pregnancy, they ordered
Carmen and her boyfriend to marry. Two years later, the couple had a second
daughter, Donna's younger sister. However, Donna's mother left her husband
soon after, fleeing to escape his drunken beatings. Since then, Donna's father
has been in and out of jail as a result, says Donna, of continuing involvement
in gang-related activities. Carmen became involved in other relationships
during Donna's elementary school years, had two sons out of wedlock, and
moved repeatedly. Between kindergarten and sixth grade, Donna attended
eight different schools. (No record data—grades, test scores, or teacher comments—are
available from these early school years.)

Since she began middle school, Donna's situation has stabilized. Carmen
has not been involved in another relationship since leaving her youngest son's
father. Further, Donna attended just one middle school and moved on with
the majority of her classmates to her high school. Donna describes her mother
as determined to keep her children in schools that she perceives as offering
the educational conditions and social setting necessary to ensure safety and

high school graduation. As she explains, "My mom really likes these schools. You know, they're like the real—she won't like me to go to school like on the South Hills or anything where they call Mexican schools because they're so mean and stuff and they don't teach right. That's what they say, so she likes it here. I do too." Consistent with Donna's description, Carmen demonstrated her advocacy over the course of this study. For example, during Donna's freshman year the family lived in a high-crime area because housing there was affordable. Donna's mother worried. Each day she woke with her children at 5:30 A.M. to drive them to the bus stop in order to ensure their safety. One year later, when Donna told her mother of an impending conflict between youths of Mexican and Vietnamese descent, Carmen came to the high school, demanded a meeting with the principal, and alerted him to the problem. "She said she'd sue if anything happened to either of her daughters," Donna explained. Carmen also regularly attends semester meetings with Donna's homeroom teacher, who has been assigned to monitor Donna's progress through high school.

Donna's perception of her mother's reliability as well as her absolute support and advocacy is a theme that ran throughout our conversations. During our first interview, for example, I asked Donna to tell me a bit about her family. She replied:

> I live with my mother only, my dad's not around, hasn't been around for almost—all my life practically. . . . I can really depend on my mom. She's very understanding and I love her so much. I do. . . . It's real nice. I don't really consider her my mom in a way, she's like a best friend. I can tell her anything, any time, anything. She would understand and stuff. My friends always tell me "God Donna, you have special mom."

In addition to citing her mother's efforts to ensure that her children attend "good schools," Donna says that her mother spends time with her children, speaking with them about her past experiences. According to Donna, Carmen's central concern is that her children not repeat her or her ex-husband's history:

> She really wants us *not* to be like her. She wants us to learn from her mistakes . . . she regrets not going to school. . . . Really, mainly, she wants us to graduate out of high school. To go out, graduate, since she didn't really do that. She wants us to be responsible.

When referring to her strong desire to graduate from high school, Donna speaks often of her mother's influence: "I'm going to graduate, that's one thing I'm determined to do. I couldn't let my mom down on that."

A final factor relevant to understanding Donna's orientation toward school is her family's precarious financial situation. Carmen has lived on public assistance since Donna's birth. Money—or lack of it—is often on Donna's mind, serving on the one hand to strengthen her resolve to finish high school and on the other to divert her attention from school. For example, both Donna and her younger sister were given a *quinceañera*, a major celebration for a 15-year-old Latina girl that serves to introduce her to the community. This event is of considerable symbolic and cultural importance for young women; thus Donna's mother viewed it as imperative. However, it is also a significant expense. In addition to a formal religious ceremony that requires gowns for the young woman and her attendants, the family hosts a party after the event. In order to save the money necessary for her sister's *quinceañera*, the family moved into Donna's maternal grandmother's one-bedroom apartment during Donna's sophomore year. After weeks of living in cramped conditions, there was a fight and Donna's grandmother insisted that the family leave. Still recovering from their recent expenditures on the *quinceañera*, the family moved to a cheap motel, where they lived for 4 months until they could find an affordable two-bedroom apartment. During this period, Donna began part-time work at McDonald's. Her desire to contribute to the family income and her worry about her mother's economic situation prompted the decision to work. While living in the motel, Donna spoke often of her depression: "I'm so happy that we're going to move. I'm tired of that place actually. It makes me feel awful." She also described her exhaustion, a state that she attributed not just to the increased responsibilities associated with her job but also to the stress she experienced due to concern about her family's precarious economic situation. Economic circumstances made it difficult for Donna to adopt the behaviors and mind set necessary to function at her academic best, generating socioeconomic borders that impeded her ability to easily make transitions between home and school.

The Responsible Donna: Familial Norms and Expectations

> To me, I'm like a second mom at home, okay? And that's a tradition. But I'm always, every time my brother says something, or mumbles something to my mom, I tell him, "be quiet" or "don't talk like that." . . . I'm like a mom to them, when my mom's not home. And even when she's home, they ask me to help them with their homework and stuff, and my mom can't do it, you know, cause she didn't go to high school. . . . I have the most responsibility in the house than anybody else.

In a barrio neighborhood, much of Donna's life is centered in a social world that blends Mexican and American traditions. At home, Donna speaks two languages, using Spanish with her young cousins and grandmother, English with her mother and siblings. Donna and her mother refer to themselves as Mexicans and Donna's mother is quite fluent in the language; however, neither has a desire to visit Mexico, follows news from that nation, or is in touch with relatives. Donna's mother is well known for the "menudo" (Mexican stew) she prepares on holidays; however, on a day-to-day basis the family eats whatever is most convenient to prepare. And while oral aspects of the Spanish language have been passed at least as far as Donna's generation, written language has not. Thus Donna takes Spanish at school partly because of her wish to acquire this aspect of the language. Further, Donna describes family practices and beliefs that she perceives as antithetical to more traditional Mexican norms concerning female behavior. In particular, Donna contrasts her grandmother's socialization patterns with those of her mother. From Donna's perspective, her mother is less traditional because she has raised her children on her own, because she advocates against dependency on males, and because she is open to discussing topics such as sexuality with her children. Carmen, for example, has told Donna that she will go with her if she needs contraception.

However, other aspects of Donna's home world are more culturally traditional. In particular, Donna holds a position of responsibility consistent with descriptions of the eldest child's role in working-class Mexican families (Delgado-Gaitan, 1987, 1994). She is given latitude to make a variety of personal decisions. In exchange, she is expected to play a significant role in the care of her younger siblings and to perform household duties.

In addition to contributing to the family income with money earned at her part-time job at McDonald's, for example, Donna helps her mother with cooking, cleaning, putting her younger brothers to bed, and other household matters. Because her mother left high school in the ninth grade, Donna is also responsible for helping her siblings with academic matters. Occasionally, Donna assists her mother with tasks that require academic skills, such as letter writing and calculating percentages. Donna is also expected to model socially responsible behavior. In addition to contributing to the family's well-being, Donna is expected to set an example for her younger sister and brothers by graduating from high school. Scholars have suggested that behaviors like Donna's help to foster interdependence in Latino families (Delgado-Gaitan, 1994); by giving support, Donna contributes to an overall feeling of collectivity. And Donna does not appear to resent but in fact takes pride in her position in the family: "My mom tells my brothers, 'You guys have to be good like Donna.' . . . I love to be like this, the oldest, because I help my mom out. It's more fun, I guess."

While many of Donna's responsibilities are defined and delegated by her mother, Donna uses discretion in outlining the steps necessary to fulfill her mother's requests. This is especially apparent in matters concerning Donna's education. Her mother expects Donna to progress toward graduation. At the same time, she allows Donna to direct and plan her education. For example, Donna plans how to address poor grades without her mother's input:

> Right now I have one F. And my mom tells me I have to raise it up, and I tell her I can handle it, I'll just take the course again. Not the whole next year, but take it again until I raise up my grades, I get more credits out of it, and then just go on to a higher level. And she tells me that's fine. . . . I do it on my own more.

Donna also makes short-term, day-to-day decisions concerning her schooling: "If I don't want to come to school, I just tell my mom. She'll ask me if I'm not feeling well, and I'll just tell her 'No mom, I just don't feel like going today.' And she'll clear it for me. Because she knows that I don't do that that often, that usually I have a good reason. I don't take advantage of that you know." Donna explains that the freedom given to her by her mother is based on evidence that she will execute her responsibilities. For example, consistent with her promise that she could "handle" the failing six-week grade described in the quote above, Donna raised her grade to a C− by the end of the semester. Further, through middle school and high school, she has earned C's and B's.

In sum, Donna executes diverse responsibilities as part of her role within a social group. Also striking, and in contrast to many European-American middle-class families in which children view chores as burdensome and deserving of financial reward (allowance), Donna sees her responsibilities as providing her with status and a sense of accomplishment.

A Parallel World: The Meaning and Practice of Friendship

> *Donna:* Every time I'm walking around the hall [I hear] "Hi Donna, hi." [I'm] looking all over, "Hi." Having a lot of friends is . . . friends are [mean] so much to me.
> *Social studies teacher:* Donna Carlyle. I really like her. She's got a great personality. And you can see she has 10 or 12 friends in here and I'm sure hundreds outside the class.

During her sophomore year, Donna was a central figure in a large Mexican-American peer group that included her younger sister, five males, her best friend, Anita, and a second friend, Carla. During every passing period Donna was accompanied by at least one friend; at lunch her peer group met every day to sit in the same spot on the outside lawn. Hugs and verbal expressions of affection—both between females and female to male—occurred during almost every interaction.

Outside school, Donna and her friends go to movies and the mall and, on special occasions, they organize group picnics and attend family celebrations. Donna plays a key role in organizing group outings, and spends hours on the telephone each night. (While her family was living in a motel, one of Donna's greatest sources of depression was that she no longer had her own phone.) Donna's friends frequently come to her home and her mother and younger sister are often part of the social activity:

> My mom knows most of my friends, my girlfriends that is. And she'll go out with us, shopping or whatever. Like last weekend, Anita and I were going shopping and we invited my mom to go. . . . My friends will talk to her about all sorts of things, like my mom, you can talk to her about guys, she likes to talk about guys. She's not like a lot of parents, really strict about that.

In short, Donna is surrounded constantly by friends, whose emotional support she considers critical during times of both happiness and hardship. She encourages actors from her family and peer worlds to commingle.

As does her family, Donna's friends blend Mexican and American traditions in their behaviors and presentations of self. For example, while English is dominant, Spanish words and phrases crop up during casual conversation. All of Donna's close friends are of Mexican descent, and while Donna could easily pass as European-American, she chooses clothing and adopts hair and makeup styles favored by many peers from her barrio. Social activities and shopping excursions typically take place in her community. Donna says that she and her friends often feel uncomfortable in the white upper-middle-class section of town where her high school is located because they feel conspicuous.

In Donna's highly social peer world, norms of behavior and accompanying values promote interdependence in the form of mutual aid and support. Predominant peer-group norms include helping one another and maintaining the group: "[At this school] we're outnumbered by the count of who our friends are, and this neighborhood is, we're outnumbered a lot, quite a bit. But not by involvement, you know what I mean? If something happened or something we all stick together. . . . When anybody meets any trouble, we are all gonna help." Loyalty and support are manifested in day-to-day activity. For example, when her friends became involved in a conflict with youths of Vietnamese descent, all of the members in Donna's peer group wore red to symbolize their solidarity.[1] Donna explained that she did not understand the full significance of wearing this color, but was willing to do so in order to

show support for her friends. Likewise, after Donna and her girlfriends organized a food booth at her school's International Day, several of Donna's male
friends approached after the sale and asked for food. Though Donna and her
girlfriends were somewhat perturbed, afterward Donna remarked that "we
should give it to them because they are our friends."

Donna's peer group is also primarily oriented toward relationships and
social activity, rather than individual achievement. Thus, among friends,
schoolwork and grades are rarely discussed:

> We just talk about guys and what our boyfriends tell us and just stuff
> like that. It's real nice to talk to them about stuff like that. (*Do you talk
> about school together?*) School? Not exactly like *schoolwork*. We talk about
> schoolwork if I need help or something, or if they need help, and they
> really want me to help them, but not really. We don't really get into
> school. We talk about the guys here but not really school.

In accord with these norms, Donna frequently appears to place social relationships ahead of her individual achievement. For example, as a tenth grader
Donna once asked me to help her finish vocabulary homework for English.
When a friend sitting near by saw Donna's paper, she asked to copy Donna's
answers. Donna gave her friend the assignment, despite the fact that it was
just half complete and due in 20 minutes. Similarly, in ninth grade Donna was
placed in a lower-track language arts course due to her low reading achievement test scores. It quickly became apparent to her teacher that Donna would
do well in a regular classroom. However, Donna decided to remain in the
course, in part so that she could remain with her friends. Donna's tendency
to arrive late for class also reflects tension between her desires to invest the
time necessary to maintain her social relationships and to adapt to the world
of the school.

Even more so than for Donna, school is not the most primary concern
of her friends. During sophomore year, for example, Anita failed several
classes and Donna's boyfriend had to attend night school in order to make up
credits he was missing for graduation. At times, aspects of their behavior—
particularly tardiness and failure to complete homework—appear consistent
with the argument that native-born youth of Mexican descent, because of
long contact with economic and political inequality, are more likely to resist
schooling (Matute-Bianchi, 1986; Ogbu, 1993; Suarez-Orozco, 1993). However, in other significant ways Donna's friends do not fit this pattern. Most
notably, they are not opposed to maintaining a basic level of school involvement and success. For example, Donna is not teased for her desire to graduate
from high school. Rather, Donna's friends expect her to fulfill this publicly
stated goal and urge her to earn at least C's in school: "If I get a bad grade,

Anita will say 'What's this D, Donna? A D? Come on!'" Further, according to Donna and consistent with my observations, members of this peer group do not actively promote or publicize poor school performance. As Donna put it, "You usually don't find out that they got a bad grade unless one of them gets grounded. . . . And also, if one of them does badly they'll just change the subject real quick. That's how you know they don't want to talk about it."

In sum, Donna's peer and family worlds are characterized by emphases on close relationships, interdependence, and support, as well as by the expectation that Donna will take the time and make the sacrifices necessary to contribute to group goals when necessary. Reflecting her experiences in these worlds, Donna brings specific skills to her school environment. These include organizational skills, a talent for identifying and addressing the needs of others, an ability to work collaboratively, and knowledge of how to involve, motivate, and support others. In addition, Donna has had experience teaching others as part of the assistance she provides in her household. While some of the things that she brings with her reflect her individual personality, others are shaped by her cultural values, beliefs, and expectations.

Others' Expectations: Student Roles and Responsibilities at Huntington High

Huntington is characterized by norms, values, and expectations that differ in fundamental ways from those in Donna's community and peer group. First, classroom relationships, while friendly, are cordial, formal, and structured around the production of traditional academic work. Second, classrooms are organized to promote and distinguish individual advancement. Thus, while responsibility is promoted and valorized, it is to be used for the sake of the individual, rather than the group. On a daily basis, the significant skills that Donna brings with her to school are rendered irrelevant and even inappropriate by aspects of her school environment. Thus, for Donna sociocultural borders are the most immediate impediment to her transitions between home and school.

Donna's seven sophomore-year classes, all in the general track at Huntington High, include physical education, typing, introduction to algebra, English, social studies, driver's education, and Spanish 5–6. With the exception of driver's ed and physical education, classroom activities in these courses are structured strictly around traditional academic content. For example, when students write they tend to analyze readings from class; when students do math they tend to address problems from a textbook. There is little multicultural content in any of the texts that Donna encounters. Further, she rarely works with supplemental materials or readings.

Donna describes her teachers as "very nice and understanding" and "real sweet." Nevertheless, Donna's sophomore-year teachers know little about her. For example, with the exception of her academic advisor, who also serves as her Spanish teacher, no adult in Donna's environment knows of the difficult living situation she faces during her sophomore year and none know that she works to supplement the family income. None of Donna's teachers know about the significant caregiver role she plays in her family, none know that she is working to be the first in her family to graduate from high school, and none (including Donna's Spanish/advisory teacher) seem to recognize Donna's curiosity about college. During the 27 class periods in which I observe Donna, she engages in extended dialogue with just one teacher, and this conversation revolves around her academic progress. Though Donna feels this teacher knows her as a person, she is aware that even he has knowledge only of her general personality rather than of her relevant background characteristics: "He knows that I ask a lot of questions, so he knows what gets me mad and what makes me frustrated. And he knows that I'm loud, that I like to talk to people."

Formalized, work-based relationships such as those described above are consistent with classroom interaction patterns that convey the idea that academic inquiry and endeavor are solitary affairs, punctuated by the display of individual knowledge or accomplishments. Two types of interaction patterns are prominent in Donna's classrooms. First, students work silently and individually, while the teacher circulates to monitor student progress and provide assistance. In typing, for example, youths spend the period at individual seats, completing typing exercises. In Spanish, students frequently work out of the textbook, answering questions at the end of a chapter or defining vocabulary. In English, students often define vocabulary, quietly working at their individual desks. In math, students frequently observe their teacher demonstrating solutions to a problem, or work silently at their seats.

Second, teachers stand at the front of the room, typically lecturing or posing questions. In the latter case, teachers typically wait for and then evaluate a response before moving forward, reflecting the "initiation-response-evaluation" pattern of classroom exchange (Mehan, 1979). In both cases, the display of individual knowledge and achievement are relevant. In general, teachers (and students) in many of Donna's classes appear to share the understanding that when teacher-student interaction occurs, a single student should provide a single, correct, answer. The result is an individual display of factual information, rather than a discussion emanating from higher-order questions or group construction of knowledge.

On a more general level, and parallelling the value placed on individual achievement and advancement, youths at Huntington are expected to take individual responsibility for directing their academic futures. For example, when planning their classes students are given a sheet that lists high school graduation requirements. Youths complete their class schedules using this sheet as a guideline, consulting with an advisory teacher as necessary. If individuals do not make an active effort to investigate classes relevant to college entry, it is unlikely that they will receive guidance and information from adults. Similarly, if a teacher recommends a class that a student feels is below his or her ability, it is up to the student to contest the teacher's decision. For example, Donna's sophomore math teacher said the following to his students as they were selecting classes for the upcoming year:

> If you circled Algebra A/B [a less advanced class], that's probably good for me. If you circled Algebra 1/2 [a more advanced course], that might be good, or might not. I may or may not agree today. Your work could improve. What I want to see over the next few months is exams with 80s, not 30s or 40s. . . . I may change some of your algebra 1/2 to A/B. Don't get mad! I'd be happy to call your mom. Feel free to come in at lunch, convince me, and we can get a program going. You've got two more months to convince me.

While information and avenues for protest are available in the environment, students must be enterprising and relatively savvy in their information or change-seeking strategies in order to find help and assistance.

For Donna, this institutional emphasis on individual responsibility creates a structural border. Without an adult to guide her, she is unable to maximize the information she receives or her academic placement. For example, though interested in college, Donna has learned little about which classes are most relevant to entry or even what college is like.

> It's hard to get information about college. Just little stuff that we hear around school and about colleges, but not really actually basic stuff about college. Maybe it's just me, maybe I just don't ask people or, I don't know what it is. Cause I do have a lot of questions. I just don't have like a person to ask, you know what I mean? Like to talk to about college. I haven't actually talked to anyone about college yet.

Similarly, as a freshman Donna took introduction to algebra, where she earned a C−. However, departmental policy requires students to pass a placement test prior to advancing to the next level of math. Donna missed passing this test by one point. Though she asked to take the placement test again, she did not aggressively pursue the matter: "I argued with him, 'Oh, come on! It's just one, let me take it over again.' And then I was gonna take it over again, but I never had a chance to. You know, school was at an end, it just like sift on through it and I just didn't have time to do it." In accord with the premium placed on individual responsibility, Donna's teacher did not remind or encourage her to try the test again.

Basically, norms, expectations, and values in Donna's school world are organized to promote individual effort, individual achievement, and individual responsibility. Neither interdependence nor interpersonal relationships—both critical elements of Donna's life outside school—are emphasized. Because individual achievement is promoted and valorized, these differences create a sociocultural border. In order to succeed in school, Donna must find a way to navigate this border on a daily basis.

Donna's Response: Keeping School in Its Place

> When I leave school I go with my mom to pick up my little brothers at school. And then from there we come back home and I clean. . . . After that I'm mostly on the phone. Usually I don't have homework. . . . I'd rather do it then [in class] than bring it home. I hate having homework, especially taking books home, that gets me so lazy. I get so lazy about taking books home.

In general, one can describe Donna's response to the sociocultural borders that separate her worlds as pragmatic. To manage the conflicts between her worlds, Donna keeps activities and behaviors in her school and community separate and tightly bounded. In both settings, Donna structures her actions and behavior in accord with characteristic norms and expectations. To accomplish this, however, Donna must restrict academic efforts to school hours; none of her friends or family members engage in academic projects outside of school. Thus, while in class Donna tries to focus and work efficiently. However, when she leaves school, her books stay behind. Thus, work left undone is left for the next day in school. Donna has no desire to move into more challenging courses, perhaps because this would jeopardize the delicate balance she now manages to maintain: "In those classes, you are going to have to study. You know that. I'm not prepared. I don't like studying actually. I hardly ever do."

In accord with her pragmatic approach to schooling, while in class Donna is well behaved. She participates in classroom activities and does the work that her teachers ask of her without complaint, resistance, or comment. Actual course content is of relatively little interest; Donna sees no overlap between her studies and her interests: "The classes I have are just typical classes that you take, math and stuff, and I just want to help people like a social worker." Further, because Donna does not do homework, her assignments are often incomplete. Nevertheless, Donna always has something to turn in and she listens politely. Thus it is not surprising that, to teachers, Donna appears as a pleasant, "consistent" student:

> *English teacher:* She's very consistent. She is consistently good. Very neat work.
>
> *Math teacher:* She's pretty consistent. I think she's pretty consistent. Not that anything we're doing is marvelous, you know, or really difficult in a way, but it takes attention to detail.
>
> *Social studies teacher:* She's getting a B right now, and I see no reason why it shouldn't end up that way unless she blows the final. She's consistent, and as you can see here, she's completed 36 of the 50 extra credit points that I allow them to earn.

The relative effectiveness of Donna's strategy, however, is contingent on her ability to focus and concentrate in class. If she cannot do this, Donna will waste precious time as she struggles to discern what is being asked of her when she turns to her written work. In the descriptions that follow, I briefly consider classroom social features that affect Donna's ability to focus. To do so, I first describe social relationships and interaction patterns in a classroom where Donna looks highly disengaged, a classroom that Donna describes as both difficult and boring. I then compare and contrast this to a classroom where Donna appears engaged, a classroom that Donna describes as fun and easy. My purpose is to illustrate how classrooms that incorporate norms and expectations similar to those found in Donna's community appear to encourage more active participation by Donna. Subsequently, Donna displays knowledge that might remain inert in a more traditionally structured classroom.

The Disengaged Donna

> I like most all my teachers, but there's a little, about one or two teachers that are really—like really boring and you have to get into the subject, if not you fall asleep. That's how I get sometimes. I'm all sleepy. There's this one teacher, he's just like—he's not interesting. Most of my teachers, they would like, talk about yourself, know things, not only just about the subject but about other things. But he's real boring. Take three apples plus two apples equals how many apples.

For Donna, particularly difficult classrooms—those in which it is hard to focus—are characterized by two features. First, relationships between teachers and students are formal and focus almost entirely on academic content. Second, teachers dominate classroom interaction with long, content-centered explanations. In these situations, Donna does not look engaged, attentive, or even interested. Rather, she struggles to maintain her academic foothold. Typically, she slips into the academic danger zone and then engages in a flurry of last-minute activity to pull her grade back to a C. Donna also quietly withdraws from much of the classroom discourse and activity, writing notes to friends or simply staring into space.

Donna's disengaged classroom self emerges often in her tenth-grade English class. Pedagogy in this class revolves around lectures, seat work, and occasional question-answer recitation reviews; students are graded largely on their written work. During the ten times I observe class, students write essays, look up definitions to long lists of vocabulary words, complete grammar exercises, read and engage in oral recitation reviews of short stories, and listen to lectures about poetic devices. In addition to the more standard sorts of short stories found in high school texts, Donna grapples with notions such as setting and sentence structure, and reads portions of *Julius Caesar* and selections of poetry.

Donna's teacher, Mr. Yana, does chat with his students, including Donna, before class begins. However, he expects students to adapt to a formal and cordial working atmosphere during class time. While laughter and quiet conversation are permitted during seat work, Yana frowns on these behaviors during lectures and classroom discussions. He initially ignores and then quickly squelches any attempts at classroom antics, as illustrated in the field note segment that follows:

Mr. Yana: Now the homework question number two, page 75 . . . question number two has two parts. What is the old conflict? And, what new conflict is the basis of the story? Now perhaps we can begin by reminding you of the plot of this story. What is the plot of this story? Ahm, Ian.

Ian: I was stretching.

Mr. Yana: Oh, I thought you wanted to answer. What's the plot of the story?

Ian: (smiling) Chee, Chee's a man. (A few students giggle) He's like a horseback man.

Mr. Yana: A horseback man?

Student: He's small and plump.

Ian: Yea, that's it, he's small and plump. And, it's like, ahm—

Mr. Yana: Well, actually you're missing the central conflict in the story Ian.

Ian: We're not done reading it are we?

Mr. Yana: What is the difference between Chee and his people? [Students laugh in response to Ian's comment]

> *Mr. Yana:* Sh-sh-sh—about custody of the daughter. That's the basic conflict. But the basis of that conflict could be traced to the setting. The customs and traditions of the parents, what we were talking about earlier.

Attempts at humor are clearly discordant with the more scholarly atmosphere Yana wants to promote. Rather, in his class interaction reflects the understandings that (1) students should listen and strive to absorb teacher explanations and (2) a single student should provide a complete answer to a teacher's question. Donna's response to these patterns is frequent disengagement. Prior to and following class Donna chats readily with her teacher. However, during class she seldom participates. During the five discussions that I observe, Donna volunteers just two answers and asks just two questions. Often, Donna tunes out, writing notes to her friends or putting her head on her desk. As illustrated in the field note below, Donna's disengagement is often surreptitious:

> *Mr. Yana:* Run-on in poetry means, simply what we just said. You will not drop your voice at the end of the line, you are forced *by* the end of the line to move on to the next line. [The teacher reads a line to demonstrate, then continues.] You do not drop your voice at the end of the line. Those lines are what we call iambic. So one stanza here is actually one sentence. Let's move on. Is there rhyme in the poem?
> *Student:* No.
> *Mr. Yana:* We see that there is no rhyme. And we call this blank verse. No end rhyme is called blank verse.
> *Donna:* [whispering to Melanie] What did he say?
> *Melanie:* I don't know.
> [Mr. Yana continues to discuss poetry. Donna borrows a pocket video game from a friend and begins to play the game behind her purse.]

Typically, Donna's more focused classroom persona reemerges after Yana concludes his discussion:

> *Mr. Yana:* OK, for your homework. Page 25. Veinte-cinco.
> *Donna:* [looks up from game] Not bad, Mr. Yana.
> [Donna returns the video game to her classmate, borrows a piece of paper, and begins her homework.]

However, after tuning in again, Donna often does not know what she is doing and may give up in despair or disgust. On two occasions as I observe, she complains that she feels sick to her stomach. This is the only class where I see Donna stop work during a free period. She receives a D both semesters. In explaining her disengagement, Donna emphasizes classroom interaction patterns: "Mr. Yana, when he talks I just can't follow what he's saying. So I just give up."

A Different Donna

> Sometimes it was really easy for me. . . . Ms. Ashton's class, she's slow because she sits there and she'll talk to us about everything. . . . She'll write what we say. . . . When I was first in there I used to help the students that need help. . . . [That class] it's funny because of the people that are in there. It's just really nice.

While Donna struggles in more traditionally organized classrooms, she tends to identify classrooms where teachers encourage peer-peer discussion, employ cooperative learning techniques, engage students in discussion, and allow time for independent work as "easy." In such classrooms I see a different Donna, a Donna who participates actively, helps her classmates, and enjoys the learning process. Donna's engaged classroom self appears often in her "Improvement" English class, a course Donna took during her freshman year.

Students are assigned to Improvement English, a remedial class, based on their eighth-grade reading national achievement scores. (Donna's eighth-grade scores are in the 30th percentile for reading and the 50th percentile for language.) The course content—in terms of both difficulty and the amount of work required—is not particularly challenging. Donna's teacher, Wendy Ashton, organizes her curriculum around short reading activities that students complete themselves and relatively simple novels that she reads aloud. (*Where the Red Fern Grows, Of Mice and Men*, and *Someone Is Hiding on Alcatraz Island* are among the novels Ashton uses.) Drawing on content from reading activities, students in Ms. Ashton's class develop vocabulary lists, write short essays, and hold frequent in-class discussions in which they are pushed to develop their descriptive abilities, make inferences, and identify various writing techniques, such as a flashback. In addition, Ashton emphasizes oral participation, auditory activities, and reading for understanding because of her belief that the way in which many classrooms are organized impedes many students from succeeding academically. During our interview, Ms. Ashton criticized teachers who she believes assume that their students arrive with well-developed reading skills and therefore do little or nothing to help their students to become good readers: "For instance, when I started *Of Mice and Men*, this one boy who came from another teacher to my class said 'Gee Ms. Ashton, you go through things.' He said 'When we were given this book in another class, all we were told to do is read the book and answer the questions she gave us on ditto sheets.' That was reading *Of Mice and Men*."

In contrast to the majority of Donna's teachers, Ashton works hard to develop relationships with her students because of her belief that it is important to earn her students' trust and affection. She seats quieter students in the front of the room "so I have a lot of eye contact and I can touch them every once in awhile, just briefly touch them, to make contact with them." She also finds moments to visit with her students briefly during work periods:

Ms. Ashton has asked the students to get out the previous evening's homework, and is moving through the room to check on who has completed their work.
Donna: I finished mine of course.
Ms. Ashton: Thank you sweetheart, you're perfect. [Ashton touches Donna on her shoulder]

As illustrated in the field note that follows, with more verbal, rambunctious students Ashton develops relationships through affectionate teasing and a good sense of humor, using these skills to push her students back on track:

Ms. Ashton's students are preparing to write an essay on how army ants have been used during history. She is working with her students to develop an essay outline [in the form of a visual map] on the chalkboard. A.J., a student sent to Ms. Ashton from another teacher after being "sent out on a daily basis for being disruptive," is sitting in the back of the room applying lotion to his legs.
Ms. Ashton: Can somebody tell me one way an army ant was used? You can tell this based on your memory or your reading. Now nobody (inaudible) while we discuss this. I want everyone's attention focused up here. Now give me one way they were used.
Naomi: Their heads were used as stitches. They used it for stitches!
Ms. Ashton: All right. [Adds this to the map on the board] All right, should you add anything to that? Would you need to explain a little bit how they did that? How did they do that?
A.J.: They were, they let the ants bite it.
Ms. Ashton: Now who is they?
A.J.: The cavemen, heh-heh. [Students laugh] The old, the people with the hurts, the boo-boos.

Ms. Ashton: (smiling) You're going to have worse than a boo-boo A.J.
 . . . Johnnie. Let's hear it Johnnie. Help this fellow out. Who made
them, who put the killer ants on the wound?
A.J.: The doctors.

Ms. Ashton explains that a good sense of humor and an ability to laugh with
her students helped to maintain the flow in her classroom: "I think it carries
me along with them. I find them funny. And they need to laugh more."

A second feature distinguishing Ms. Ashton's class from others is its emphasis on group displays of knowledge. Discussions occur frequently; further,
students are allowed to respond to and build on each other's comments.
Moreover, Ashton does not frown on unconventional answers but allows students to express themselves. Therefore, her students' personalities are very
visible in the classroom, as they laugh, tease, and encourage one another while
moving through academic material. As reflected in the field note segment below, Donna responds favorably to this situation, participating actively:

[Students are discussing a question from a reading. They've been asked
to describe what life in a fictional setting in the reading was like.]
Ms. Ashton: A. J. talk.
A.J.: Everyone was always happy.
Ms. Ashton: And why would they be happy?
A.J.: Because! They were.
Naomi: No, because, because they thought they could do whatever
      they wanted to, and it was like a really pretty place.
Donna: It was beautiful.
A.J.: I have something to add to that. There was electricity, and wash-
      ing machines, and plumbing, and medicine. But there was no cars,
      TVs, radios, phones . . . girls, pretty girls.
Ms. Ashton: And according to him what was life on Earth like?
A.J.: H-E-double hockey sticks.
Ms. Ashton: Ruben, what was life on Earth like?
Donna: I have one.
Ms. Ashton: Ruben, I need to hear you loud and clear honey, whatever
      you have for what life on Earth was like. What its problems were.
      [Ruben replies inaudibly]
Ms. Ashton: And what other problems did he face living in Manhattan?
Donna: He didn't have no friends.
Naomi: He didn't make money.
Donna: He didn't make that much money.
A.J.: He didn't make kids.

It appears that Donna is able to understand Ms. Ashton's explanations and wants to be part of the class. She participates eagerly and actively.

A third factor relevant to understanding this class is Ashton's emphasis on eliciting and supporting students' academic voices. Ashton believes that teachers should not only provide their students with content, but also be willing to expend the effort necessary to push them academically: "They're in here to learn, and I'm not going to let them—to me, I might as well let them put their head down on the table, if I let them get by with 'I don't know.'" During the five times I observe Ashton's class, I see her push students who answer "I don't know" to attempt an answer four times and to expand on their answers 23 times. The example below is typical:

> *Ms. Ashton:* Would somebody volunteer to tell me what they think needs to be answered for number one.
>
> *Donna:* For what, number one? (Ms. Ashton nods) OK, Charlie didn't believe in a place called Verna, and he thought that he tricked them.
>
> *Ms. Ashton:* And you were going to list what life on Verna was like . . .
>
> *Donna:* OK, everyone is smiling and happy . . . on Verna.
>
> *Ms. Ashton:* Where are we talking about?
>
> *Donna:* On Verna, OK? And there was no TV, radios, or telephones.
>
> *A.J.:* (quietly) Cars.
>
> *Donna:* Or cars or anything like that. That's all I put. Well I put all kinds of things but that's all I'm going to have.
>
> *Ms. Ashton:* Well let's hear what else you have, because there were a number of lines there. Anyone who does not have anything that Donna has, and you have blanks, you know what I want you to do.
>
> *Donna:* OK.
>
> *Ms. Ashton:* Go ahead, sweetheart.
>
> *Donna:* Life on Verna was simple and . . . that's it.
>
> *Ms. Ashton:* Anybody else have anything to add to it?

Studies concerned with creating classroom environments conducive to the achievement of Latino youths indicate that collaborative learning and a sense of belonging to the classroom community are critical (Losey, 1995). In Improvement English, interdependence is encouraged as students engage in joint discussions, and social relationships are cultivated. Consistent with this, in Ms. Ashton's class, Donna looks engaged. As illustrated in the transcripts above, Donna frequently and eagerly contributes to classroom discussion, stays focused, listens when necessary, and works when given the opportunity.

One could raise the point that the differences observed in Donna are due purely to differences in the difficulty of these two courses. While this

explanation is possible and may contribute to Donna's response, a second example offers additional indication that differences in the organizational and
interactive features of a classroom are also relevant. As a freshman, Donna
attended a highly regimented mathematics class in which students spent almost all of their time in their seats, listening to teacher explanations. Often
tuning out of the classroom discussion, Donna appeared resistant in the eyes
of this math teacher: "You know, last year I didn't have any feeling that she
couldn't do, do the work. I had the feeling that she just wasn't, as is the case
with many many kids. . . . Just really refusing." One year later, Donna participates in this same teacher's revised introduction to algebra course. Though
the difficulty level of the course is the same, the content is presented in a
different manner. Some of the new activities involve group projects. In this
situation, Donna appears quite different to her teacher: mature, engaged, and
willing to contribute. As he saw it, "This year the course is different, but she's
different also. . . . It's just a willingness, a willingness, willingness . . . she's in
her team there, and when we're outside you know they're going to be working
together. . . . She's right up there with them, and contributing, and seems to
be very pleased with being able to contribute, from what I can see."

CONCLUSION

Donna exemplifies a student who manages transitions, but only with difficulty, as she moves across the sociocultural and socioeconomic borders between home and school. Her teachers' comments as well as her steady progress toward high school graduation indicate that she has made significant and
successful attempts to adapt to the norms and values of her school environment. At the same time, however, it is apparent that Donna finds border
crossing both exhausting and difficult, and at times she appears vulnerable to
disengagement. This vulnerability was especially apparent during a period
when Donna's family was homeless and socioeconomic borders were salient.
During this time, Donna not only struggled to maintain her academic standards but also complained of symptoms indicative of stress: exhaustion,
stomachache, and headache. Even during periods when Donna's economic
situation was more stable, her fluctuating grades, particularly in classes like
the tenth-grade English course described in the preceding section, reveal that
it is a struggle to juggle the demands of her two worlds. Donna's effort to
both maintain her pivotal role in a highly social peer group and conform to
an individualistic school environment is a significant source of the tension she
experiences. Donna and her friends are not opposed to school involvement;
however, there are times where the norms and assumptions that underlie
school practice conflict with their desire to develop personalized relationships

and the expectation that individuals will place the needs of the group above their own desires. But even after Donna enters a classroom and focuses attention on what she must do to succeed, she may experience discomfort as she grapples with interaction patterns and expectations that differ from those mastered in her home. Though Donna generally manages this situation, classroom climate can affect her overall level of participation, attention, and interest in academic work.

It is important to note that Donna receives very little help or assistance from school personnel as she struggles to cross the borders between home and school. She does not ask for a great deal. Donna wants to know about her postgraduate opportunities and she wants someone to provide her with a glimpse into the collegiate world. Donna would like also for adults to recognize and appreciate what will be for her and her family a significant accomplishment: graduation from high school. Used to operating in a relational and interdependent world, Donna would welcome and benefit from stronger relationships with school adults. However, she lacks the energy to bring these relationships about on her own.

Donna brings many abilities to school that are highly relevant to the work world. Organizational and planning experience, collaborative skills, leadership capabilities, and a history of contributing to group efforts are among some of these capabilities. Yet, for the most part these abilities are not called on during the school day. We are not suggesting that schools reorganize to match the norms and expectations characteristic of students' communities. Given the diverse nature of most student bodies, this would be impossible. Further, this position is inconsistent with our general belief in the value of developing bicultural abilities. However, Donna's case illustrates that schools often focus too narrowly, and thereby miss an opportunity to let students with diverse types of expertise teach through example. Adults too miss out. Donna, like many other students who remain invisible in formalized school environments, has much to teach about maintaining family and friendships, supporting others, and balancing priorities.

NOTE

1. Red is the color typically used to symbolize loyalty to "Norteño" gang groups. According to the youths with whom I spoke, Norteños are oriented, among other things, toward a Chicano life-style that blends American and Mexican behaviors as well as practices particular to Chicanos as a group.

6

SONIA GONZALES

ON CRAZINESS

Mexicans are more crazier than white people. It's—we have like different kinds of thinking I guess, I don't know. Like we want to do everything—it's like they [whites] take everything slowly you know. You know they take everything slow, and I don't know it's just that they think about the future more and stuff. And us, you know what happens, happens. And it's just meant to happen. And it's like we do crazy things, and we never think about the consequences that might happen. . . . Right now it's like if I keep on acting the way I am, I don't know what I'm going to do—end up in the streets, sweeping floors. I don't want to do that, and maybe if I get my act together I'll go to college, you know. I want to get a degree.

It is a warm spring day, and I wait, worrying and wondering, as a current of young men and women move without comment around my adult body.[1] It is passing period at Explorer High School. I look around. The center of the campus is normally eerie, quiet, the silence punctuated only by the echoing steps of students scurrying to and from the administrative building and the squawks of walkie-talkies on the belts of campus security people. Now, it is flooded with almost 1,400 young bodies moving between classes. I see the standard clumps: groups of Mexican immigrants, speaking Spanish; groups of neighborhood youth—mostly European-American; fewer students of Asian descent—mostly Vietnamese immigrants. I do not see the body I am looking for.

I have an appointment to see Sonia Gonzales, a popular sophomore student of Mexican descent who speaks above. I first met Sonia in April 1990, when recruiting Latino students for this study. I became interested in Sonia's experience at Explorer, for her academic performance plummeted on entering this environment. During middle school, Sonia earned mostly B's and C's, finishing with 2.33 and 2.17 grade point averages (GPAs) during her seventh and eighth grade years. During her freshman year, she failed six of the 12

118

courses she took (for a 0.58 GPA overall). While Sonia's eighth-grade California Test of Basic Skills (CTBS) scores were not high (49th percentile in mathematics, 43rd percentile in language, 29th percentile in reading), they were not so low that they made me wonder if she could do her academic work.

Over the next 14 months, the markers of Sonia's engagement did not improve. During the first semester of her sophomore year, she failed five out of six classes, passing only driver's education with a D−. Her absences during the same 90-day period ranged from a high of 30 days missed in English, her least favorite class, to 12 in Life Science, her favorite course. Yet these official markers of disengagement hid another peculiarity. During the period spent with Sonia, I saw her academic performance and verbal self-presentation fluctuate. Indeed, during the 10 hours that I spent interviewing Sonia and the approximately 40 hours I spent with her in classrooms, I saw two selves emerge. The first and most dominant is a "crazy" self who believes in spontaneity and defiance of parental and school authority, a self who equates being Mexican with social and academic failure and sees the sociocultural borders between community and school worlds as insurmountable. The second and nearly submerged is a "schoolgirl" self who worries about her grades, speaks of attending college, and believes that youths of Mexican descent can follow a difficult but navigable path to academic and professional success.

I continue to wait, hopeful but worried, in our prearranged meeting place. I had looked for Sonia after her first-period algebra class, but her teacher informed me with a question in his voice that she did not show up for class. As the warning bell rings for second period, Sonia arrives from the wrong direction, her notebook clutched in front of her chin, her body pressed close to the side of her female companion, her brown eyes, rimmed with dark eyeliner, watchful. She is smiling. "We went out for breakfast," she laughs. Sonia's crazy self has arrived.

Where Is Sonia Coming From?

Sonia leaves her home in a well-kept, working-class barrio for Explorer around 7:00 A.M. every school day. At home, Sonia lives with her father, mother, younger sister (5 years Sonia's junior), uncle, and maternal grandparents. Sonia's father, a production worker, and her mother, a cannery worker, emigrated to the United States from Guadalajara, Mexico, in their teens. Arriving during a manufacturing boom, Sonia's father quickly found work and eventually was able to purchase the family home. While both of Sonia's parents were raised in Mexico, her mother's family has been connected to Mostaza since the early 1940s, when Sonia's grandfather moved there to support his then-young bride and his children. Sonia was born in the United States when her mother was 16. As Sonia sees it, while she and her parents are U.S.

citizens, much of the family's heart remains in Mexico: "Our family, it's like, all of our family is like always into Mexican stuff. Like we're always talking about going to Mexico, we're always talking about going to Mexican parties, everything, all, everything. Any free chance that we get, any vacations, we want to go to Mexico." At home, Sonia speaks Spanish exclusively. Family vacations revolve around trips to Guadalajara. During the holidays, celebrations incorporate Mexican traditions. In all, Sonia has been to Mexico five times. Sonia also describes her parents as attempting to socialize her to behaviors they associate with proper Mexican female comportment. As Sonia sees it, "This is practically all the Mexicans: A lady shouldn't go out at night, a lady shouldn't be out in cars with all these guys, a lady shouldn't be doing—like a lady shouldn't be smoking, a lady shouldn't be drinking, a lady shouldn't . . . you know. She should just stick to her house." Sonia—like most of her friends—is not allowed to go out of the house on weekends or after school hours unless chaperoned by a friend's older sibling.

Like her parents, Sonia has maintained a strong, emotional commitment to her Mexican identity. She sums this up succinctly in her comparison of American and Mexican cultures:

> Right here it's like totally different, it's a totally different culture. Right here, you know, everything's like, very sad looking. I don't know, it's sad. Over there [in Mexico] out in the streets you can see everybody happy, being friends, just talking to one another . . . everybody talks to everybody over there . . . everybody respects one another over there in Mexico. Over here it's like, nobody gives a damn about nobody else, it's just like they're only looking to themselves.

Sonia's current friends, mostly Mexican immigrants and first-generation Mexican Americans, share her pro-Mexico orientation. They prefer speaking Spanish, prefer Mexican music, prefer dancing at mostly Mexican parties, and are fiercely critical of Mexican-descent students who hide their ability to speak Spanish or otherwise appear to deny their culture. Sonia sums up this viewpoint:

> That's what I hate. It's like, some people, they're Mexican, they have Mexican blood inside of them, but they were born here. That doesn't make a difference, they're still Mexican, I think. And like they say, "No, I'm not Mexican." And like, they know how to speak Spanish and everything and they try to tell you "Oh, I don't speak Spanish." And you try to talk to them in Spanish and they go "I don't understand what you're saying." They try to deny their culture.

According to Sonia, she and her friends also express their pro-Mexican orientation through affiliation and friendship with "Sureño" gang members. Sureños embrace several neighborhood gangs oriented, among other things, toward the assertion and preservation of the Spanish language and Mexican culture. As a group, Sonia and her female friends are consistently critical of just one aspect of their cultural heritage—traditional Latino conceptions of proper female adolescent behavior. Feeling that restrictions on dating and freedom of movement are inappropriate for young females in America, Sonia and her friends spend quite a bit of time designing schemes and carrying out plans in order to evade their parents' wishes.

Sonia's parents' place in history, particularly their immigrant status, is reflected in the lessons they teach her. For example, Sonia's interviews suggest that her parents manifest what Marcelo and Carola Suarez-Orozco (1993) term "the immigrants' dual frame of reference," in which "immigrants are constantly comparing and contrasting their current lot in the host society against their previous experiences and expectations in the country of origin."

> My parents said that they prefer to be poor here, than being poor in Mexico. Cause the poverty over there is scary. It's different. Right here, being poor here, over there it's like being rich. And it's like, over there, it's really ugly, you know, it's scary. You see these little kids out in the street, you know, no clothes whatsoever, you know, all dirty. They're small begging out in the streets because there's nothing, there's no money. And there's people dying.

Further, Sonia's mother also appears to manifest classic immigrant beliefs about education. (According to Sonia, her father has little involvement in her education.) For example, according to Sonia her mother believes that education is key to professional and economic success in America: "My mom, she's always trying to encourage me. She's always telling me 'Go to school, try to be someone in life. Get a good education cause if you get a good education you get a good job, a good paying job' and everything."

Sonia's mother's beliefs concerning schooling are reflected in the ways that she has attempted to support Sonia's education. For example, based on the recommendations of middle-school teachers, she made Sonia attend Explorer. Sonia also describes her mother as constantly asking if Sonia has completed her homework and consistently encouraging her to graduate from high school. At the same time, because Sonia's mother did not graduate, she cannot offer assistance with homework. Further, she has not contacted the school about Sonia's declining performance, perhaps because of fears related to cross-cultural communication. (Sonia's mother does not speak English.) As

Sonia's grades have plummeted, Sonia says that her mother has alternated between pleading with Sonia to do her homework, yelling at Sonia for destroying her future, and throwing her hands up in despair. Sonia's mother has not shown Sonia's father Sonia's high school report cards, because she is afraid of his possibly violent reaction.

In light of Sonia's academic history, Sonia says that her current educational performance is particularly upsetting and incomprehensible to her mother. As an elementary student, Sonia attended a bilingual school near her home. Her elementary school record indicates steady progress. For example, her teachers cite her excellent conduct and study habits, with her third-grade teacher commenting "Very good student" and her fifth-grade teacher "Sonia is a student with a lot of ability" and "I want great things for her." She earned A's and B's in all subject areas, with the exception of handwriting. Entering as a Spanish speaker, Sonia was classified fluent English proficient by the fourth grade. During her first year of middle school—sixth grade—Sonia continued to excel, earning A's and B's. Her grades fell slightly (to B's and C's) in the seventh and eighth grades, because, according to Sonia, she became involved with a peer group that was not academically oriented. Nevertheless, most of her middle-school teachers (21 out of 24) continued to cite her excellent conduct and six (out of the ten who commented) her acceptable preparation. Over her three years in middle school, only three teachers mentioned incomplete assignments, and four inadequate preparation. Sonia's CTBS scores also indicate competence. In the fourth grade, she scored at the 46th percentile in reading, the 36th percentile in language, and the 37th percentile in math. By the seventh grade, while her reading score fell to the 38th percentile, her scores increased to the 55th percentile in language and the 61st percentile in math.

In sum, Sonia comes to school with a pro-Mexico orientation, supported by both friends and family. She also remembers a successful early school history. In addition, according to Sonia, her family is not critical of the American opportunity structure. Rather, they have aspirations for Sonia, encourage her to apply herself to education, and compare and contrast the economic situation in the United States favorably to that of Mexico.

Sonia's "Crazy" Self

> It's like we all have these—I mean we're young, and we have all these crazy ideas you know. All of a sudden we come to school, we come to school, come to study and everything, and then all of a sudden we have this great idea.

Sonia's crazy self—the self who values spontaneity, fun, and danger; the self who cuts, drinks, and parties, sometimes with gang members—is Sonia's public identity. In four interviews, Sonia used the word crazy 7 times to describe herself, 16 times to characterize individual friends, 16 times to refer to herself and her peers ("we"), and 6 times to characterize Mexicans as a group. Sonia's crazy self skipped 23 out of 180 school days over her sophomore year, and missed 62 periods of English over the same time period. Sonia's crazy self also became increasingly dominant over her first two years of high school, with her grades falling steadily and her absences increasing up to the end of the first semester of sophomore year.

With me, Sonia tries to keep her crazy self under control. She attends school. She arrives on time for classes. Yet, Sonia's crazy self reveals itself in uncompleted homework, borrowed pencils and paper, and friendly teasing and interaction with peers.

It reveals itself during passing period, for example, as Sonia laughed when her best friend Maria informed us, "I have to go, I'll be late to class." Sonia commented, "I don't know what's wrong with her, all of a sudden worrying about being late." It reveals itself during lunchtime, when Sonia's friends open her fat white notebook, overflowing with papers. A pile of uncompleted worksheets, tucked haphazardly into a back pocket, spills onto the table. "Look at all this work Sonia hasn't done!" It reveals itself in the steady decline in Sonia's academic performance. Sonia's highest semester grade to the end of her sophomore year was a C+ in physical education (P.E.). She had earned just 50 credits by the end of her sophomore year. In all, 225 are required to graduate.

Finally, Sonia's crazy self reveals itself in the bravado with which Sonia speaks of defying authority, of throwing caution to the wind: "White girls, they're like 'Oh my mom's going to do this' and they're all scared, and you know they don't like to cut and everything. . . . I mean, my parents are the same way and everything, but it's like, I don't listen to them. Cause sometimes I go 'Well, if they're gonna beat me up or something, I might as well have fun!'"

In explaining craziness, Sonia speaks in psychological terms. She conceives of craziness as a powerful state of being, as a psychological characteristic that reflects and emanates from cultural differences. For her, craziness differentiates Mexican-descent adolescents (and African Americans) from their European-American peers. Thus, for Sonia European Americans are "calm" and "careful" while Mexicans "don't care about what we do" because "us Mexicans are more daring." Mexicans, in her view, are also more spontaneous: "We never plan like one day ahead or something, we just do it"; "We are always looking for action." This translates into behaviors that preclude aca-

demic success, most notably skipping class and failing to complete assignments: "Us Mexicans, we like 'Oh, we don't care if we do our homework' or
whatever." For Sonia, these differences are significant and immutable sociocultural borders:

> For them [whites] to fit in it's so hard. I think it's very hard for them
> because like us Mexicans think of their people —they're like more at
> calm, they're careful. And it's like us, we don't care, we don't care about
> what we do or whatever, and white people it's like they're more cautious
> of what they do, what people might think. (*How about if you wanted to
> hang out with white people, what would be the barriers for you?*) Oh my gosh,
> I just couldn't do that because they're just much too quiet, too calm,
> two different cultures, personalities, different. I just couldn't.

Interestingly, Sonia's crazy behavior is not noticeably different from that of
many European-American teens. In general, for Sonia craziness in practice
consists of a variety of experimental behaviors in which adolescents of all
backgrounds tend to engage: sneaking out at night, partying, drinking, and
cutting. Although Sonia occasionally sees a gun, goes along with friends as
they steal alcohol, and knows gang members, her involvement in these sorts
of activities is the exception rather than the rule. Nevertheless, Sonia is emphatic in her belief that European Americans cannot fit into her social world:
"It's not so much that we wouldn't accept you guys, it's just so much that I
don't think—they won't, white people wouldn't be willing to do what us Mexicans do, you know?"

I considered a variety of factors in trying to understand Sonia's craziness.
First, and most obvious, it is possible that Sonia no longer has the ability to
do her academic work. However, Sonia's academic performance and behavior
during one period indicates this is not the case. For six weeks during her sophomore year, Sonia was in a fight with her two best friends. During this period,
Sonia presented a "schoolgirl" self. She attended class regularly, receiving the
second highest grade (A−) in Life Science, and passed five out of six classes
with a 2.06 GPA overall.

Second, it is possible that Sonia does not believe schoolwork would pay
off. Again, however, this explanation is unsatisfactory in light of Sonia's interview data. During our conversations Sonia equated education with a good job
on three separate occasions and also said that this belief keeps her in school:
"Well, sometimes I just feel like dropping out and forgetting everything. But
then I think about it and I go 'Nope, not worth it.' Because at the long run I
have to, you know, stay here, I have to come to school so I can get a good
education and if I want to get a good job. So that's what keeps me going,
my future." Sonia also gave ideological responses when speaking about the

American social structure: "When you give it all you got, and you try, it's like, whatever culture you are, whatever color you are, it doesn't matter. Cause there's always a lot of opportunities. You could take that person down to court if they're prejudiced. So that's nothing that could get in your way." Further, Sonia did not criticize or tease her Latina friends who were relatively successful in school and expressed admiration for the students some call "schoolgirls": "Some girls and boys that are really good at school, they call them schoolboys, schoolgirls, stuff like that. I don't see no reason to be embarrassed because I think it's good, I mean, I'd like to be a schoolgirl myself, you know, I want good grades. I mean they're showing that they know more than the person that's putting them down."

Third, it is possible that Sonia simply does not care about school performance. This explanation also seems simplistic. For one thing, Sonia expressed interest in college during three different interviews. She also spoke often of her worries about her grades, future economic opportunities, and her desire to finish school:

> My mom was talking to me the other day and she got mad at me because I got my report card and I got F's. And she sits down and she talks to me and she goes "If you don't want to go to school, just quit." I know it hurts her but you know, I don't want to quit yet. I don't want to quit, 'cause one thing I want to get more education. And I want to get a good job. And then later on get a family, you know.

There were also moments when Sonia revealed a schoolgirl self, demonstrating care for academic performance. In Life Science, for example, Sonia was once the last student to finish a test on vertebrates, working in great concentration and occasionally muttering "I don't know what he's trying to do here." In a foods class, Sonia and a tablemate were completing their "management sheet," a worksheet that asks students to detail how they will divide, manage, and carry out cooking tasks. Sonia asked her partner: "Try to make it better so we can get 20 points this time" and then added, "We got all the points for the last sheet." Perhaps most significant, when Sonia was counseled out of Explorer at the end of her junior year, she enrolled in independent study, completing her work and continuing on to her senior year.

In the end, it appeared that Sonia's craziness most reflects the ideology of a peer group to which Sonia pledges allegiance. While Sonia describes craziness as a psychological characteristic emanating from cultural factors, in practice it is highly social. First, craziness is one component that Sonia perceives as integral to her popularity: "I have all kinds of friends, cause they know I'm crazy and everything, but I always listen to people and everything so, I have all kinds of friends." Second, from Sonia's perspective it is essential to have friends present in order for craziness to occur: "If I wouldn't have any friends here, I think there'd be nothing else better to do than just do my work. But since my friends are here it's like, OK, let's go over here and cut." As mentioned previously, Sonia's grades and attendance improved markedly during a period when she was in a fight with her two best friends. Thus, Sonia's record data support her verbal assertions.

However, to say simply that Sonia's ideology emanates from her peer world is to ignore the context in which she operates. It is critical to consider how Sonia's day-to-day experiences may shape her conclusion that the sociocultural differences between Mexican-descent and European-American youths are impassable social borders. In considering Sonia's school world, it becomes apparent that various school practices and policies work to confirm, rather than challenge, her convictions that Mexican-descent and European-American youths are fundamentally different. Further, aspects of the environment, most notably meanings that emanate from disciplinary policies and structural borders, combine to communicate the meanings that Sonia herself asserts: Latino youths are irredeemable and destined for academic and societal marginalization. Finally, Sonia's classroom experiences suggest that academic success is contingent on the ability to adhere to rules and follow directions, behaviors Sonia has come to perceive as characteristic of European Americans.

Reinforcing Sociocultural Borders: Lessons on Social Divisions

Ivan, ESL tutor, Explorer graduate: I mean there's two Explorers, the Explorer that is seen or presented by the administration, and the Explorer in reality. And Explorer's divided into the white people Explorer, college-bound students—you know Cloverbrook—and the students that are bused in. This is a divided school.

As a freshman, Sonia moved into an environment caught up in significant social change. Prior to court-ordered desegregation, Explorer's student body was 81.8% European-American, with the majority of these students middle- and upper-middle-class. Five years later, by the time Sonia is a sophomore, the enrollment of youth of color has jumped from 18.2 to 57.8%; 30.6% of the student body qualifies for free or reduced price lunch. The majority of Explorer's new students are of Mexican descent; in all, Latino students make up 40.6% of Explorer's student body.

However, while students at Explorer attend school with youths from varying backgrounds, they enter a highly segregated environment when they arrive at school. Particularly relevant to Sonia, Explorer's more than 400 English as a second language (ESL) (355 of them Latino) students are in their own track. Academic and social divisions are repeated in the English-speaking environment. Advanced courses are dominated by European Americans, while fluent-English-speaking (FEP) Latinos are concentrated in general and remedial classes. (When Sonia is a sophomore, Latinos make up 22.8 percent of Explorer's FEP population but 7.6 percent of the accelerated English track.) A similar pattern characterizes Explorer's math and science classrooms. Explorer's staff is also overwhelmingly European-American; during Sonia's first two years of high school all of her teachers were European-American. Policies both amplify and attach status to this academic differentiation. Most notably, high-achieving ESL students are shut out of the honor society (CSF) because they cannot take the classes that qualify them for admission.

Such divisions take on added significance when one realizes that school policies foster social as well as academic segregation. For example, the daily bulletin that alerts students to school activities and scholarship possibilities is read and posted in English. At lunch time, students who qualify for free or reduced-price lunch line up inside the school cafeteria for hot meals, as lines for youths who buy hamburgers, pizza, and other popular fare are located in the outside courtyard. Because of the strong association between socioeconomic status and ethnic background in the Explorer area, youths of color— the majority of them Spanish-speaking—dominate the dimly lit cafeteria. European-American students dominate the central outdoor courtyard, the most visible area of the school. As a youth who prefers to speak Spanish, wears bright lipstick and heavy eyeliner, and teases her hair, Sonia marks herself clearly as a member of Mostaza's Latino community. As such, though English-speaking and able to purchase lunch outside, Sonia says that her place in Explorer's social system was clear when she arrived: "Because mostly at lunch time you see Mexicans in the cafeteria, white people here, and blacks— you could see . . . you could see the groups right away." She and her friends eat lunch in the cafeteria, with Explorer's immigrant Latino students.

According to Explorer's principal, the school's explicit mission is to integrate its new students into the student body. Given this mission, one might expect a set of concentrated and targeted efforts to address both the academic and the social differentiation described above. However, even as adults verbalize concerns about student behavior and express the desire for integration, there is a notable absence of effort directed toward academic empowerment or social inclusion. In both their general approach to Explorer's Latino population as a whole, and their specific response to Sonia's craziness in particular, adults communicate their tacit acceptance of the divisions that permeate Explorer's environment.

First, for example, despite the fact that 58% of Explorer students are youths of color, and many come from families where neither parent has attended college, there are no mentoring or targeted college recruitment efforts in place. Latinos and African Americans at local universities and businesses have no formal connections with Explorer students, nor do youths from Explorer visit colleges with diverse populations. Thus, Sonia and her classmates are not made aware of the many Latinos in the area who have succeeded both academically and professionally. Further, Explorer is not connected to national programs targeted toward the college enrollment of youths of color, such as Upward Bound. Rather, individuals are expected to research these and other opportunities on their own. (Limited information about college scholarships can be attained by going to a career center tucked in the back corner of the library.) Sonia is keenly aware that she lacks information relative to her European-American classmates: "Sometimes it's so hard because I think about it, about going to college, you need [to meet] so many requirements and I go 'What's the big difference between the state and UC system?' I don't understand any of that. And it's scary too 'cause I hear other students say 'Well, I'm going to UC' or whatever, and I go [to myself] 'What's that?' You know, I want to know!" In not providing information relevant to higher education, Explorer contributes to producing a structural border that impedes Sonia's connection to school. As Sonia observes which groups of students appear to have relevant information, she also has more reason to believe that European Americans "have their act together" while Latinos do not.

A second factor relevant to communicating tacit acceptance of the idea that European Americans and Latinos are differentially suited for academic endeavor is Explorer's traditional curriculum, which emphasizes European history and literature. During the days we spent in classrooms at Explorer, matters related to cultural or economic diversity were not discussed in any in-depth way. Seeking to check the representativeness of our experiences, we asked four students (two Latinas, one Vietnamese immigrant, and one African American) explicitly whether they had encountered curriculum relevant to their heritage during their first two years of high school. All said that their exposure to such content was minimal to nonexistent. According to Sonia, for example, just one teacher presented content relevant to her ethnicity. Further, from Sonia's perspective this teacher emphasized negative social statistics (e.g., the correlation between ethnic background and poverty, teen pregnancy):

> Like last year, Mr. Kula. It's like he used to say all this and that. But he was always, everything bad was [about] Hispanics, blacks. All of us Latino. Us, you know. I mean, I understand 'cause there's a big majority of Hispanics and Blacks that are not doing that good? But there's a lot of them that. . . . So we felt right there that he was discriminating [against] us, you know, he's prejudiced.

In her first two years of high school, despite enrollment in a world history course both years, Sonia did not consider the works or accomplishments of people of color, nor did she discuss mechanisms that work to generate and promote social divisions.

Third and finally, tacit acceptance of academic divisions between Latino and European-American youths is personalized for Sonia in that adults pay little attention to her academic decline. Despite the fact that Sonia entered Explorer as a relatively successful middle-school student, she had no conversation with any school official about her rate of academic progress. Further, according to Sonia, just one teacher "got on my case" during her sophomore year, telling her that she was capable of more. This same individual, her favorite teacher, was the sole teacher who noted and praised Sonia's added academic effort when her grades rose during the six-week period referred to previously.

Consistent with the above, Sonia feels that Explorer's adults generally operate and act on lowered expectations for Latinos. In her experience, such expectations are communicated in two primary ways. First, says Sonia, adults appear to distance themselves from youths like Sonia, who signal allegiance to Latino culture through their dress and makeup:

> It's like once they see a Mexican right away, you know, especially when they dressed like this [like me], you know. . . . I wear a lot of eyeliner or something, you know, we look scary looking sometimes, you know? I guess that's the way teachers are, you know. The first impression has a lot to say about a person, you know. But, they should always look at what a person has. They have to talk to that person, get to know that person.

Second, though Sonia feels that the majority of her teachers treat her with respect, some communicate that they have given up on her and her Latina friends:

> *Sonia:* Most teachers, you know, white teachers, some of them are kind of prejudiced. Kind of prejudiced.
> *Interviewer:* What makes you know that?
> *Sonia:* It's probably the way they look at you, the way they talk, you know, when they're talking about something like when they talk about the people who are going to drop out. . . . And then Mr. Kula, when he's talking about teenage pregnancy or something like that. He turns around and he looked at us. It's like, he tries to look around the whole room so we won't notice but like he mostly tries

to get it through our heads, you know. Sometimes I think he's prejudiced.

Though adults appear to ignore Sonia's academic performance they nevertheless convince her, through looks and glances, that they view her as dangerous and destined for academic failure. Though Sonia signals lack of interest in school, teacher expectations are nevertheless salient. For example, she heaps praise on the one teacher who noticed and praised her improved grades.

Confirming Sonia's Vision: Explorer's Disciplinary System

In addition to entering a highly segregated environment, Sonia and her friends work in a setting characterized by tight social control. Teachers perceive behavioral changes in Explorer's new student population, expressing worry about low skills, student hostility, lack of parental involvement, and student immaturity. In addition, nearly 60% of the faculty listed disrespect for authority as their primary concern in a survey conducted during Sonia's sophomore year. These teachers' worries reached their height soon after Sonia's arrival at Explorer, when a stabbing incident occurred. Though the incident involved a Latino adolescent who came from off-campus to the school in search of a rival gang member, this incident was perceived as further evidence that the school was out of control. In response, those in charge of discipline implemented a set of practices designed to control and manage their increasingly diverse student body. Meant to assure safety, this plan also works effectively to support the idea that Explorer's Latino students are dangerous and irredeemable.

Increased reconnaissance and surveillance, organized around monitoring student activity during passing periods and lunch time and identifying students operating as "key players" in the environment, are the first means by which Explorer adults control the student body. Students' movements are closely monitored and strictly controlled by campus assistants, who patrol the campus and communicate by walkie-talkie. Adults in this role generally do not communicate with youths during the lunch hour and passing period, but rather watch and monitor student movement. Youths seen on campus during classroom hours are immediately referred to Saturday school.

Though these tactics affect all students, certain policies make it clear that the administration is particularly concerned about the activities of Latinos. Soon after the stabbing incident, colors associated with Latino gangs were banned from campus. Students wearing two or more pieces of red or blue—the colors associated with rival Latino gangs—were called into the discipline office and given one warning. According to the discipline principal, this "colors campaign" was integral to an effort to identify "major players" on campus. Based on the students who visited his office, the discipline principal compiled a list of names. Those seen as defiant were quickly expelled, the remainder watched carefully.

Explorer's system of school-level surveillance is complemented by classroom disciplinary mechanisms that ensure quick removal from the classroom of youths perceived as disobedient. Teachers have the prerogative to remove students from the classroom at any time, sending them to "in-school suspension." According to the principal of discipline, students sent to his office as a result of such classroom conflicts face certain reprisal, typically Saturday school or, in severe instances, suspension: "I support teachers. That's very, very important to me. . . . I'm one of those guys that thinks that schools or institutions of any kind run better when there's a hatchet man." Again, these aspects of Explorer's environment affect all individuals. However, statistics indicate that Latinos are more commonly subject to these efforts to control. For example, data on out-of-school suspensions confirm that Latinos are disproportionately subject to disciplinary action. Further, Latinos are 92.3% of those suspended for "defiant or disruptive behavior," the second most commonly cited reason for student suspension (behind threatening or causing physical injury).

Though frequently absent, Sonia does not wander the campus during passing period, does not wear colors, and has not been subject to disciplinary action due to conflicts with peers or misbehavior in class. Nevertheless, during our interviews Sonia referred to the feeling of being watched on three occasions. If her descriptions are accurate, than the disciplinary staff develops its sense of whom to watch not only by noting who wears colors, but also through knowledge of a youth's friends and associates:

> Mr. Clarkson? He's an asshole. He used to be at Brookvale High. He knows Ralph [Sonia's friend's boyfriend] really good, he used to be like a real troublemaker and that's why they kicked him out of Brookvale. Ralph, like when he used to come pick us up at the beginning of the school year, he [the principal] came up to us and then he goes—he came to our table during lunch time—he goes "Hmm, I can see you guys are really popular around here, you guys are really known." And he goes "Erica, I've heard a lot about you. Sonia, I heard a lot about you." Mr. Clarkson, it's like he'd be watching . . . he's always keeping an eye on us.

Though Sonia has no significant discipline record, she views this surveillance as an indication that she has been predefined as crazy: "Cause you know how we build up our reputation since last year, cause they always look at the people who behave bad. They're always watching them, cause they always follow in their same footsteps."

The emphasis on controlling and removing youths perceived as disobedient or dangerous, combined with the seeming acceptance of the academic and social divisions that permeate Explorer's environment, communicates the idea that Latinos are different and irredeemable. Sonia sees many Latinos thrown out of school because they are perceived as troublemakers and no Mexican-descent individuals are held up as role models, either by the school or in the curriculum. Her disengagement from school, along with that of her close friends, goes generally unremarked. Given this set of conditions, there are no reasons for Sonia to question her conclusion that youth of Mexican and European-American descent are fundamentally different.

Classroom Lessons: Constructing Whiteness

> Like white people, they really think about what they're going to do, they're like more serious, more shy. You know, they're more serious about what they're going to do.

In a previous section, I described Sonia's conviction that youths of Mexican descent are "crazy." As indicated in the quote above, Sonia is equally emphatic when voicing ideas about "white" psychology and behavior. Sonia perceives European Americans as quiet, calm, careful, and cautious by nature.

As Sonia has no close friends of European-American descent, and has little contact with European Americans after returning to her home, her primary source of information about them comes from her day-to-day experiences in high school. However, it is not likely that Sonia draws her conclusions from interactions. During lunch and passing period, Sonia spends her time exclusively with Latinos and African Americans. During class, the conversations that she holds with European Americans are brief and revolve around the task at hand. As Sonia explains, "I mean, I talk to them and say 'What are you doing?' or, you know, talk about school, talk about the class. But it's not like we're talking about our friends or anything like that." In sum, Sonia knows few European Americans, and the relationships that she does have do not lend themselves to the degree of knowledge that she asserts above.

However, Sonia's conclusions about European Americans are completely consistent with her observations of who is willing to adopt the behaviors necessary for success in the academic classrooms that she attends. During her sophomore year, Sonia enrolls in six classes, four of them academic. In the latter, interaction patterns and tasks combine to corroborate Sonia's belief that calm, quiet, care, and caution are essential to academic success.

First, in three of her four academic classrooms, Sonia spends the majority of her time in virtual silence, her only interactions consisting of brief comments or asides to peers. In English, for example, Sonia does seatwork, completing worksheets and answering short-answer questions from her textbook. Students are threatened with in-school suspension for speaking during silent reading or seat work: "You can't talk in there cause if you talk you go to in-school suspension. . . . It's strict and there's hardly ever group work in there, so nobody's talking in there, just we read, read, read and that's all we do." In Math and World History, Sonia spends most of the period listening silently as a teacher demonstrates, lectures, and poses questions. Students either take notes or remain silent unless called on. Those who do not are quickly reprimanded: "All right, we're going to play a third-grade game. I hear your voice, and you're out." At times, even note-taking is highly directed, with the teacher stopping at key points to tell students what to write down: "Here is another term to note. Pugachev. He started a peasant uprising. Write down that the peasants hated their masters." "This is what you need to know. Catherine the Great was not Russian, she was German. She expanded the empire and power. She didn't solve the domestic problems."

Second, in all of Sonia's academic classrooms, activities convey the idea that care and caution, critical for the memorization of detail, are essential to successful academic work. While the content in Sonia's classrooms varies significantly, in general the emphasis is on learning facts, definitions, specific answers, and prescribed problem-solving procedures. In World History, for example, for a test on the medieval period, students are expected to name the predominant architectural style and to define terms such as nave, buttress, gargoyle, king, knight, vassal, serf, peasant, and lord. In Life Science, students regularly complete long worksheets focused on intricate biological detail. One period, for example, Sonia works half-heartedly on an assignment that revolves around 39 questions about algae. Here, she peruses her text for answers to questions such as: What can be the smallest size of algae? What are the large algae plants called? List four things that all algae have in common.

No class that I attend with Sonia on a regular basis significantly challenges her conclusions about the type of mind set that typifies those who succeed academically in an American public high school. Indeed, in the majority of instances my observations support what she claims about the behavior of the more school-oriented peers enrolled in her general track courses. In order to meet the behavioral expectations in most of these classrooms, they do have to stay "calm." They do have to stay "quiet." They do have to be "careful." Sonia notes that European-American peers conform to these norms, and is aware that European Americans earn better grades than she and her Latino peers. This may help to explain why Sonia concludes that European Americans are more psychologically suited for constrained situations and that sociocultural differences are, in fact, impassable social borders.

What Matters for Sonia? Some Preliminary Insights

The preceding sections emphasize the difficulties Sonia has with regard to school, and school features that support her beliefs about sociocultural differences. However, while Sonia's grades might indicate that nothing any teacher does can make any difference and my analysis might suggest that Sonia's classrooms are all alike, this is not entirely the case. Sonia distinguishes between her classrooms and her evaluations of their relative worth are reflected in her attendance data.

Sonia describes her best classes as those in which teachers work to develop positive working relationships with students. In classrooms characterized by depersonalized teacher-student relationships and unfamiliar subject matter, Sonia explains, it is not only dull but also not possible to get help when it is needed. For example, when explaining why English is her least favorite class Sonia complains about her teacher's distant pedagogical style: "Sometimes I really don't understand. 'Cause sometimes we have to read like old English literature and stuff, and that's really hard to understand. He never talks about the stories. He just lets you read them." In contrast, in classrooms where Sonia feels that the teacher knows something about her and where students are allowed to work together on projects, Sonia enjoys herself more and feels confident that she can do well if she applies herself. Sonia has two sophomore-year classes—Foods and Life Science—that meet these general criteria. From our perspective, Life Science is the more beneficial in that the teacher, Mr. Ingalls, continually encourages Sonia to make academic efforts.

Life Science is in many respects similar to Sonia's other classrooms: Students work out of textbooks, defining vocabulary words and completing questions at the end of chapters. The questions Ingalls poses do occasionally require students to think, for example, "Describe the coloration pattern on the upper and lower body surfaces of a frog. How is this an adaptive advantage?" "What does the frog's eye have that we lack? How is the eye position an advantage?" However, as in most of her other classrooms, Sonia spends much of her time in Life Science writing and regurgitating facts.

Nevertheless, says Sonia, Life Science is the highlight of her academic day. Looking more closely at the course, it is apparent that Life Science differs from Sonia's other courses in three respects. First, Ingalls makes an effort to develop personalized and respectful work relationships with his students. Second, he encourages students to work together and help one another. And third, he personally and persistently urges Sonia to make academic efforts.

Ingalls rarely lectures. Rather, he spends his time communicating with students, circulating among them as they work in groups of two or four at lab tables on written work or occasional laboratory exercises. Ingalls feels that positive communication is critical for establishing the type of atmosphere that allows teaching to occur: "There are people that can be a combination of bad experiences in many things. But I've always tried to find something about everyone. . . . It helps that they know that there's something good about themselves, because they may not hear it for years."

Ingalls's strategy for fostering positive relationships between himself and his diverse students combines personalized interchange, affectionate bantering, and frank self-expression. Ingalls watches his students, observing and remembering what is important to them. For example, of all Sonia's teachers Ingalls is the only one who frequently uses the little Spanish he knows to greet Sonia and her friends. Ingalls also teases. With Sonia and her friends, who often chat about their love lives in class, this often involves ribbing them about their constant emphasis on social relationships, as reflected in the following quote: "Get to work. I'm not grading you on your social hour. Your love life is a D−!" Finally, Ingalls expresses his feelings and perceptions. If he is feeling tired and grumpy, he says so: "The stress, I mean sometimes I have to come back the next day and apologize to the kids and say 'I'm sorry, there was just things yesterday that I didn't like and I didn't know how to handle them' and go on about my business. You know, it's just like my wife at home." As Ingalls sees it, verbalizing feelings helps students "know where I'm coming from, and most of them accept when I say things that I'm not giving them a song and a dance and a story."

It is clear that Sonia enjoys the personalized nature of Ingalls's class. During interviews, for example, she fondly recalls classroom interchanges that she found amusing, as below:

> Mr. Ingalls just goes—when we start speaking to him in Spanish . . .
> we're all like telling him "Hi Mr. Ingalls, how are you today?" [in Spanish]. . . . He's all "Blah, blah, blah, blah." (laughs) He's all "blah, blah, blah, blah." He starts laughing, you know. "Yeah, whatever you guys say."

Sonia also enjoys Ingalls's class because her friends are enrolled and because the organization of the class allows her to talk with them as she works.

It is important to say, however, that Ingalls's classroom is academic as well as social. Ingalls prods his students to incorporate pro-academic behaviors into their lives. During the six times I visit Ingalls's classroom with Sonia, for example, I see him pull her toward academic work again and again without asking her to hide or submerge her highly social self. It is fine with Ingalls if Sonia and her friends chat about a sister's wedding dress or problems with a boyfriend, but the group has to make progress on their academic work. At one point, he separates them. Ingalls is also the only teacher I see who comments on and encourages the rise in Sonia's grades described previously:

> Sonia is working on a worksheet. Ingalls drifts by with his latest grade printout.
> *Ingalls:*   I want to show you this. You're only missing your cartoon packet, and you're two points from an A. I want you to get that in. Ingalls leaves.
> *Sonia:*   [chuckles and turns to researcher] You know what? He's come by to tell me my grade every other day!

Consistent with these observations, according to Sonia, Ingalls challenges her to reason about the academic material she encounters:

> You ask him a question and like most teachers just give you the answer. And like when you ask him a question he makes you think about the question, and then he gives you clues and then you have to figure it out yourself. . . . I like that, cause he makes you think.

In all, Sonia feels, Ingalls expects something of her and appreciates her potential: "He knows that I could do better if I tried, I know he knows that. 'Cause he's always telling me, encouraging me to do my work because he knows I could do better than that."

Though in the end she failed Life Science, during interviews and casual conversations Sonia says repeatedly that it matters that Ingalls did not discount her as a student and that he noticed the academic efforts she did make. She also attended Life Science more regularly than any other class, despite the fact that it fell directly after lunch—a convenient time to leave school. (In all, Sonia missed 28 out of 180 days in Life Science over the course of her sophomore year, compared with 62 days in English, her least favorite class.) It is also important to note that Ingalls showed Sonia that a European-American teacher can reveal a sense of humor and a capacity for emotion much like her own. As Ingalls negotiated the sociocultural borders between Sonia's social world and the calm, serious academic world of the classroom, he did the most of any of the teachers to force Sonia to reconsider stereotypical notions about who is likely to do what.

REFLECTION

Enrolled in the general track of her high school, Sonia has become increasingly involved in "crazy" behavior that she defines as characteristic of what it means to be Mexican. Part of a highly social peer group whose members spend significant periods of time away from school, Sonia skips classes, does not do homework, and consequently fails the majority of her classes. At the same time, Sonia reveals some interest in the very "schoolgirl" behaviors that her crazy self rejects as well as faith in the American opportunity structure. Thus, Sonia is not clearly and consistently oppositional. Rather, she appears to embrace stereotypes, making them her own even as she questions their generalizability. For her, cultural differences are unbridgeable social borders.

Sonia's perceptions of sociocultural borders cannot be fully examined without consideration of the definitions and meanings that permeate her school environment. Situated in a school where disciplinary practices support Sonia's view that Mexican-descent youth are psychologically prone to "screwing up," navigating an environment in which adults appear to keep a safe distance from Latino students even as they attempt to watch and circumscribe their behavior, there is no discourse present to challenge the meanings that Sonia and her peers accept and reproduce. It is notable, for example, that Sonia can practice the most academically harmful aspects of her crazy self relatively unfettered. Her truancy and academic failure are ignored. Sonia thus discovers that the school officials with whom she most often has contact make many efforts to watch and identify behavioral weaknesses in Latinos, and little effort to identify or nurture academic capabilities.

It is important to note that some features of Sonia's ideology and behavior are inconsistent not with learning and education, but rather with proper academic comportment as defined by the school. Sonia shows a preference for activities that require risk-taking and spontaneity, for example. Both are behaviors integral to work that requires creative thinking. Sonia also shows a capacity for analysis, as she notices patterns in her environment and seeks to construct and assert theories that enable her to make sense of what she sees. Finally, Sonia orients toward collaborative activities, demonstrating an ability to work with others to plan and organize social activities. However, within classrooms Sonia encounters a narrow conception of learning; here, neither creativity nor analysis nor collaborative skills are relevant. This reinforces Sonia's idea that academically successful European-American classmates must be different from herself. Otherwise, Sonia reasons, they would not be able to endure the behaviors and activities required for school success.

In sum, the conclusions Sonia draws and her behavior are consistent with meanings conveyed by the environment in which she operates. For Sonia, therefore, there are no clear challenges to the sociocultural borders she perceives.

NOTE

1. An earlier version of this chapter appears in Davidson (1996).

7

ROBERT HIRSCHMAN

I was born in Canada, Winnipeg Manitoba, and I left there when I was two. I lived with my mother until I was nine and then she passed away and I live with my grandparents now. I've been living there since I was about nine. We left my father when I was two. And I've had no contact with him. I've been living in Adobe Viejo for about—almost 11 years now . . . and I went to Darrow Junior High School and Larkin Elementary and I lived in Texas for a year in Corpus Christi and San Antonio with my mother—when I was seven—from six to seven. And I've lived in Nevada for a really short time. And I like to draw, I guess that's one of my strong points is my artistic skill. And I'm reasonably competent in geometry, and I like creative writing and I also enjoy cycling. That's my exercise. Cycling and racquet ball—things like that. And that's basically it. It's not a most exciting life.

This brief, matter-of-factly delivered life summary was my first introduction to Robert. It followed from my question, "Tell me a little bit about yourself." Robert's view of a not very exciting life is contrary indeed to the way he is perceived by teachers, students, his grandparents, and most everyone else with whom he has contact. In fact, the principal at Onyx Ridge High School selected Robert as one of the students to be included in our study because, as she said, "he is such an unusual and interesting character." It soon became clear that Robert is not the kind of student who blends easily into the throng of 1,100 students at Onyx Ridge High School. Rather, his reputation as "odd, unusual, quirky, brilliant, immature, and a classic underachiever" is widespread among both students and faculty. The mention of Robert's name to administrative staff, counselors, teachers, and other students unfailingly elicits raised eyebrows and upwardly rolling eyes. Although it is clear that most everyone likes Robert and finds him interesting and engaging, it is equally clear that he is an enigma to most of the people he knows. Failing to perform academically as he "should," constantly asking questions that he "shouldn't," and frequently challenging the reasons for policies and procedures, Robert has caused many of the adults in this school environment to throw up their hands in despair. In this relatively new, upper-middle-class school where 80% of the students go on to four-year colleges, almost everyone (parents, teachers, and students) feels privileged to be a part of the community; Robert's nonconformity is baffling. His failing grades, consistent refusal to complete homework assignments, and outspoken commentary on the mediocrity of education juxtaposed with his regular attendance, animated class participation, and general compliance with behavioral norms leave many teachers and his grandparents frustrated and despairing. In general, adults in Robert's life feel thwarted in their attempts to persuade him to do what they believe is best. Robert's math teacher exemplifies this view.

> Hey, he's got a personal vendetta against doing homework when [according to Robert] you don't need to and he figures it isn't for him. But, for as bright as he is, he is not very bright as to what is happening on the outside. This is the thing that really bothers me about it. Last year his intermediate algebra teacher would come to me and said, "What's with this kid?" And I'd say, "I know, I know." And I guess the second semester last year in intermediate algebra he decided he wasn't going to do homework and ended up failing it. (*And he has a supportive family?*) Oh, yeah. But what can they do? There is very little they can do at this particular point because he is pretty much determined to fail.

In selecting students for this book we did not initially include Robert since his story seemed too extreme. However, as we talked with teachers and other school personnel, we were surprised by people's immediate recognition of the patterns Robert exhibits. Further, when teachers read descriptions of Robert they are quick to point out that they too have known students whose actions and behaviors defy explanation. While there are many stereotypic low-achieving students—those who receive low grades, exhibit disruptive behavior, and accumulate tardies and truancies—there are also a good number of students like Robert who seem, for no obvious reason, to resist normal academic expectations, that is, completing homework assignments, exhibiting a desire to achieve, and so forth. Although teachers speak frequently of students who "should be doing better than they are," youths like Robert stand out because of the enormous gap between their obvious ability and their dismal academic achievement. For example, Robert's consistent 90th percentile test scores, verbal acuity, and energetic class participation contrast starkly with his failing grades, thus making him highly visible in the Onyx Ridge school environment. No one knows what is wrong. The standard explanations—troubles at home, uninterested parents, a deviant peer group, inadequate school resources, boring or unconcerned teachers, lack of school support—do not appear to apply. Robert's grandparents have consistently kept in contact with the school and have besieged school personnel with pleas for help in getting Robert on the "right track." Robert's older brother, Allen, now a successful college student, also attended Onyx Ridge High School and was an excellent student. Robert admires his brother, whom he describes as his best friend. Further, Robert's friends have clearly defined long-range educational goals (i.e., going to college) and, for the most part, they all receive good grades. As Robert says, "I'm in the advanced track and so people who are here are mostly school-oriented and spend a lot of their time trying to get good grades."

Teachers too have tried unsuccessfully to persuade Robert to conform to the academic expectations of the school. And it is not as if Robert doesn't like many of his teachers. As he says, "Some of my favorite all-time teachers of my life are here at this school." No one, however, has been successful in attempts to convince Robert of the necessity of maintaining a strong academic record. Repeated attempts to impact his behavior or to come up with a plausible reason as to why this bright and talented student is not doing well have failed. A good number of teachers say that Robert simply *chooses* not to do his work. "It's his choice. There is nothing we can do." Nevertheless, teachers are frustrated and in some cases angry. They resent Robert's outspoken comments and overall defiance. As a result, they adhere rigidly (and righteously) to school standards and policies to measure his progress. Elements of the school environment, considered to be academically excellent, are not questioned. As one teacher said, "If this kid wants to fail, it's up to him." However, Robert's case illustrates vividly the way in which structural borders, emanating largely from differences in expectations for how schools as institutions should operate, hinder his involvement. In essence, there is not a match between Robert's view and that of the school's with respect to what education should be.

FROM COOPERATIVE TO CONTENTIOUS: A DRAMATIC SHIFT

Information in Robert's cumulative record file about his early elementary school years (grades K–3) is sparse. His first-grade report card contains checks for "very good progress" and "good progress" in all areas, including citizenship. "Has made great progress in reading" is the only handwritten teacher comment we find. A speech and language report indicates Robert's need for "speech therapy" due to his difficulty with the phoneme *r*. The report also states that Robert is in the 75th percentile in both receptive and expressive language and lists "attentiveness" as a behavior strength. No records exist from Robert's second-grade year when he attended school in Corpus Christi, Texas. In December of third grade, having returned to Adobe Viejo, Robert is identified for the Gifted and Talented Education Program (GATE). The evaluation report for GATE lists his IQ at 136 and intellectual functioning as "very superior."

Robert's third-grade California Test of Basic Skills (CTBS) scores in math, language, and reading are 99th, 98th, and 94th percentile respectfully. In January of third grade, speech therapy is again recommended for Robert due to his continued distortion of the r phoneme. "Very bright" and "cooperative" are descriptions we find in this report. Exactly one year later (January of Robert's fourth-grade year) Robert is removed from the speech therapy program due to "his lack of motivation and progress." The report states: "Continues to substitute w for r. Attitude and attendance problems necessitate dropping from speech for the present."

A perusal of Robert's records suggests that the middle of his fourth-grade year marks a shift in his school performance and attitude. While his report card continues to indicate marks of excellent and very good in almost all academic subjects ("needs to read more" is the only suggestion with respect to academics), a downward decline in personal development is evident. For example, we find numerous checks for "needs improvement" in areas such as "exercises self-discipline," and "accepts responsibility for completing assignments." By the end of fourth grade a dramatic change is evident. "Needs to improve" is the box checked for all areas of personal development and 22 tardies and 27 absences stand out. There is no mention in Robert's file that his mother died in the spring of this year.

Robert's standardized test scores in the fifth grade remain high—96th, 97th, and 82nd percentile in math, language, and reading. However, comments by Robert's fifth- and sixth-grade teachers indicate his need to improve "self-discipline" in the classroom and on the playground. In subject area progress, three marks of "excellent" contrast with 16 marks of "excellent" he received in the fourth grade. By the end of sixth grade, a pattern of academic decline is evident and Robert's cumulative record folder, the only written documentation of his experiences in elementary school, is transferred to the junior high school he will attend. It contains no mention of his mother's death, no suggestion of the type of assistance or support he might need, no inference regarding his increasing lack of attention to school, and no clue to anyone at the junior high that two years previously he experienced one of the most profound tragedies possible for a 9-year-old child. In a school district renowned for its supplemental services—counseling, speech and hearing therapy, attention to learning and behaviorally disabled students, a focus on individual needs—it is ironic that the same amount of concern and assistance that Robert received for the incorrect pronunciation of the r phoneme was not provided to help him deal with issues surrounding his mother's death. Psychosocial borders were clearly in place and yet it appears that there were not only no means of identifying the difficulties that Robert faced but also no services to meet his needs. Expectations for the types of intervention and assistance that schools should provide apparently did not include death.

Not surprisingly, comments by Robert's junior high school teachers indicate increasing trouble. Teachers' remarks focus exclusively on descriptions of Robert's behavior—no one speculates as to its cause. "Missing assignments; needs to improve; should concentrate on work and not on other students' business; disruptive behavior at times; needs to watch talking; final grade of F possible unless test grades improve; needs to follow directions; citizenship is an N (needs to improve) at this time." A referral from one of Robert's seventh-grade teachers exemplifies the tone of most of the comments contained in his folder: "Constant disruptive behavior! Will not or cannot behave himself. Talks constantly. Plays. Distracts other students. Oblivious to corrections. Detriment to class."

The tenor of these statements is punitive and angry. It is clear that teachers are frustrated by Robert's failure to comply with norms of behavior expected in the school environment. There is no indication, however, of any attempted intervention (except periodically banishing Robert to the principal's office, where he is detained for disruptive behavior). Although we do not know if there were efforts by individuals to assist Robert, teachers' written comments imply blame and exasperation. Further, there is nothing in Robert's file that would orient future teachers or counselors toward a compassionate or problem-solving view of dealing with this child. It is easy to imagine that perusal of his file by a teacher or counselor would probably produce an "Oh, god, this is going to be a problem kid" response. However, despite his disruptive behavior and generally low grades, Robert's CTBS test scores remain in the 90th percentile. His records also include notes from his grandparents documenting their concern and requesting conferences. Finally, in October of his eighth-grade year, a memorandum from his counselor to all of his teachers exemplifies her attempt to galvanize school resources.

> Robert's grandfather is very concerned about his grades and behavior. He would like a meeting with all of us and Robert on Wednesday, October 29 at 2:30 in the conference room. I hope that you can be there; it should be over in 30–40 minutes. If you can't attend, please give me any information or insights, suggestions, observations that might help. Thanks!

There is nothing in Robert's records that discusses the outcome of this meeting. However, in January and February referrals for misbehavior continue to dot his file, and in March, teachers' comments on his student progress report continue to document missing assignments and misbehavior. In

February of the same school year a phone message from Robert's counselor, apparently taken by a secretary, says, "Concern with grandson's problem— gave names of 3 psychologists." There is no indication of who took this message, who provided the referrals, or any subsequent action that was taken. In fact, the message, written on a small scrap of paper, is essentially buried in his file. However, a second telephone message (also inconspicuous), dated March 25, provides a clue to what might actually be wrong. "*Message to Laura* (Robert's counselor). Please call Dr. Harker after 10. Robert depressed. Not accepting mom's death."

We have no idea if the substance of this message was transmitted to any of Robert's teachers or considered in attempts to help this youth. However Robert's April progress report (except for physical education) indicates little improvement. F's in English, Science, and Math are offset only slightly with C's in Nutrition and U.S. History. Teachers' comments remain negative. "Still not turning in homework; talking is a problem; too disturbing; fails to come to class."

In April of his eighth-grade year, four years after his mother's death, an "Intervention Plan for At Risk Students" is filed as a result of Robert's failure to acquire the credits necessary for promotion to the ninth grade. The plan calls for tutoring in math and suggests that his homework be supervised. A comment, "Robert has the potential to do much better," is redundant. This form also notes that a decision to promote Robert to ninth grade will be delayed pending the receipt of his summer school grades. During the last two months of his eighth-grade year, angry teacher referrals continue. "I found Robert fighting after school behind the pool. Robert was throwing punches and behaving like an animal. I saw Robert physically assault Joey Cutter. [Teacher Referral]"

In ninth grade (apparently having successfully completed summer school), Robert's grades continue to be erratic. A C in Art one grading period is followed by a B the next. In Spanish his grade fluctuates between a D and F. Teachers' comments remain consistent—"missing assignments, too much talking, very little effort, needs to mind his own business."

At the end of ninth grade Robert's cumulative record file, now bursting with negative comments evidencing teachers' frustrations and anger at this uncooperative student, is transferred to Onyx Ridge High School. While it is certainly improbable that high school teachers would review incoming files, it is not unlikely that they might eventually turn to Robert's records for information to help explain the inconsistencies between his ability and his grades. Again, however, the file contains no information to help teachers understand the difficulties Robert faced during his early school years and no speculation as to why he had difficulty. There are no recommendations for pedagogical or personal approaches that might assist Robert. Nor is there anything to orient teachers to a humanistic or compassionate view of Robert's past circumstances. Rather, *everything* in the file alerts teachers to a "problem" youth, destined to disrupt their lives and create problems. The one phone message that suggests that he might be having difficulty resolving issues around his mother's death is markedly inconspicuous. It is highly probable that anyone reviewing the file would miss this note. The negative comments dominate. Not surprisingly, none of Robert's high school teachers had knowledge of the circumstances by which he had come to live with his grandparents. Only two teachers were aware that his mother had died.

It appears that intervention strategies to assist Robert in elementary and junior high school focused entirely on helping him to acquire adequate study skills and complete his homework (except for early speech therapy). His identification as an "at-risk" student occurred long after signs of distress were apparent and help seems to have been targeted at symptoms rather than causes. While structures and services to assist students were in place in Robert's elementary and middle-school environments, they did not match his needs. Robert appears to have received no help with respect to the psychosocial borders he faced as a result of his mother's death. Further, it appears as if structural borders arose as a result of teachers' attitudes and their focus on Robert's behavior rather than its cause.

"GALVANIZING MY FEELINGS FOR MYSELF"

In many ways Robert is the ideal informant for a study of students' perceptions of school. Outgoing, articulate, and obviously delighted at the opportunity to express his views, Robert often voiced reluctance at ending our conversations. Toward the end of each interview he unfailingly said he'd like to stay longer and on more than one occasion he asked if he could wait while I interviewed another student and then talk with me again.

During the two years that I knew Robert his appearance changed dramatically. My first introduction was to a small-framed, wiry, and physically immature looking 17-year-old whose dark eyes and big smile accentuated his heavy braces and missing front-side teeth. Heavily moussed, dark brown hair was slicked back on the sides and crew cut on top. I thought perhaps that Robert identified with a particular group but soon learned that he preferred moving casually among many. By the end of his senior year Robert was a much more mature young man. Several inches taller, braces off, missing teeth replaced, and dark brown hair dyed black (now worn long on top and shaved on the sides), Robert expressed a newfound self-confidence. "My maturity at the beginning of this year was less than it is now, and I think the amount of time that I've had to be a little bit introspective has galvanized my feelings for myself. . . . Oh, I'm very happy. I got my braces off Thursday and new teeth—those weren't real. And I'm also going to the prom. Yeah, things are working great."

Although willing and eager to expound on just about any topic, Robert inevitably turns the conversation to art. In fact, it is clear that "being an artist" is the theme that most dominates Robert's life and thoughts. Outside of school, Robert spends a good deal of his time painting in his garage studio, which was assembled with the help and support of his grandparents. He reports that conversations with close friends are typically about art and he describes spending hours on the telephone discussing art projects with Jeffrey Chambers [pseud.], a practicing artist in Georgia. Robert met Mr. Chambers two years earlier at a comic book convention in Adobe Viejo. He describes going directly to Artist's Alley where all the artists hang out. Apparently Mr. Chambers expressed an interest in Robert's work and as a result they began communicating on a regular basis.

Robert's goal of becoming a professional artist remained unchanged during the time that I knew him.

> (*You know what you're going to do?*) I know it's going to be art related, that I'm going to be working in a studio with my friend or in a different studio in commercial art. Hopefully by that time I'll have made at least some sort of name for myself. I'll either be working doing covers for albums or comic books or whatever or movie posters hopefully. . . . That's about it. That's all I can really be sure of.

During our first interviews Robert talked about his plans to apply to the University of California but by the end of his senior year he had chosen instead to attend the Southeast School of Design—a prestigious, four-year liberal arts institution. It is not unlikely that Robert began considering other university options as it became increasingly clear that his "failing grades" pattern would undoubtedly limit his choices. Unfortunately, my last interview with Robert revealed that his plans for the future continued to be threatened by his dismal high school record. It was not until his final grades were reported (two days before graduation) that he or anyone else knew if he would graduate. "Teetering on the edge" is a theme in Robert's life that creates frustration and despair for adults concerned with his well-being and his future life chances.

But how do Robert's views compare with those of his teachers and his grandparents? How does he think and feel about his school experience? What meaning does he give to his days at Onyx Ridge High School? And how do his views fit with his future goals?

"LOOKING FOR VARIATION": SCHOOL AS AN INSTITUTION

It's so, so fixed, so linear. There's no leeway for variation at all, and for me, as you can tell, I work at variation every day and so I try to go for as much change as possible. . . . [School] is set for some type of everyman, sort of some person with mediocre mental acuity who is working on going to college—the classic well-rounded person that you never find. If you do, they are [so] exceedingly bland that you don't even want to spend any time speaking with them. The school is made for that type of person. It leans a little bit toward the lower, toward someone who's just barely making it. I think that's what school's geared for.

Robert's treatise on the mediocrity of schooling illustrates vividly the lack of match between his expectations for what learning should be and those of the school. At the same time, there are many things about Onyx Ridge High School that Robert specifically likes—the overall school atmosphere, social interaction with peers, teachers he considers excellent. In fact, he rejected outright his counselor's attempt to persuade him to attend Adobe Viejo Performing Arts School. Robert is adamant that he does not want to leave Onyx Ridge. But to many, Robert's view of a positive school environment seems ironic given his academic performance.

Robert's high school records indicate a cumulative grade point average (GPA) of 1.62. The range, 1.29 to a 1.86, shows little variation from one semester to the next. The exceptions are grades he earned in two summer school classes (2.5 and 4.0) he was required to take to make up for classes he failed. With respect to his grades there appear to be no particular patterns— an A in Art one year is followed by a D in Commercial Art the next. Nor do Robert's feelings about a teacher appear to impact his performance. For example, he describes his junior and senior English teachers as both superb but he received a C in one class and an F in the other. However, despite his poor achievement his test scores throughout high school remain high—the 90th percentile in vocabulary, reading comprehension, language expression, and concept application; the 80th percentile in spelling; and the 70th percentile in language mechanics and math computation. And much to his delight, a score of 1,200 on the college entrance exam earned him a scholarship to the Southeast School of Design (contingent, of course, on his graduation from high school). Robert's account of his own behavior is telling. "There's a lot of laziness involved. Based on the theory that if I don't like it and it's not very intriguing, I'm not going to push myself very hard to engage in it. As far as art is concerned, as long as it's basically related to art, I'll attack it with more fervor than I would say something related to science."

During his junior year, I questioned Robert extensively about his favorite and least favorite class. My purpose was to try to identify possible structural borders at the classroom level that were impeding his ability to succeed in this school environment. Despite his self-identification as an artist and his clear interest in the subject matter, Robert identified Art as his least favorite class. My surprise elicited the following reply.

> The class itself I think is a poor art class . . . poor assignments and cer-
> tainly not much enthusiasm [from the teacher]. . . . I've never seen any-
> thing by this teacher that I thought was any good at all. I've seen
> students in the class that brought better art pieces than he ever has. . . .
> I really don't have much respect for him as an artist. So that really
> affects my judgment of the class. I don't think he teaches anything I
> didn't already learn in ninth-grade art class. And it's almost like busy
> work for art. Which is really a disappointment.

Robert's description illustrates once again a lack of match between what he expects and what he receives with respect to instruction. Further, there are other reasons Robert expresses disdain for this particular teacher. His detailed description of a specific class interaction provides a flavor of the types of problems he encounters.

> He assigned three illustrations of a stool. I did an illustration. . . . I
> stood above it [the stool] and tried to get a different angle and he was
> anything but supportive of my changes. . . . Then the next assignment
> was a distortion and to make your illustration look as a stool that's been
> distorted. . . . So I had two legs going up like two female legs going per-
> pendicular to the—and two male legs going perpendicular . . . and he
> said it was too suggestive, so then I made it so the legs themselves were
> about mid-thigh and he said it was still too suggestive. So then I
> decided to start drawing the stool like Georgia O'Keefe and he said,
> "Robert, why don't you just do it this way?" and he showed me a pic-
> ture that a student had already done.
>   I didn't think that was really supportive of originality, when they
> suggest that somebody else do an assignment the same way it's been
> done. The same way. This person got an A on the assignment and then
> I told him no thanks, and I started doing a different illustration that had
> the metal top of the stool . . . and I got called down to the counseling
> office and it turned out that he'd given me a referral and said I was
> trying to change the assignments and thought I was being disruptive
> in class.

This description suggests that Robert's ideas and the teacher's, with respect to what learning should be, do not match. Robert's statement also provides an almost visceral sense of the art teacher's reaction to Robert. While Robert's logic about the irrationality of the teacher makes imminent sense, we can also imagine the level of frustration that this teacher experienced interacting with a student who basically did not respect his work (as an artist or as a teacher). Robert's continued description makes it apparent that there was a history to their relationship.

> I had to write him a letter to ask him to allow me to be in his class this year because he had thrown me out last year. So I wrote him a letter and he thought the letter was excellently written and he asked Miss Quince [Robert's English teacher] if the letter was mine and she said, "Oh yeah, definitely."
>
> I have a friend who was in the class last year, who he [the teacher] thought was the greatest artist ever. I airbrushed a cover for him and he turned it in and coach thought it was the best piece of the year.
>
> And then I had that piece in my portfolio and I showed him my portfolio in the beginning of this year and he asked me, "What's this doing in here?" and I said "Oh, I did that," and he said, "Didn't Jason do that?" and I said "No, I airbrushed it for him." . . . And I brought in a new piece that I had just done of a girl's face and he said, "Oh, did Jason do that too?" . . . And every time I bring in a piece of art work of my own, he like hints at the fact that it looks kind of like what Jason does or something.

A problem in communication and a breakdown in trust appear to have evoked a power struggle between Robert and Mr. Malloy. The teacher, wedded to the belief that Robert did not do his own work, seems intent on acquiring Robert's compliance, while Robert describes actions he knows will goad the teacher into reacting negatively. Neither the teacher nor Robert appears to have the skills to negotiate an understanding, a reasonable plan of proceeding, or a way to move beyond their negative view of "the other." The structural borders that result make it impossible for Robert to engage positively in learning. Rather than being viewed as a promising young artist in an environment where people support his strengths and encourage his development, Robert is perceived (at least by this teacher) as recalcitrant and uncooperative. Robert's relationship with this teacher limits seriously his ability to pursue work and feel successful in an area he loves. The problem is further exacerbated by the fact there are few art courses and few art teachers at Onyx Ridge High School. In this school, as well as many others, the arts are marginalized relative to academic subjects. For Robert, structural borders result from differences in view about what is important and what subject matter is appropriate.

However, Art is not the only subject in which Robert has difficulty. His description of a math class (his least favorite subject) again suggests that Robert's nonconformity is particularly irritating to the teacher whose orientation is to press for his compliance.

> Math, actually I'm not supposed to be helping the students because I don't follow the equations, so when I start to explain my method to students, they usually get confused, cause they're trying to learn the equation, and I show them how to not use the equation. (*So the teacher doesn't like you to help?*) No, she doesn't. She likes me to do the work but when it comes to explaining how I got the answer, she lets me take a seat. And she says, "No, no, you have to explain it by the formula."

While Robert's descriptions illuminate his reaction to rigid pedagogical methods, they also invoke empathy for teachers who are disconcerted and frustrated by this highly verbal and facile young man. Robert, however, does not view himself as rebellious and sees clearly differences between himself and those students who purposively disrupt class.

> If one purposely goes out to, like, um, disrupt, and not follow the rules, I mean, me, I follow the rules, it's just my own interpretation of the rules. For others, it can be really detrimental, not just to them, but to the other students in the school. Some people come to school thinking, like, it's a challenge, not like a learning challenge, but like a personal challenge. They work really hard to defy the teachers and to try to get away with almost anything. Seems kind of bizarre.

In sharp contrast to descriptions of Art and Math, Robert's comments about English are animated and positive. The combination of his intrinsic interest in literature and excellent teachers appears to be critical to his positive views. Further, Robert's comments match those of other students in our study who talk specifically about classroom features (i.e., relationships with teachers, curriculum, pedagogy, and classroom organization) that support their involvement in learning (Phelan, Davidson, & Cao, 1992). For example, Robert talks about the advantages of a classroom organization that supports students' working in groups. His comments mirror those of researchers who detail the benefits of cooperative learning groups (Sharan, 1980; Sharan & Shachar, 1988; Slavin, 1989).

> She read names and it was kind of luck of the draw. You could end up in a group of people you despise . . . but at the end of the year people had to go to the front of the room and give a short speech on what the year meant to them, and I don't think I've ever seen more people cry in a group. The harmony—because working together and then even some people, even the stupidest idea wouldn't be overlooked. Everybody seemed to be like a valid contributor to the classroom.

While Robert's description is testimony to the bonds that can form when students work together, he also talks about other pedagogical methods that serve to draw students in and connect them with the substance of Miss Quince's class.

> Throughout the year there was a little game to be able to recall exactly where [a particular quote or idea] that it came from, the idea. People would be yelling it out in the classroom because someone would bring up an idea and it would be, "I know where that's from," and people would be working together looking through books trying to find quotes, drawing banners of puritanical ideas, stuff like that, doing things that made the class work.

Miss Owens, Robert's senior English teacher, also engages students actively in learning but her style is quite different from that of Miss Quince. Robert's description illuminates the importance of teachers who display enthusiasm for subject matter content.

> In Miss Owens's class it's less so that way [students openly calling out in class], but there's still a certain bond you feel because in the reading groups you still could help each other work and even though she lectures a tremendous amount—I don't know what her class would be if she weren't lecturing. . . . She gets everybody involved. She's so amazingly energetic toward literature. I've never seen anybody be so excited about literature—her veins stand out on her neck and she gets really excited and she makes weird voices and she jumps up and grabs the table and hits the books and she's really an energetic lit teacher. . . . Everybody, everybody pays attention to her. Everybody seems really engaged.

Robert's extended discussion of English teachers at Onyx Ridge remind us that excellent teachers may well possess very different styles and methods. The common factor to which Robert repeatedly alludes is the ability of teachers to create environments in which students feel connected—with the class-room, the teacher, the curriculum, and their peers.

Despite Robert's feelings that he has had excellent English teachers, he does not always do well academically. While English is the only class in which Robert earns a C his senior year (D's and F's in all other classes result in a cumulative GPA of 1.86 the first semester and 1.29 the second), the previous year he received F's in English although he expressed strong and positive feelings about his teacher. Both he and Miss Quince (his junior-year English teacher) agreed that his failing grades resulted specifically from his failure to complete and submit assigned work. However, there is no doubt in Miss Quince's mind that Robert is intrinsically interested in the subject matter. His own description is telling.

> I think I'll always be thoroughly interested in reading literature. I'm so intrigued by and involved in English lit currently as I was last year with American lit, because it relates to one of the [good] classes, but also I find it really interesting. I spent days just trying to memorize Hamlet's speeches, Lake's poems, Wordsworth, quotable rhymes, things of this sort. . . . I find it really interesting. Other people look at me like I'm crazy. (*You mean you do all of that work and still don't get a good grade?*) Oh, it doesn't translate over. Those aren't necessarily class-related items. I find it interesting. I can recite the first 18 lines of Canterbury Tales to you in Middle English. I memorized Hamlet's "To Be or not to Be," though I'm sure any decent actor can do that.

According to Robert, English also provides him with the opportunity to use his imagination, to draw on personal experiences, and to formulate ideas in a coherent fashion. "Like English, . . . a lot of my writing I can be creative with or relate my own personal experiences or even if I can't it's also a challenge to formulate your ideas in a coherent format where you put it on paper and you make sense and . . . it's well thought out and things of this sort. I find that interesting." In this subject area there is at least a partial match between Robert's ideas of appropriate subject matter content and what is taught. However, his descriptions also exemplify the wide range of literature in which he is generally interested.

> Do you know Walter Austin? (*No.*) It's kind of carefree, basically bubble gum type of fiction. The kind that is not really mentally engaging, it's fun to read, nice stories, stuff like that. And then I also like reading literature like heavy duty, like *Moby Dick*. I've read that a couple of times. I've read the whole Tolken series at least 13 times. . . . Every English assignment I read at least once and then if I'm interested I'll

even try to memorize it. I'll read it enough times so that I've got it practically memorized for the next month and then after that it slips into
the recesses of my memory. But it's interesting.

Robert's interviews are laced with superlative comments about the English
teachers at Onyx Ridge High School. "I think the English department here
is easily its [the school's] strongest point. Definitely." Robert's assessment of
the English department is consistent with other data we obtained about this
school.

"Why Should I Be Doing This?"

"I think that a lot of stress is put on the teacher–student relationship [as
opposed] to person-to-person. I think that people would be tremendously
more pleased with the class if they were actually able to see their teacher as a
person rather than as a fixture, part of an institution." Robert's comments
reflect his desire for personal relationships with teachers. His feelings mirror
those of other students in our study who talk repeatedly about the importance
of teachers who demonstrate explicitly that they care about students as individuals (Phelan et al., 1992). However, having teachers who care doesn't necessarily mean that Robert performs well academically. On the other hand,
having teachers who don't care appears to assure his failure.

Perhaps most telling with respect to Robert's school performance is his
view that schoolwork is completely unrelated to his future. At the beginning
of his senior year he is adamant that none of his classes relate in any way to
his future.

> (*Do you see your classes here related in any way to your future?*) [Pause]
> Definitely not. I had to think about that one to make sure I had to go
> through the whole list and be positive that none of them related, but I
> would on the whole say that none of them had absolutely anything to
> do with what I'm going to do the second I get off this campus.

However, later in the year, having been in a graphics arts class for several
months, he is able to talk explicitly about the importance of class content that
he perceives as relevant.

> Graphics—that's one of the few classes that I actually enjoy because
> it's—that's the one class here that actually relates to something I'm
> going to be doing because it's the printing of art work and things of
> that sort. I have to understand the demands that the printer's going to

make on the art work as I intend to be working in commercial so I think I need to realize exactly under what parameters I need to work.

An interesting feature of Robert's Graphics class is that the instructor, unlike his Art teacher, is flexible in modulating class policies. For example, standard procedures call for students to work for several weeks in each of three graphic arts areas—printing, silk screening, and photography. Robert's six-week grade for printing was an A. During this time he designed and produced his own business cards. On the first interim report of the second six-week period his grade dropped to a C—silk screening was not something that he enjoyed. However, instead of insisting that he complete the silk screening block, the teacher allowed him to return to printing and offset and encouraged further development of his skills in these areas. As Robert says: "I jumped at it and got my grade back up to an A. It gives you kind of an idea how I behave. If it's interesting and I find it enjoyable, I'll run with it. If it does nothing for me, it's like, 'I'll give it back to you, thank you very much.'"

This teacher's flexibility in modulating class policies makes it possible for Robert not only to earn a respectable grade, but also to develop skills in an area he perceives as directly relevant to his future. In this case there is a match between Robert's expectations of what school should be and what he actually encounters in the classroom.

We find the theme of "why should I be doing this?" throughout Robert's interviews—for example, he describes his misgivings about the educational relevance of homework:

> You stare at the paper and you wonder, "Why exactly am I doing this? Oh, busy work. Now I remember why I had to do it because for some odd reason the teacher actually wanted to correct something." It's either a state of masochism or somebody who believes in basically the theory behind homework, and I guess for really intelligent people the need for homework is very little. For others the need to do homework as a memorizational technique and things of this sort, I'm sure it's a great help. To make it a standard and something to be graded upon, that's of questionable merit.

Robert's comments bear remarkable similarity to issues raised in the literature on the values and benefits of homework policies generally (Earle, 1992; Olympia, Sheridan, & Jensen, 1994; Thomas, 1993).

Robert is not unaware that his general views on homework fly in the face of teachers' expectations, school policy, and general beliefs about what it takes to be academically successful. What is clear is that Robert believes homework should relate to learning. In contrast, the primary concern of many of his teachers seems to be compliance to homework expectations. Nevertheless, Robert is very much aware that his failure to comply with school expectations is a major problem with respect to his grades.

> I think the homework policies are probably the one thing I have trouble with . . . because they're counted as a large chunk of your grade and some of my teachers say, "If you don't do 50% of the homework you don't pass the course." For me, if 50% of the homework was interesting I would be amazed. (*And you leave it at school?*) It's like a bad job. You really don't want to take it home.

While Robert describes homework policies as particularly troublesome, his questions about the importance and rationale behind such practices are not unlike his questions about other aspects of the educational process. There is no doubt that Robert has an unrelenting determination to question the reasons why things are done.

What Could Have Been Different?

Over the period of 2 years of our study, a nagging question persisted: What could have made Robert's school experience successful? I asked him this question repeatedly, in different ways, at different times. Interestingly, Robert expresses the view that he is responsible for his school failure. Although he has developed elaborate reasons as to why he does not choose to conform to standard academic expectations, he nevertheless believes that he is accountable. As he says: "A lot of it's personal choice. It's a personal lack of decision that allows me to feel very comfortable about not doing anything. I think it's very rare to find someone who actually decided to be an underachiever." Robert's view of the situation is not much different from that of most of his teachers. Is it possible that Robert has merely internalized beliefs about his failure that are perpetuated by adults in his school environment?

As I continued to talk with Robert, he did however mention specific modifications that might have increased his chances for success.

> I'd rather have independent art, you know. I'd rather have a free period where I could go home and do whatever I wanted to on a piece of art board and bring it to class and have him grade it and then just get my credit that way.
>
> In class, he could tell me what assignments he wants throughout the year, like "I want you to do an abstract art and pencil piece," and I'd go home and I'd do it and I'd do something that I'd much more enjoy than laboring over what I tend to call stool samples. He heard me say

that actually, that's another reason why I think he has mixed feelings about me. . . . I would like to learn how to be a professional artist and he doesn't teach it.

Robert's description illustrates the types of possible arrangements that might have altered his direction. However, at no time is Robert included in a conversation about alternative possibilities. Rather, school officials work diligently to obtain Robert's compliance to existing expectations. Despite the school's lack of flexibility, Robert initiates, on his own, contacts he believes will be beneficial.

I have assignments from a professional artist in Atlanta. . . . He's got an 800 number and I can call him—I call him up all the time and get assignments and send him my work to critique. (*And the school?*) They don't acknowledge it but that's not really what I'm looking for. The credit itself is really unimportant to me. It's the actual learning. As far as I am personally concerned—for me, the graduate and the diploma, college and everything of that sort are simply technicalities. As long as I am able to learn something, actually palatable knowledge, just to be able to walk away with it and say, "I know this and I can reuse it, totally utilize it for myself," then I feel like I've learned something.

This statement illustrates Robert's intrinsic motivation to learn in the context of a school environment where extrinsic rewards are paramount. However, it seems not to have occurred to Robert that the structure of his school experience could have been different. In fact, he professes an overall positive view of the help he has received. For example, he says "I think everybody at this school did the best they could. It sounds like that would make a great epithet."

My continued probing about other things that could increase Robert's chances for academic success elicit similar responses. For example, when I ask Robert if he would have earned higher grades in the regular rather than the advanced academic track, he replies:

No, I would have had more free time [in the regular track]. I think my practices would have been exactly the same. I think they would be exactly the same in AP as well. In AP I would be doing more work but probably receiving the exact same grades. . . . I couldn't really imagine working 24 hours a day, seven days a week, full-bore, trying to bring myself up to the highest grade possible.

Further, Robert believes that he has been lucky to have had many good teachers. His comments not only reflect this view; they also provide an elaborated definition of a "good teacher."

When you go into a classroom and the teacher is going through a process, a study process, as if all the variables are already accounted for, and nothing will change within this process and if something does then we can just ignore it and keep going on head first. And it's kind of a daily chore that's not really enjoyable. It doesn't give you anything—all it does is take away. . . .

Where there's more than just you participating, when it's the teacher participating with you and the students participating with you—anyone participating with you, it becomes interesting because you learn something about that person. . . .

And to find a really good teacher, an interesting teacher, a creative teacher—that's definitely difficult to find. We have a lot of them in this school. We're really really lucky.

Apparently teachers feel less than fortunate in their dealings with Robert. Although all acknowledge his aptitude and ability, no one—even those whom he likes a lot—seems able to affect consistently his compliance to academic norms. Likewise, Robert is clear that good teachers do not necessarily mean that he will perform according to conventional measures of success.

(*Just because they're a good teacher doesn't make it so you get an A in the class?*) No, not at all. It makes it fun to be in the class and it definitely makes it enjoyable and the in-class writing and some of the essays that I do are a lot more fun, a lot more interesting, and whenever you have personal writing or anything that requires a certain amount of inter-jection of personal experiences you always feel a little bit closer to the teacher and you open up communications to the teacher a lot easier. (*But for you it doesn't necessarily translate into . . .*) No, it hardly translates into better grades. (*What would make a difference?*) Nothing. That's just me. I'm really odd that way.

While Robert's statements support the general view that he has *chosen* to fail, his counselor speculates on other possible reasons.

He just doesn't do his homework. And I don't know that he knows why except that a lot of times—a lot of times with very intelligent kids they go through and get through a lot of elementary school and junior high just on general knowledge, intelligence, and good family background. And they get through and—it catches up with them by junior high and high school and then all of a sudden someone throws geometry. . . . And maybe part of it is his older brother who was so successful and that was part of it to begin with. (*What happened to his parents?*) Actually I

can't remember. He and I have never talked about it. I think his older
brother may have told me.

While this particular counselor considers possibilities for Robert's lack of
success beyond the fact that he merely chooses to fail, her emphasis (and
blame) is nevertheless on Robert. We know, however, that large caseloads,
limited time, and institutional expectations often preclude counselors' attention to family history or students' life circumstances outside of school. Further, Robert's counselor, like other adults, simply does not consider or acknowledge the fact that elements in the school environment (i.e., structural
borders emanating from differences in expectations for how schools should
operate) may well impede Robert's chances for success.

INTEREST AND DIVERSITY:
AVOIDING "WELL-ROUNDED" FRIENDS

"I think that the biggest link [between worlds] is between school and
friends, because that's where you meet most of your friends while you're a
student, is through school. That's how I met all of my friends. That's definitely the biggest link." As Robert moves from class to class, it is apparent that
he is well known among his peers. Extroverted, gregarious, and outgoing, he
seems to know and talk to everyone. "Hey Robert, what's up." "Hey Robert,
you look great." (This particular day Robert is wearing a suit as his economics
teacher has invited him to be a speaker for a community business luncheon.)
In his Graphics class, where students move freely around the room, Robert
introduces me to nearly everyone—he also describes students' projects and
engages each person and the teacher in conversation. My observations suggest that Robert's interactions with his peers are easy, friendly, and uninhibited. But Robert describes more unusual interactions as well. For example,
simply walking between classes or hanging out at lunch provides him with the
opportunity to expand his repertoire of interactive styles.

> Walking down the halls at school I act like an idiot and I do it well
> enough to forget the rest of the day. Some of my conversations with
> people—some people would look at this as making myself feel superior,
> but I change the mode of the conversation so rapidly so many times in
> just a few sentences that people are wondering and are going, "What?"
> and I go "exactly" and then I walk off. I say things, little things like
> "What's the question again?" or say something like, "Can I ask you a
> question?" I think those people are just wondering, saying "Ok, what's
> going on here?" and then I'll yell something like "I must be in the front

row," something totally wild and people go "Okay, this boy is weird," and then I go off in peals of laughter which relieves any tension I may have had.

(*So it's one of the ways to relieve tension?*) Oh, yeah, being an idiot, you'd be amazed at how well it works. . . . Everything I do I try to make it as conscious as possible. . . . Acting like an idiot makes everybody realize just how idiotic they themselves are. Be totally petty and it makes everyone realize just how petty things are. Whenever you act to one extreme of a problem it always makes everyone realize just how small the problem really is.

But such shenanigans are not confined to daily routines in school. For example, his description of providing a "community service" to other students while taking the SAT exam also provides a colorful example of his personality.

At the SAT [test] the people were stressing and I was sitting here and I was almost done with my test and I have five more questions on the English side, and I looked around and people were just biting their nails and one guy snapped his pencil from stress. And I was going "What are you people doing?" and I stood up in the classroom and I yelled out like a big yodel in the middle of the test taking place, and everybody looked at me and I sat back down and finished taking my test. And people were going, "What the hell is going on?"

I did it with a straight face. I'm pretty good at doing that and sat back down with my straight face, picked up my pencil and continued taking the test. Some people snickered and there was like a general air of relaxation. I felt better because I felt I had done a community service or something like that.

Although we certainly do not know the underlying motivation for such actions, Robert's own explanations reveal an unusual degree of self-awareness. His well-formulated and analytical comments suggest that he ponders regularly the reasons for his actions. But whatever the reasons, it is clear that unlike many adolescents who spend a great deal of energy trying to "fit in," Robert consciously made an effort to "stand out."

While Robert confirms that he has "lots and lots of acquaintances," he talks distinctly about having only a few close friends. "I have a really small group of friends. I guess I'm not interested in having tons of friends. I like to be really close with my friends that I have—say I have three or four really good friends. . . . I have a lot of acquaintances." During the 1½ years that I knew Robert, his "small group of friends" remained the same. It seems as if he found a group of young people to whom he could relate—as he said, who "agree with you the way you are." But according to Miss Quince, his much favored junior-year English teacher, this was not always the case.

> When he came here he physically was really runt like. He was tiny, he was missing teeth, he had bad skin, and he was what the kids called a poser or a wannabe. For all of his intelligence, he was emotionally and socially, very immature. . . . He did not have any mechanisms for inter-acting other than a pedantic way or a kind of a looking up. So he would follow kids around. He would at football games, be down on the side-lines looking up—I mean literally—just following athletes who were ready to play. He was so enamored of them. And he would go from group to group to group—during his sophomore year [the first year of high school] he was hanging with the gang kids cause he was looking for belonging anywhere he could. So he started wearing these rags— these gang kind of things in his back pocket. And he started wearing his colors, his shirt, combing his hair—just bizarre stuff and then he shifted from that group to the punks for awhile and pierced his nose and pierced his ears. . . . And then he shifted from there to, god where did he go, to the surfers, he was in with the surfers. . . . [Now] he is beginning to come into his own [he has a more stable group of friends] as he finds some direction for his art work.

Although Miss Quince sees Robert's ability to establish a stable friendship group as a positive development, she also describes Robert's friends as "really peculiar kids. They are very odd. You'd see these guys and worry." But from Robert's perspective, the fact that his friends are "unusual" is a characteristic to which he is drawn. The following statement illuminates his view.

> I think that my friends themselves, I find people interesting that are strong. There's one thing that disgusts me more than anything on the whole face of the planet would be a well-rounded person. They are an anathema. They're the worst type of person. I mean to me a bland, well-rounded, it worries me that there's actually people like that on this planet. . . .
> The day I heard the term I knew it only boded ill for myself. Well-rounded is just, ugh, it means, thoroughly mediocre. Well-rounded means that they have no edges, no sharpness, reminds me of a blob of jello and you just think to yourself, "how can this be anything but bad?" . . . A well-rounded person means that you are successful at being mediocre. It's like you're trying to work toward—regression toward the mean.

Robert perceives his friends as being far from the "mean." And like Robert, all are involved in some aspect of the arts, a common denominator that, not surprisingly, draws them together. Robert's description of their conversations also suggests that they share a common interest in simply being together and exploring ideas.

> We talk about art basically, that's about it—art. . . . Every once in a while we have the deep, profound discussions at nighttime about, I don't know, just really bizarre discussions and we continue for about two and a half hours talking about nothing and everything. (*Give me an example.*) Um, like one night, a while ago, I had all three of my friends spend the night . . . it was about . . . life imitating art, or art imitating life, that's what it was about. And one of my friends, he's in the AP Art History, and he was describing like, things that he learned in school, and applying them in our discussion, and stuff like that. It was really neat.

Although Robert's close friends are primarily European-American, he is very much aware of the racially mixed student population and expresses adamantly his preference for being in a heterogeneous environment. At the same time, he comments on the difficulty of forming close friendships with students who live on the other side of town.

> I think it would be disgusting to come to this school every day and just see the exact same people over and over again. It doesn't reflect society at all. . . . There's people here who I would like to spend more time with, like Jesse Cooper. He's one of my friends. I couldn't think of anybody cooler to hang out with. He lifts weights and he runs and he listens to the same kind of music as I do. I find him really interesting. The only reason he's not my best friend is because he doesn't live around here. I wouldn't be able to spend the amount of time that I spend with my best friends. That's really the only reason I don't have more friends of an ethnic or a socioeconomic mix is just because the area I live in.

Robert's comments about students who are different from himself stand in stark contrast to those of Ryan. While Ryan appears fearful of particular groups, Robert appears to embrace a view that prizes diversity.

Overall it appears as if Robert (like many other adolescents) struggled to find his place among peers at Onyx Ridge High School. Miss Quince's comments suggest that he did not have an easy time finding a peer group to whom he could comfortably relate. However, there is no question that, over time,

Robert built a unique and distinctive reputation and he became well known, highly visible, and connected to the Onyx Ridge peer world.

ON DISHARMONY WHEN WORLDS COMBINE

"The most disharmony that I think most any student can suffer is when they mix their worlds [family, school, and peer worlds] together. Keeping them as individual as possible I think is the best ploy I've come up with." This statement reflects Robert's attempt to separate as much as possible his home and school worlds. However, unlike students who keep their worlds apart because of perceived differences (e.g., Trinh), Robert's efforts stem from the fact that values and expectations of his family and school are very much the same. All agree that academic achievement is critical and all believe that Robert has a problem.

Robert is the sixth and last child to be raised by his grandparents. Having raised four of their own children, they assumed responsibility for 9-year-old Robert and his 12-year-old brother following the death of their daughter. Robert's early school records document his grandparent's consistent involvement in his education. Unlike Trinh's parents, who rarely cross the border into her school environment, Robert's grandparents have regularly communicated with school personnel (i.e., requesting conferences, calling teachers, etc.) and involved themselves in school affairs (i.e., chaperoning school events, attending college information seminars, etc.). As a high school student, Robert rails against their efforts. (*So they really look for opportunities to involve themselves in school?*) "Yes. And I keep saying, 'No, no, let's just leave school at school,' and they don't seem willing because all their five other charges brought school home."

Robert's attempts to keep his family and school worlds separate in part results from his positive feelings for his grandparents. Comments throughout his interviews illustrate affection, commitment, and the gratitude he feels for their efforts. "I think there's nobody else who's ever helped me more than my grandparents."

It is not surprising that Robert's feelings for his family and his inability to meet their expectations with respect to school achievement creates distress—he responds by keeping his worlds as separate as possible. While he realizes that he is not living up to their expectations, he also empathizes with their position.

> I don't feel any pressures except basically from my grandparents. And I think that pressure, and I'm sure they'll be more than willing to confirm this, is for my own well-being. . . .

> Basically, they're worried about me and I try to allay their worries as much as possible. I try to tell them "Don't worry, it's okay, I'll take care of it." The thing is, what worries me most, the reason it's the most stress, because it feels like I'm causing them distress. . . . I think also their being Jewish grandparents, I'm sure they'd land on something else that would cause them certain amounts of distress. I feel quite safe about that. I have no doubt in my mind they would worry about at least one thing.

Despite his grandparents' concern about his school performance, they try in many ways to accommodate his interest in art. Unlike some parents who restrict favored activities in order to obtain children's compliance, Robert's grandparents support his artistic pursuits.

In my last interview with Robert he reported that his grandparents were increasingly positive about his decision to attend the Southeast School of Design. As Robert began to more clearly delineate his future path, he was able to build bridges between his world and the world of his grandparents.

CONGRUENT WORLDS: TRANSITIONS RESISTED

We have characterized Robert as a student whose worlds are similar—with respect to values, beliefs, and expectations—but who was unable to meet even minimal requirements for school success. Robert's teachers and counselors say he has failed—a 1.27 cumulative grade point average, refusal to conform to school policies (e.g., homework completion), overly gregarious and confrontational in classes, not enough credits to graduate from high school—the evidence is damning. This is a student whom teachers and others describe as purposefully choosing *not* to "succeed." "He's tried to get by and it's going to catch up with him" were his counselors words two weeks prior to graduation when it became clear that Robert would not graduate with his peers.

But what about Robert's apparent failure? Bottom-line measures of achievement (i.e., standardized test scores) place him above the 95th percentile in almost all academic areas. His SAT scores, though not dramatic, are such that he would qualify for most universities in the country. And what about critical thinking, ability to solve problems, analyze situations, and galvanize learning opportunities? It seems to us that Robert's comments on the structure of schooling, his treatises on the mediocrity of education, and his descriptions of educators' orientation to "push towards the mean" are not dissimilar to analyses by some of the most prominent scholars, policymakers, and educators in the country.

Contrary to teachers' descriptions, our observations of Robert over a period of 2 years reveal a young man who has grown and matured socially, has developed meaningful friendships with peers and adults, has spent long hours developing his artistic talents, has read widely, and has demonstrated the ability not only to investigate but also to extend his access to a variety of learning situations. We know of no other students who sought out and developed a relationship with a professional in a field in which they are interested and willingly and enthusiastically completed assignments to be critiqued.

Nevertheless, Robert has been defined as a failure—not only are many of his teachers' comments negative; the most damning evidence is that he will not graduate from high school with his peers. Lacking a small number of credits for graduation, Robert plans to attend summer school to complete the courses neccessary for graduation so that he can attend the Southeast School of Design. From our perspective it appears as if Robert's entire schooling process has provided him with little assistance with respect to academic, social, or emotional growth. Rather, a good deal of energy and effort have been directed at acquiring his compliance, his conformity, and his acquiescence. This is a youth who has been left to build his own developmental ledges, his own academic opportunities, his own markers for success. This is a student who, failing to conform, has essentially been left to fend for himself. From our perspective it is actually quite remarkable that he appears not to have internalized the message that he is a failure.

It appears that during Robert's elementary school years he faced psychosocial borders emanating from his mother's death. Expected to leave this tragedy "outside the classroom door," Robert apparently developed a resistant attitude toward school expectations and norms that probably carried into junior high and high school. This case also illustrates vividly the presence of structural borders that emanate largely from contrasting conceptions of what learning should be. Robert's ideas and beliefs seem almost diametrically opposed to those of educators in his school environment.

We cannot help but wonder if Robert's story would have been one of publicly acknowledged success (rather than one of generalized failure) had the tremendous efforts directed at his compliance been redirected toward his growth. What is apparent is that Robert's expectations for what learning should be and what the school as an institution should look like are fundamentally different from those held by school authorities.

8

CARMELITA ABELLO

This is my first full day of accompanying Carmelita Abello throughout her day at Huntington High School. I have interviewed her once previously and I am now anxious to observe her classes, meet her teachers, and talk with her about her reactions to school. As we leave first-period freshman English, she answers my questions briefly. "Tell me about Mrs. Zooey." "Was this a typical class?" "How do you feel about the things you are reading?" Carmelita's answers are thoughtful but she does not elaborate without my encouragement and probing. Her reserved manner mirrors the comments of many of her teachers who describe Carmelita variously as quiet and shy, self-confident and assured. According to Mrs. Manley, Carmelita's freshman and sophomore history teacher, "She is very quiet and sweet, and there is no doubt that she will go to an excellent college."

As we head toward Carmelita's second-period German class she is joined by Laurie and Li Hua, her two best friends. While all are dressed in commonly seen Huntington high school attire—walking-length shorts, long-sleeved cotton shirts with tails tied in front, athletic shoes, thick socks, and backpacks slung loosely over their shoulders—I note how different these three young women are from each other. Carmelita's lovely oval face, chiseled Filipina features, and thick black braid extending almost to her waist contrast dramatically with her friend Laurie's large frame, blond hair, and blue eyes set in an almost perfectly round, Scandinavian face. Li Hua, the third member of this tightly knit group, is a tall, large-boned, Japanese-American girl whose serious expression reveals little of what Carmelita later describes as a very pessimistic and gloomy outlook.

As Carmelita greets her friends, I watch as her manner changes dramatically. Moving among the crowded halls of Huntington High School, Carmelita's quiet and reserve drop away to reveal an animated, giggly, laughing, gregarious teenager. While I cannot hear clearly the entire conversation, there is no question that these three young women form an exceptionally intimate friendship group. Watching them together in the few minutes between classes provides me with a glimpse of Carmelita's often hidden extroverted and interactive side. With me not far behind, Laurie heads towards her math class while Li Hua and Carmelita, still deeply engrossed in conversation, enter Mrs. Moore's beginning German class for the second period of the day.

BEGINNING AT HOME: MODELING MOVES, ENCOURAGING TRANSITIONS

(*Tagalog is the language you speak at home?*) I feel more comfortable cause that's the language I've used with them [my parents] all my life. And you know, just like if my friend asks me to speak Tagalog with them I wouldn't feel comfortable because I've always talked English with them.

For Carmelita, moving among her Filipino family, her ethnically mixed peer group, and her culturally diverse urban high school is accomplished with comfort and ease. Speaking Tagalog with her parents, switching to English with her friends, and studying German at school is, for Carmelita, patterned and routine. She laughs when she tells me her friends have noticed a Tagalog accent (discernible at no other time) when she occasionally speaks English with her parents. Her family's Filipino background, their adherence to Filipino customs and ways, and their strong emphasis on interdependence and family cohesion seem only to enhance Carmelita's ability to move easily between home and school. Unlike Trinh, who describes internal conflict and ambivalence about her cultural heritage and works diligently to hide aspects of her Vietnamese background, Carmelita expresses appreciation and respect for her parents and talks openly about her deep connections to her extended Filipino family, with whom she has maintained close contact despite her many moves. A physicist, Carmelita's father has worked in countries around the world. As Carmelita says, "Well I didn't really grow up anywhere because we were moving every two years. My dad is a scientist so he would do research in one country or he'd teach in another, so I've been to like—this is my eighth school."

Born in the Philippines, Carmelita moved to Denmark when she was 3 months old. Two years later the Abellos returned to the Philippines, then to the United States for a number of years, to Germany for 2 years when Carmelita was 7, back once again to the Philippines, and finally to the United States, where the family has been for 5 years. Carmelita's well-educated, upper-middle-class parents have themselves navigated a variety of cultural milieus with apparent success. Likewise, many of her extended family members move comfortably in diverse settings and across cultural borders. Most are professional people who have also obtained graduate level degrees. "My family is clearly intellectual. I've got a lot of engineers and doctors and lawyers. All of my cousins have gone on to graduate school."

Carmelita is an only child, and her relationship with her parents is characterized by warmth, support, and mutual respect. While friends are important, Carmelita often spends time with her family on weekends—church on Saturday night or Sunday, shopping, seeing a movie, visiting her uncle in Neville, or just hanging out at home.

> We don't really consciously go, "we have to be together as a family." It's just the way they [my parents] were raised and the way they believe and stuff. . . . They come from big families, you know, there were six children and stuff, so. Yeah, so, we don't really consciously go—"well we have to stay close so we have to do things together," we just do.

Nor is Carmelita reluctant to talk about her parents—their background and beliefs—with her friends at school. In fact, she muses often about how lucky she is in comparison with many students whose relationships with their parents seem problematic.

> American kids really hate their parents. . . . Their parents aren't really that bad you know, they just kind of misinterpret them. And they don't really talk that much [with their parents], that's the problem. Because they assume their parents are a certain way, their parents assume that their children are a certain way.

Carmelita's descriptions over a period of 2 years suggest that her parents not only provide a great deal of support but also encourage open discussions about issues such as school work, family decisions, friends, and dating.

> We got into this big discussion in the car the other day. (*Just you and your mom and dad?*) Yeah, and I said, well you know if anyone is ever going to date me, they're not going to date me with a chaperone you know, and we were just kind of joking but I think they're just going to loosen up on it. (*And they were laughing too?*) Yeah, I guess if they trust the guy they'll let me, but the first date should be like at home and with my parents and stuff so they can get to know him, but after that I said I want to go with him alone. [laughing] (*It sounds like they have a good sense of humor.*) Yeah they do. I can really talk to my parents. . . . I mean I can't keep secrets from them.

However, conflicts do occur and Carmelita is consciously aware that contention arises not only because of parent/adolescent developmental issues but also because of cultural factors. As she says, "I have a lot of conflict with my parents too because they're from the Philippines and everything is really strict." However, according to Carmelita, the fact that her parents are strict and their expectations are high is not particularly problematic. "It doesn't really bother me that my parents are strict because, I mean, that's all I've known." While Carmelita and her parents don't necessarily always agree, differences are most often negotiated. For example, her family did, in fact, modify their stance on dating following a number of discussions and her reminder to them that in 2 years she would be on her own at college. "After awhile they start thinking about what I said and stuff, or sometimes they don't, sometimes they still stick to their rules."

By the end of her sophomore year, Carmelita described her parents as "loosening up." They had begun to lift such restrictions as not going to the mall with friends and not driving with peers who had recently obtained their drivers' licenses. However, being informed of her whereabouts, knowing her friends' parents, and maintaining a strict curfew remained important rules. For the most part, Carmelita had little trouble complying with their wishes given the open communication, lengthy discussions, and mutual respect that typifies her relationship with her parents. "Yeah—well, I tell them everything you know, even though I don't mean to. I just bring it out. I don't know, I feel like I need to tell them because I want to just get it out of the way."

With respect to school, Carmelita's parents are interested, supportive, and involved though not necessarily in traditionally defined ways. While their expectations are that Carmelita will attend college, they do not pressure her to make perfect grades.

> Well they don't really, they don't push me or anything, but they're also aware of my limitations and they expect me to get good grades you know. But not—if I can't get all A's they don't ground me or anything. They more or less ask me what's going on in the classes and how they can help.

Their involvement and concern about school is also illustrated by their routine inquiries and obvious interest in school-related matters. As Carmelita says:

> After every test they go, "so how did you do?" and "was it easy?" . . . They ask me about schoolwork, and that's their way of getting involved in it. Instead of just going, you got an F, you'd better study harder and stuff, they don't tell me what to do, they just ask me what is going on and what's going wrong, how can we help, and how can you improve, you know.

Carmelita also talks appreciatively about her parents' orientation to listen to her opinions. She says they are quick to empathize when she describes teachers with whom she is having difficulty.

> I told them about my biology teacher, my dad says he's a dork. [laughing] He's a scientist so he might—you know—he pushes me in the science direction and when I get a teacher that doesn't know anything about science he kind of gets disappointed. But he tutors me in science. . . . Usually I'll just hand him the book and he'll explain it to me.

While obviously concerned about what happens in school, Carmelita's parents are not inclined to contact teachers or other school officials unless they feel that there is a major problem. Only once, in junior high, does Carmelita remember her father directly objecting to what happened in school. "This teacher would mark something wrong and I'd know it was right and I'd bring it to my dad and my dad said, 'yeah, it's right,' so he'd make an appointment and go and talk to the teacher and told this teacher, 'it's right.'"

There is no question that Carmelita's parents place a high value on education and are committed to providing as much support as possible with respect to making sure that Carmelita succeeds in school. Their own experience in various cultural settings increases their conviction that border crossings can be smooth and they explicitly encourage Carmelita to adopt behaviors that will ease her way. For example, communicating with teachers is a strategy they suggest. "They keep up with all the stuff that's happening to me in school . . . so you know if my grades are slipping in one class then they'll go and try to help me with that class. Just asking me what I'm having a hard time with and telling me to talk to my teacher and stuff."

Carmelita's close connection to her parents and her pride in her Filipino heritage are prominent themes in all of our discussions. From her perspective, her parents' positive attitudes about education, her father's knowledge as a researcher and physicist, extensive cross-cultural experiences, and her parents' overall support and concern are important factors is easing her transitions between home and school.

FROM HOME TO SCHOOL: EFFORTLESS MOVES

Even though Carmelita is one of only three Filipino youth at Huntington High School, she blends in effortlessly in this culturally and ethnically diverse environment where over half of the student population is Asian Mexican-American, and Latino. What distinguishes Carmelita is her excellent academic record and teachers' perceptions that she is a highly motivated

and intrinsically interested learner. As Mrs. Manley, her freshman and sophomore history teacher says:

> She is very religious about doing her work. She's just a super neat gal.
> She just comes in and "what's there to do?" and then she comes up
> with ideas of her own and adds to them . . . she is very dependable as a
> student and she has a big future ahead of her. She has very supportive
> parents.

Carmelita's own comments about education support teachers' views about her
intrinsic motivation to learn. "Yeah, I am going to go to college, but not really
for having a career and stuff. I think, I just want to go to college to just, for
studying cause I like studying. I just want to learn more things and I think if
you go to college you can just enrich yourself."

A 4.0 grade point average, high standardized test scores (99th, 95th, and
94th percentile in math, language, and reading her freshman year), and repeated teacher comments of "excellent conduct, attitude, high responsibility"
mark Carmelita's cumulative record file. Further, many of her teachers believe
that her family and cultural background are assets that positively affect her
attitude, motivation, and orientation toward school. Mrs. Manley is particularly positive about the wealth of cultural experience that Carmelita brings
to class.

> She has a really great background [being from the Philippines]. . . . (*Do*
> *you know her parents?*) I have met them. (*What about parent expectations?*)
> Oh, I am sure they are very high. Father is a physicist and he writes me
> a note every once in a while and tells me about something you know
> that she is working on and you can just see the support coming in. . . .
> And it's amazing because with her ethnic background she has lived in
> the Philippines and she can tell stories in the class about—they have
> some kind of thing that they do over there, one of those religious cere-
> mony things where people actually take nails and pound them into their
> own hand redoing the crucifixion and things like this. She's seen things
> like this and so she has a big cultural background of things that are
> unknown over here that she can add to the class.

Mrs. Manley, herself a world traveler, greatly values cross-cultural experience and incorporates her own knowledge of other cultures into her curriculum. While some students find Mrs. Manley's classes rigidly structured and
difficult, Carmelita speaks highly of her efforts:

> She's really enthusiastic about helping us to learn and she has a lot of experience in other countries so she tells us about the things that we don't actually have in the book. (*She draws from things outside of just the textbook?*) Yeah, and she makes it a lot more interesting. I don't know if other people agree with me, but I like her class. It's real interesting.

However, it is interesting to note that Mrs. Manley does not necessarily evince such enthusiasm for all of her culturally diverse students, particularly those in her regular track classes. Espousing a classic deficit view (Bereiter & Engelmann, 1966; Deutsch, 1967; Hess & Shipman, 1965), she believes that many of her lower-achieving students are not only unmotivated academically but also that their families are uninterested in their education.

> My other classes are just very . . . they don't want to learn anything. That's very hard. That's very difficult because what you want to do, somebody wants to interrupt you and not let you do it because they want to stop the process and I don't want to stop the process. . . . The difference between the accelerated and the average is just enormous. And the difference between the average and the low who might be just a slow learner is very different because the average ones are the ones that could do it but don't want to. And lots of parents that don't care whether they do it or not. There is a lot of difference in that middle group.

In contrast, Mrs. Manley responds approvingly to those characteristics about Carmelita that match her own values and beliefs about what is important. That Carmelita's parents are well-educated, well-traveled, and involved and concerned about their daughter's education are positive attributes from Mrs. Manley's standpoint. Further, Mrs. Manley confided to me that she would give anything to have had the types of overseas opportunities the Abellos have had.

During her freshman and sophomore years, Carmelita and Mrs. Manley developed a close relationship. Mrs. Manley saw Carmelita as a student with a great deal to contribute and she specifically provided opportunities for her to do so. Further, she made a point of letting Carmelita know that her cultural heritage was an asset to be valued. As a result, Carmelita felt she was an important and valuable contributor to the classroom discourse. In essence, Mrs. Manley made it easy for Carmelita to move from home to school by encouraging her to bring valued aspects of her home life and heritage into the classroom.

Almost all of Carmelita's other teachers also described her as extremely strong academically, although none drew as extensively on her background knowledge about Filipino customs and ways as did Mrs. Manley. Many of her teachers also note her generally reserved and quiet demeanor in classes. As Mr. Cao, her sophomore English teacher says,

> Carmelita . . . very talented woman. Sometimes she should be more verbal in class. . . . She has good ideas but I guess she just doesn't choose to share them. But she has good ideas when she gets drawn in. Maybe some of her heritage. I don't know how traditional her family is. She's friendly outside of class though. When she's in the classroom and comes by with her friends, she's bubbly. She's very lively. So, maybe the system.

Interestingly, Mr. Cao speculated that Carmelita's reserve might well result from the rigid way in which most high school classes are structured. He described Carmelita as much more verbal when she was involved in small-group work, a behavior we too observed. In general, Carmelita seemed uncomfortable competing for the floor during whole-class discussions and in such situations she usually chose not to participate. Her own description of the few opportunities in which she was able to work with others confirmed Cao's suspicions about the structure of most of her classes.

> (*What about other kids in the class? Does that make a difference at all?*) Not really. Well they don't let us talk or anything like that, so I don't really pay attention to the other students. (*You don't have any classes in which you are encouraged to work together?*) Choir and PE. (*But not any of the academic subjects?*) Not really. Well sometimes in Mrs. Manley we have a project—a group project. . . . (*Do you like that?*) Yeah, I like working with other people.

While Carmelita likes some teachers better than others, like Ryan, she maintains consistently high grades across subject areas. At the same time, she is sensitive and discerning about what constitutes good teaching: "I think if the teacher does something more than just taking things out of the book or something. If she includes the students in everything I think that's really fun. . . . Yeah, not just lecturing and stuff."

Similarly, Carmelita's description of her sophomore biology teacher illustrates well the reasons for her withdrawal from class participation.

> Well, like my biology teacher, I don't really know him and he's kind of . . . he presents this front like he's really tough and not really approachable you know. So when you have a teacher like that, that doesn't really know you, and you don't really know him, you kind of back away and

you don't really want to ask questions in class, and you just don't want
to participate a lot because you don't know when he's going to—how
he's going to react. . . . He doesn't really connect well with the class.

Further, this teacher's inability to share his own personal experiences, his in-
timidating manner, and his monotonous classes do little to actively engage
Carmelita in the subject matter content. Carmelita's description illustrates
reasons why even excellent students become turned off from learning.

He doesn't really bring in his personal experience when he's teaching,
he does it from the book. So when you ask him a question he goes "well
it's in the book, go read it." . . . Do worksheets, we read the chapter, and
he lectures, and then we see a movie, we do a lab, and then we have
a test. So it's the same thing every week, every week, so it's kind of
monotonous.

In contrast, Carmelita is very much aware of teachers who are able to
move into students' worlds. From her perspective, having teachers with whom
she can connect makes school a much more meaningful place to be. Carmelita
describes Mr. Cao, her sophomore English teacher, as an important person
with respect to easing her transitions between home and school.

One time Trinh and I went there after school to make up a test. And
we just start talking and it was—I think we started talking about half an
hour you know—just about life and everything you know. So he, I
guess he knows. It sounds like he remembers . . . most of the stuff he
knows about me. I think it's better when you know the teacher and
the teacher really knows you. You kind of connect more. And it kind
of—you can talk to the teacher without being intimidated or kind of
approach them better.

Carmelita's general self-confidence as well as her skill in assessing others' border-crossing capabilities impact the way in which she views and defines difficult classroom situations. For example, in contrast to Mr. Cao and Mrs. Manley, Mrs. Zooey's arbitrary and disrespectful behavior toward students' in
Carmelita's freshman English class serves only to affirm Carmelita's feeling
about what she herself believes. "Well she changes her mind a lot and all that.
She doesn't like anyone. . . . If she asks, how do you feel about this, and then
you write an essay on it, she'll put a comment on it, 'I don't really believe you
feel that way.' . . . She thinks—she wants us to feel what she feels." Carmelita's
awareness of Mrs. Zooey's inability to enter meaningfully into the worlds of
her students leaves her critical of the teacher rather than with self-doubt. Ac-

cording to Carmelita, Mrs. Zooey's remarks are not only insensitive; they also demonstrate her lack of respect for other cultural groups.

> [She's] not really racist, but she's so—just the way she talks you know. If she's talking about a bad neighborhood or something, she'll say, "the black kids." The whites are all in the good neighborhoods and stuff. She always says that. And then just stuff, she'll just—whenever we talk about bad people, she'll mention blacks and gangs.

However, Carmelita is also aware that Mrs. Zooey's feelings toward her are not entirely positive. Mrs. Zooey's comments to us confirm Carmelita's view.

> She is a funny little girl. I think she is smart, yeah. . . . She and Li Hua and Laurie and another girl whose name I can't remember are very close knit. And they talk a lot amongst each other but they never really talk to me or anybody else in the class. They are more kind of removed. You know how some kids do that. They have no relationship with the teacher whatsoever.

Mrs. Zooey's view is that students must be the ones to cultivate a relationship with the teacher. What she failed to consider or explore were Carmelita's reasons for avoiding closer contact.

Aside from Mrs. Zooey, who seemed distressed by Carmelita's lack of interest in developing a relationship, all of her teachers commented on her excellent academic work, her positive class demeanor, and their confidence that she would surely go to an excellent university. While most of her teachers did not know her parents, they nevertheless perceived them as supportive and involved. However, aside from Mrs. Manley, none were attentive to the differences in the sociocultural components of Carmelita's family and school worlds. The fact that Carmelita's parents are upper-middle-class and well-educated, have traveled a great deal, and are perceived by teachers as involved in their daughter's education coincides with teachers' views of what is important for school success. While Carmelita's feelings about her teachers are mixed, overall she feels valued and affirmed in her high school classes. At the school level, however, there are a number of circumstances that make her educational experience less than optimal. For example, because of cutbacks in funding, the school district has eliminated counselors, a loss that Carmelita specifically feels.

> We don't have a counselor. (*How do you feel about that?*) I think we should have one, because I know a lot of my friends are really troubled and last year we had one. Actually two of my friends were like thinking

of killing themselves and that was really hard on me. . . . (*So there's no place you can go here for help?*) You have peer counselors but that doesn't really help because they're not really professional counselors. I mean it's nice to talk to a friend and all that, that's your age, but you still need a professional.

Sworn to secrecy and yet feeling a tremendous amount of responsibility for her friends, Carmelita feels caught. Turning to her parents who do call the school, Carmelita nevertheless feels frustrated and alone without the availability of school counselors or other programs and services to which she can turn. While Carmelita does not herself describe psychosocial borders, she is certainly impacted by the psychological and emotional needs of her friends.

Further, Carmelita's description confirms other students' comments about the lack of assistance and information they receive with respect to future educational and work opportunities. While Huntington does have a college and career center, for the most part students are left to seek out information on their own. In talking about the center, Carmelita says, "There's not really any questions you can ask, you just get brochures and stuff. And sometimes some colleges will come here at lunchtime and they'll meet with you and answer any questions you have. That's about it. I mean most of the college research I do is on my own."

Without high school counselors, students meet one period a week with a mixed-age cohort of peers and one teacher in what is called the ASSIST Program. Ostensibly this class was developed to help students with scheduling, course selection, college information, and other general types of assistance traditionally provided by high school counselors. The plan is for students to have the same ASSIST teacher throughout their four years in high school in order to provide continuity with respect to the teacher as well as other students. Unfortunately, in many of the ASSIST classes we attended students were given little help and often were left on their own to chat with peers or complete homework. In many cases teachers knew little about students who had been in their ASSIST class for as long as 2 years. According to Carmelita, in ASSIST she received only the most basic of information. "Basically what they [ASSIST teachers] tell us is what classes to take and what your GPA should be, but that's about it. And they do it for the UC system and the state system so they don't really give you other—[about] private colleges and stuff."

Further, the information that Carmelita did receive was often conflicting or simply incorrect. For example, unable to take a science class her freshman year, Carmelita had planned to take biology in summer school. Her ASSIST teacher told her this was not possible though later she learned that what he said was incorrect. Looking back at the end of her sophomore year, she reflected on the situation:

> Well I just got so many conflicting stories and they just—[I] listened to my ASSIST Teacher and it turned out he was wrong but—oh well. I'm not really bitter about it 'cause I think I'm learning. I think I should have taken it in summer school but it doesn't really matter to me anymore.

For Carmelita, selecting appropriate classes and obtaining information about colleges was possible because of her own initiative and ability to seek out information. We worried, however, because we knew that an error in course selection or inability to access accurate college information could, in fact, have significant ramifications for her future. Like many other students at Huntington High, Carmelita received little assistance in these important areas.

Overall, Carmelita's transitions between home and school appear to be little affected by less than optimal circumstances in her high school environment. An excellent student, well thought of by her teachers, praised (at least occasionally) for her culturally rich background, Carmelita appears to move effortlessly between her worlds. Her experiences illuminate well the classroom and school factors that facilitate her moves as well as circumstances that could make her transitions easier.

PRACTICING BORDER-CROSSING SKILLS: SELECTING PEERS AND ACTIVITIES

(*Which one [club] do you like best?*) International Club, 'cause it's really fun. (*Tell me about it?*) Well, the point of the club is actually to bring I guess races together and, you know, understand people.

Carmelita's choice of clubs and her desire to be involved highlight her orientation toward working and interacting with and learning about people different from herself. We watched as she purposively sought out ways to broaden her experiences, connect with diverse peers, and hone her border-crossing skills. Easing into extracurricular activities her freshman year, Carmelita joined the girl's volleyball team and by March began attending lunch meetings of the International Club. Her own ease in border crossing seemed to orient her first toward a club whose expressed purpose was to promote understanding and interaction among students from diverse cultural backgrounds.

By November of her sophomore year, Carmelita had added Science Club, Club Med (for future medical students), California Scholarship Federation, and Barristers (a law club) to her list of activities. In the spring she was elected to a minor student government position and talked about her plans to include even more activities the following year. Confident in her ability to cross borders with ease, Carmelita wanted to be involved specifically in ways that make a difference.

> When I was running for Supreme court, I was kind of mad that I didn't run for a higher office, like I really wanted to get involved. I found out the Supreme court you vote for stuff, but that's not really important . . . so that's not really making an impact. I want to make an impact.

While Carmelita described her involvement in clubs as a way of connecting with others, her descriptions also indicate that she was motivated to involve herself in activities that emphasize social responsibility.

> They have a new club called the YEH, Youth Ending Hunger and they had Amnesty International. And then next year I think I'm going to [also] join the Leo Club. I didn't know what the Leo Club was. I thought it was just for spirit, but Leo club is for helping the homeless and doing various community service works, so I'm going to do that.

As mentioned earlier, Carmelita and her two close friends, Li Hua and Laurie, formed a tight friendship group that was part of a larger, loosely configured group of culturally diverse students. When together, Carmelita, Laurie, and Li Hua seemed uninhibited and even their teachers noted the dramatic shift in their behavior.

> *Mrs. Manley: Freshman English:* She [Carmelita] is very quiet and sweet except when she is with her two good friends, Li Hua and Laurie. Then I simply can't believe the difference—more talkative. Sometimes she gets silly and reverts to being a ninth grader but not very often. She acts older. But then when she and Li Hua get together they can be very very silly.

These three friends also shared an affinity for music and talked a great deal about their hopes and dreams for launching music careers. As Carmelita describes:

> Well, I'm really involved with music, so I write songs and I take piano lessons and I sing. . . . Yeah, I really am trying to pursue a music career.

I've always been interested in music. I started singing when I was 3 and I started playing piano when I was 5 and I started writing songs when I was 5, so it kind of just developed into this thing where I want to go into music.

However, early in my conversations with these three young women it became evident that a major and increasingly significant difference between Carmelita and her friends—one that would eventually sever their close connection—was the nature of their relationship with their parents. While Carmelita described her family as supportive of her interest in music (as long as she intended to go to college), both Laurie and Li Hua talked of their parents' disdain and disapproval of music as an appropriate career pursuit. As Carmelita said:

Well my friend—the reason her mom gave [for not supporting her interest in music] is because it would be embarrassing to have a daughter that's pursuing a music career because her two older sisters are being engineers and one of them's going to be a lawyer or accountant or something like that. Yeah and you know that's really stupid. . . . I have lawyers and doctors for cousins and you know my parents were telling me, you know you should go for what you want, don't look at what other people say because you know we support you. We think you should go for this. So I'm really glad my parents really support me on this.

Further, the differences went beyond Laurie and Li Hua's feelings about music. Carmelita's close relationship with her family made it difficult for her to join with Laurie and Li Hua as they recounted conflicts and described friction in their homes. As Carmelita said, "I tell my mom everything you know. I'm all, 'oh my friend has this crazy mother' and all that. And so my mom like knows all my friends' problems."

As her freshman year progressed, Carmelita became increasingly disturbed by the negative attitude of her friends.

They're just kind of—they're very idealized. Like they have an idea of what they want the world to be. What really bugs me sometimes is they complain but they never do anything about it you know. And I'm the kind of person who's kind of positive and I want to. I don't complain unless I know I can do something about it, you know. So that kind of put the split in us at first. . . . They have a lot of problems at home and stuff. So I mean they don't really—I don't know they're always just depressed and stuff.

While the Abellos were concerned about the effect of Laurie and Li Hua's negative attitudes on Carmelita, they intervened only by encouraging their daughter to become more involved in school activities. By the fall of her sophomore year, Carmelita had created some distance between herself and these two friends. Her busy schedule (club meetings four days of the week) kept her from the close lunchtime association she had enjoyed with her friends for much of her freshman year. At the same time, moving away from Laurie and Li Hua was a slow and often painful process. For several months Carmelita talked often about her feelings of loyalty and her increasing realization that she did not want such a close relationship with peers whose attitudes about family and school were antithetical to her own.

> 'Cause they'd just start talking about how they hated their parents and they couldn't wait until they were 18 so they could move out. And another thing, I mean, they used to be pretty much into school, you know, and they used to be honor students, and now they just don't care about school anymore. If they could they'd probably drop out.

When the core values between Carmelita's worlds became too disparate, she adapted by creating distance between herself and her friends. Further, what became clear was that Laurie and Li Hua, unlike Carmelita, were having increasing difficulty in crossing borders between home and school. For Carmelita, transitions remained smooth. Further, her involvement in extracurricular school activities served to foster friendships with peers with whom she had more in common and whose attitudes were more congruent with her own.

> (*Who are some of your other friends?*) Like Elizabeth was on the right side and Ramona on the left. Mostly I've been hanging around them a lot more than with Li Hua and Laurie, 'cause they're more in my clubs you know and they just—they're more fun. I can talk to them more I guess, because sometimes when I talk to Li Hua and Laurie they have different views and everything.

By December of her sophomore year, Carmelita had essentially severed her close ties with Laurie and Li Hua. However, her orientation continued to be toward building friendships with culturally diverse peers. Joanna (Filipina-American), Trinh (Vietnamese-American), and Jessica (European-American) became her closest companions and the larger peer group of which they were a part was diverse as well.

It's sort of like a mixture of different groups. . . . It's one big group but there's clusters. (*Your friends.*) There's a couple of Hispanic friends, half Hispanic, half German. And another one that's I don't know what she is. I think she's German, I think. Oh no, she's British. She was born in Britain and her dad is British, so that makes her half British. Okay, anyway, and then let's see. Someone else is Italian.

Given the diversity that Carmelita describes, it is interesting to note that these students seldom talk about race and ethnicity. According to Carmelita, "You're not really conscious of it [ethnicity]. I mean if you're friends with someone you don't really go, 'gee you're a different color.'" At the same time, she does mention incidents that bring thoughts of ethnicity to the fore.

I mean usually I don't think about it [being Filipina]. Just sometimes somebody will go—make a racist remark and that's when I'll remember, "gee, I'm not like them, you know." . . . It's not like I'm not proud of my heritage. I just, I don't really think about it.

Carmelita's overall ease in navigating different worlds seems to make her particularly sensitive to borders that do exist in the Huntington High School environment. While school personnel express pride in the ostensibly smooth relationships among the school's culturally and ethnically diverse population, many students have quite a different view. As Carmelita explained:

I mean it's racially mixed considering like who you have in your school but the groups aren't racially mixed. . . . You get kind of discrimination from all sides you know. From whites and from a lot of Mexicans you know, cause they really hate Asians. . . . There's a lot of discrimination in this school.

While Carmelita is acutely aware of borders that exist in the Huntington High School environment, it is likely that her transitions remain smooth partly because of her view of herself in relationship to the discrimination she observes. As she says, "Actually most people hate Asians here, they really make fun of Asians." However, she is clear that being Filipino is quite different from being Asian.

I don't really feel grouped in that [Asian] because I'm Filipino and everyone considers that Filipinos, we have our own thing, you know. Because Filipinos—people don't consider us Asians, people don't consider us anything but Filipinos. So, and I'm practically the only Filipino in the school. I mean there's like two others that I know of.

From Carmelita's perspective, her high school peers do not attach the same derogatory meanings or manifest the same negative attitudes and behaviors toward Filipinos that they do toward Asians. Thus, for Carmelita, meanings about her ethnicity are depoliticized and her descriptions more accurately depict boundaries rather than borders between herself and other students. As a result, Carmelita does not feel compelled to embrace Trinh's strategy of hiding aspects of who she is in order to protect herself from peers' negative attitudes and behaviors. From Carmelita's perspective, she is outside the circle of discrimination she sees directed toward her Asian peers.

By the end of sophomore year, Carmelita's peer group included a fairly loosely configured, culturally diverse group of students who had in common a positive orientation toward school and a commitment to obtaining good grades and participating in school activities and events. Most described themselves as college-bound and almost all were interested in ensuring their chances of attending an excellent university.

As her sophomore year drew to a close, Carmelita was clear that the reconfiguration of her peer group was an extremely important factor in assuring the continuation of smooth transitions between her family, peer, and school worlds.

FINAL REFLECTIONS

An excellent student, well integrated into various aspects of the school culture and comfortable with her parent's involvement and support, Carmelita is one of only four students in our study who describe different worlds and smooth transitions. While these patterns appear somewhat exceptional, we think it is important to highlight family as well as school features that make smooth transitions possible and allow students like Carmelita to navigate different worlds with no apparent distress.

In Carmelita's case, her parents have consistently modeled border-crossing strategies and they have also provided opportunities for Carmelita to acquire such skills herself. Living and working in countries around the world, maintaining relationships with culturally diverse family and friends, and traveling regularly between the Philippines and the United States all provide Carmelita with experience in adapting to varieties of peoples and situations. Further, the educational and socioeconomic status of Carmelita's parents and their overall positive orientation toward school give them the cultural capital necessary to support Carmelita's transitions. Unlike many immigrant parents who are unfamiliar with the American educational system and know little about navigating the complexities of American schools, Carmelita's parents are well informed and savvy about the necessary steps to ensure her educational success. Finally, Carmelita's parents seem to be able to negotiate standards of conduct that continue to honor traditional Filipino customs and ways but also allow Carmelita to comfortably navigate the teenage cultural scene at Huntington High School.

Carmelita's school world also plays an important role in easing her transitions between home and school. Consistently positive feedback from her teachers, classes in which she is made to feel that her cultural background is an asset to be valued, some teachers with whom she feels connected, and at least some classes in which she is academically challenged serve to enhance Carmelita's overall positive orientation toward school. Further, as one of only three Filipino students at Huntington, Carmelita does not personally encounter the blatant racism she observes directed at her Asian peers. For Carmelita, boundaries between student groups have not become borders since meanings about her ethnicity, from her perspective, appear to be neutral. Finally, solid connections and support from family and friends provide Carmelita with a buffer to classroom- and school-level factors that are less than optimal.

We suspect that personal characteristics also play an important role in Carmelita's ability to adapt to different settings with ease. Such attributes as flexibility in her relationships with others, her orientation to reach out for new opportunities, her ability to form friendships with a diverse group of peers, and her skill at working through issues with her parents all contribute to the breadth of strategies she has available to move comfortably between her worlds.

9

IDENTIFYING BORDERS,
BUILDING BRIDGES

> An analogy for this model might be (before learning about it) trying to read a map with the paper stuck right on your forehead and covering your eyes. After learning about the model it is like reading a map with the paper at a comfortable and readable distance away.
>
> Natalie, High School Junior

We began this book by pointing out that the negotiation of varied social worlds is a critical feature of students' day-to-day lives. However, as Natalie states above, it is often difficult to distance oneself sufficiently in order to discern processes and patterns in the transitions we and others make. In presenting the Students' Multiple Worlds Model and illustrating a variety of transition types, we have sought to remove the map from our faces in order to contribute a more holistic view of the contexts and characteristics of American adolescence.

We operate out of the firm philosophical position that differences are an asset, not only because they contribute to the continued evolution of our national culture but also because they can help generate the conflicts so critical to our nation's democratic system. For this reason we believe that opportunities for students to experience movement across diverse worlds and to reflect on their own and others' transition and adaptation patterns should be integral to the school curriculum. Border crossing is a skill that should be fostered in all youth.

At the same time, we are concerned that differences are often used to legitimize the silencing of others with less political, economic, or social power. The cases we present illustrate the way in which boundaries between students' worlds frequently function as politicized borders that children and youth avoid or cross only with difficulty. Further, we find that students frequently receive little help in their efforts to cross borders and few opportunities to develop border-crossing skills or to analyze and deconstruct the borders that exist in their school environment or the broader society. To further extend our discussion of these issues, in this final chapter we look at common themes, problems, and pressures that arise for youths in each category type. In so doing, we question common assumptions held about youths—both those who are regarded as "successful" and those perceived as "problematic."

In the second section of this chapter we discuss the application of the Students' Multiple Worlds Model to practice. Drawing on data from our own work with teachers, graduate students, and high school youths, we discuss our efforts and those of others to reduce borders between students and teachers, between students and their peers, and between students' home and school worlds. We conclude by considering the ways in which the Students' Multiple Worlds Model can be used to guide the development of curriculum and instruction for the specific purpose of creating border-transformative classrooms—that is, classrooms in which teachers challenge the borders between their adult/academic and adolescent/social worlds by creating personalized relationships and by providing encouragement, insight, and knowledge necessary for students to analyze and transform borders into boundaries—not only in their own worlds but also in the larger society (Davidson, 1992).

ADAPTATION TYPES: COMMON THEMES

The seven cases we present illustrate six transition and adaptation patterns that we have identified among high school youths. Here we present a brief summary and description of the common attributes of each category type. This analysis is based on information obtained from interviews with all 55 students in our study.

Type I: Congruent Worlds/Smooth Transitions

For Type I youth, values, beliefs, and expectations are the same across their family, peer, and school worlds. While the circumstances of students' daily contexts change, for the most part transitions are smooth and uncomplicated. This does not mean that students act exactly the same way or discuss the same things with teachers, friends, and family members, but rather that commonalties among worlds override differences.

For many Type I youth, family values include an orientation toward the future, family cohesiveness, academic achievement or doing the "best one can," and conformity to white, middle- to upper-middle-class standards of behavior (as described by Spindler, Spindler, Trueba, & Williams, 1990). Likewise, friends and teachers reinforce the value of effort and achievement with respect to schoolwork and involvement in extracurricular activities and sports. In many instances the actors in these students' lives move across the boundaries of their worlds—friends go to each other's homes, are in the same classes at school, and participate in the same extracurricular activities and events. Parents are active in school affairs, rarely miss teacher conferences, volunteer for parent organizations, and support and attend school sports and drama events. Moving between home and school with proficiency and skill, the parents of Type I youth pave the way for their children's smooth transitions by serving as models for boundary-crossing behaviors.

Type I youth are those with whom teachers often feel the most comfortable—these students rarely cause problems or exhibit behaviors that are worrisome or disruptive. Teachers perceive these students as "being on the right track" or, as one of Ryan's teachers said, "programmed for success." In essence, Type I youth exhibit cultural characteristics that are comprehensible and values and beliefs that are in line with those of teachers and schools. Further, because these students participate actively, behave appropriately, and show effort with respect to their academic work, teachers are understandably relieved to have them in their classes. Type I students (and their parents) are recognized, praised, and reinforced for having the attributes valued in school settings.

While congruent worlds and smooth transitions imply harmony and compatibility, this does not mean necessarily that students' lives are without pressures and stress. In fact, pervasive high academic and social expectations across students' worlds frequently leave them feeling overwhelmed. Yet it is exactly these students who are perceived by teachers and others as well adjusted and least in need.

While Type I students often do not exhibit characteristics traditionally associated with "at-risk" youth, many talk about the tremendous pressure they feel—from family, peers, and teachers—to achieve, to perform, and to maintain high grades. Anxiety about the future and fear that they will not live up to the expectations of those around them leads to behaviors that most educators do not intend to foster. For example, many of these students describe their emphasis on "learning to play the game" rather than learning to learn. Others report their inability or their lack of inclination to remember content material following exams. Further, some students say they worry so much about their classroom performance that their ability to concentrate is obstructed. Perhaps most alarming, however, are students' reports of their decreasing intrinsic interest in learning and their increasing concern with obtaining high grades and test scores.

The stress felt by Type I students can have social and emotional costs as well. For example, some students say that their preoccupation with grades leads to competitive behavior with friends. Other students talk about how worthless they feel when they receive less-than-perfect scores. Often these students express discomfort with behaviors they have adopted in order to succeed.

Only recently have educators and other professionals working with youths become cognizant and concerned about the psychosocial costs that may result from students' obsession with high grades and test scores. Further, there is increasing speculation (and some evidence) about the possible relationship of academic pressure to emotional and physical symptoms—depression, anxiety, illness, substance abuse, suicide. For example, in 1990, the Palo Alto Youth Council surveyed students at its two city high schools. The summary report contains the following comments:

> It is not surprising that 85% of the respondents plan to go on to a four-year college after graduation. However, this quest for academic excellence does not seem to be without some potentially dangerous side effects. Ninety-five percent of the respondents claimed that academic stress manifests itself by worrying about grades, trying to meet parental and self expectations, trying to get into the best college, achieving athletically and having little or no social life. Also of concern should be the number of these young people who ignore and/or accept their feelings of exhaustion, general unhappiness, depression, school phobia, and drug/alcohol use as a result of this stress. (Burnett, 1990–1991, p. 2)

Even more alarming are suggestions that pressure and stress are associated with increases in suicide rates among young adults. For example, Wetzel (1989) states: "Experts and laypersons alike associate increases in the suicide rate with competitive pressures for success, to the decline of the nuclear family, and more generally, to ennui—an increased sense of aloneness and depression in our society" (p. 29).

In our study, almost all Type I students talk about the tremendous pressure they feel to succeed. Interestingly, a number of Type I students also report that they worry about their friends with respect to suicide threats, depression, substance abuse, family problems, and high-risk sexual behaviors. While Type I youth describe congruent worlds and smooth transitions, many face psychosocial borders that are concealed.

Finally, while congruent worlds and smooth transitions imply comfort and ease with respect to home/school transitions, these patterns should also alert educators to the possible difficulties that these youths face in connecting and relating to peers unlike themselves. It is these students in particular who have little opportunity or reason to practice or acquire border-crossing skills. Isolated from students in other socioeconomic or ethnic groups, Type I students are particularly at-risk for developing spurious ideas and stereotypes about others. In our study, we find that some Type I students are uninterested in knowing, interacting, or working with students who achieve at different levels, who are culturally or ethnically diverse, or who are in other ways perceived as "different." Constantly reinforced for their "on-track" behaviors, Type I students can be quick to denigrate divergent actions by others. In a sense, their view is limited and bounded by the congruency of their worlds.

With the tremendous day-to-day demands of teaching and the large numbers of students to whom teachers must respond, it is not surprising that students who appear to be doing well (academically and socially) can be overlooked. Further, predominant values in school settings (i.e., academic success, achievement, and future orientation) can serve to obscure potential developmental needs and problems of students that result from differential adaptation to standards of excellence. Finally, many high school teachers and counselors serve as brokers for the university system and thus emphasize repeatedly the advantage of advanced-level classes, the importance of high grades, the need to elevate AP and SAT scores, and the necessity of enrolling in special classes to do so. While setting high standards and encouraging academic excellence are certainly worthy educational goals, it may be important as well for educators to give attention to identifying and assisting students who experience undue pressure to succeed, as well as emphasizing educational goals beyond those that are outcome-based. The findings here suggest that striving for "success" (in terms of grades and test scores) can have serious psychosocial costs.

Type II: Different Worlds/Border Crossings Managed

The circumstances of Type II students are characterized by differences in the sociocultural components of their worlds—in other words, values, beliefs, and expectations emanating from culture, ethnicity, religion, socioeconomic status, or geographic location (i.e., urban/suburban/rural differences) may be quite different at home than at school. Regardless of differences, Type II students' perceptions of borders between worlds does not prevent them from managing crossings or adapting to different settings. However, this does not mean that crossings are made without discomfort and stress.

For example, we find that many high-achieving minority youth, who are common to this type, are forced to deny fundamental aspects of their personal and ethnic identities. This is illuminated by these youths' efforts to keep the actors in their worlds separate, and the tremendous discomfort they feel when unable to do so. This could also be true of students who perceive their families to be different because of socioeconomic status or religion. Reluctant to have friends come to their homes and acutely uncomfortable when their parents show up at school, these youths' concerns center on cultural characteristics that they perceive as marking them as different and less worthy. Coupled with the obligation that many of these students feel to uphold family values and traditions, many feel conflicted as they attempt to accommodate to the prominent values and norms within their peer and school settings. Because teachers often perceive these students as successfully assimilated and well adjusted, the conflicts and difficulties they feel can be overlooked or discounted as inconsequential. Teachers' beliefs that students "fit in," do well academically, and present few problems preclude their attention to important aspects of individuals' lives—namely, the energy and effort required to navigate different worlds successfully.

Type II students are often an enigma to their teachers, who have no knowledge of their family or cultural backgrounds or the reasons for their success. Moreover, stereotypes about particular cultural groups often influence teachers' perceptions. If these students fail to speak up aggressively and often (which is not unusual), teachers attribute their quiet and self-effacing demeanor to cultural group characteristics. For example, some teachers in our study express surprise that Hispanic youth are actually in high-track classes while others automatically assume that Asian students are perfectly well assimilated. Type II students' invisibility as individuals is illuminated by teacher descriptions that expose their lack of even the most fundamental knowledge about students' backgrounds—for example, the portrayal of Trinh as a model "Chinese" student.

Often a Type II student is one of a few (if not the only) minority students in high-track classes. Many feel isolated and alone. Their comments suggest that without friends with whom they can talk they have no way to test the reality of their perceptions about feeling different (and often inadequate). Not only are they hesitant to voice contradictory ideas and opinions, they are also reluctant to participate in day-to-day classroom discussions, feeling compelled to hide their ethnic and racial selves. This dynamic is discussed by scholars who suggest that stigmatized individuals who become aware of the prejudice of others may avoid aggressive participation in group discussions (Hiltz & Turroff, 1993).

Our interviews with Type II students suggest that the pressures they feel and their resulting fear of speaking up emanate both from their perceptions of classmates' prejudices and their knowledge of differential power relationships in the classroom. Several formal studies have illustrated that social categories pervade social interactions and that individuals from stigmatized groups who are alone are more likely to be evaluated harshly by majority individuals (Fiske & Taylor, 1978; Kanter, 1977; Taylor, Fiske, Etcoff, & Ruderman, 1978). As illuminated in the case studies of Trinh and Patricia, many Type II students sense that their advanced track classmates devalue difference. Further, because Type II students frequently come from families in which they will be the first to attend college, they often do not have the same access to information and resources as many of their peers. Feeling inadequate because of their lack of knowledge, students become anxious, which in turn appears to inhibit their verbal participation in class. (See Davidson, 1996, for further discussion of these issues.)

The educational and emotional ramifications of "hiding oneself" are significant. In classes, students' silent responses can prevent them from obtaining help or assistance. Further, students' limited participation restricts the possibility for the exchange of diverse ideas, thus inhibiting the liveliness and richness possible in classroom contexts. And finally, when students remain silent, bridges to friendship and understanding are less likely to be made—thus impacting negatively both minority and majority youth.

"Hiding oneself" has emotional costs as well. African-American and Latino authors and professionals, reflecting on their experiences in school, speak powerfully to the dynamics that operate (Gray, 1985; Neira, 1988; Rodriguez, 1982). As Neira (1988) says:

> When trying to live in two different worlds, one is in peril of not belonging to either of them. One is left in a state of confusion. . . . Being put in the position of changing one's character every morning and afternoon to adapt to two different worlds endangers one's identity. (p. 337)

When students attempt to overcome feelings of isolation by "fitting in," there is the danger that they may feel it necessary to devalue aspects of their home and community cultures—thus causing them to sever important links to emotional support. Finally, silence precludes students from challenging conventional stereotypes, for example, that they are unworthy, not as smart, less deserving.

An examination of the circumstances and perceptions of Type II youths brings to the fore how critical it is for educators to move beyond common stereotypes of high-achieving minority youth in order to be able to understand the pressures and problems these students face as they move from home to school.

Type III: Different Worlds/Border Crossings Difficult

In this category, like the former, students define their family, peer, and school worlds as distinct. They say they must adjust and reorient as they move across worlds and among contexts. However, unlike students who manage to make these adjustments successfully, Type III youth find transitions difficult. For these youths, border crossing often involves friction and discomfort and, in some cases, is possible only under particular conditions. For example, students who do well in one class may fail all others. Some of these students, like

Donna, do poorly in classes where the teacher's interaction style, the students' role, or the learning activity are oppositional to norms within the students' peer or family worlds. Other Type III youth describe their comfort and ease at school and with peers, but are essentially estranged from their parents. In these cases, parents' values and beliefs are frequently more traditional, more religious, or more constrained than those of their children, making adaptation to their home world difficult and conflictual.

This category type often includes adolescents on the brink between success and failure, involvement and disengagement, commitment and apathy. While many of these youths express a desire to do well academically, they nevertheless seem to be at a loss about the steps they should take to improve their chances of success. Many are apprehensive about graduating from high school and express worry and concern about a future they feel is uncertain.

In our study, almost all Type III youth say that their parents very much want them to succeed and pressure them to do well in school by repeatedly emphasizing the importance of education with respect to creating better life chances. At the same time, many of the parents of Type III youth have limited educational backgrounds themselves and thus do not have the expertise to assist their children either with schoolwork or with managing the educational system generally. These families lack what Bourdieu and Passeron (1977) refer to as cultural capital.

With respect to school, a common theme expressed by Type III youth is their frustration and worry about not understanding course content material. Comprehension difficulties appear to arise from a number of sources. For immigrant students, language problems, as well as lack of access to individualized teacher assistance, can create tremendous strain. For others, skill levels are low and pedagogical styles are unsuited to meet their needs. These students say that their comprehension difficulties are exacerbated by course content they find boring as well as their perception of teachers' low expectations. As a result, students manifest various types of passive and active opposition to schooling in order to cope with the frustrations they feel. Inability to concentrate, tuning out, and withdrawing quietly from the classroom, the teacher, and other students are all consequences that can occur. Still other students adopt more overtly oppositional responses such as copying a friend's work, creating disruptions in class, or engaging in antagonistic behavior toward teachers. Many of these youths believe that teachers feel they are incapable of doing the work or that they willfully choose not to do so. Further, they feel that teachers care little about their overall concerns.

Type III students are also highly sensitive to school and classroom contextual issues. While most students care about their relationships with teachers and school institutions, many overlook negative situations. In contrast, the negotiation strategies teachers adopt to help connect Type III youth to school are critical. Later we describe some of the pedagogical features that these youths say are particularly important to their success.

Finally, many Type III youth deal with serious outside pulls on their lives. For example, some students talk about the severe socioeconomic circumstances of their families as a factor that works against their full engagement in school. Often having to work to help provide support for their families, these youths are burdened with worries about such basic needs as food and shelter, not only for themselves, but also for their parents and siblings. Other Type III youth discuss family conflicts that are severe enough to divert their attention from school. And finally, some students mention major household tasks such as child care or family business responsibilities that take a great deal of their energy and time.

While students across groups face a variety of problems, Type III youth appear to be particularly vulnerable to circumstances that divert their attention from school. There is little question that these are some of the students for whom classroom and school climate conditions can make the difference between staying in school or dropping out.

Type IV: Different Worlds/Border Crossings Resisted

For Type IV youth, values, beliefs, and expectations are so discordant across their worlds that border crossing is resisted or impossible. When border crossing is attempted, it is frequently so painful that, over time, these youths develop reasons and rationales to protect themselves against further distress. In such cases, borders are viewed as insurmountable and students actively or passively resist attempts to embrace other worlds. For example, some Type IV youths say that school is irrelevant to their lives. Other students immerse themselves in the world of peers, where group norms devalue school success. Rather than moving from one setting to another, blending elements of all, these students remain constrained by borders they perceive as rigid and impenetrable.

Unable to navigate borders, many Type IV youths have, for the most part, given up on school. These youths are burdened with the knowledge that their chances of graduating from high school are remote and their futures bleak. They say that their attempts to do well in school create anxiety and stress. As a result, they adopt strategies to deal with the pressures they feel. Some Type IV youth orient toward situations where support is found and away from circumstances that exacerbate their discomfort. For example, skipping school to be with supportive peers is, from their perspective, a positive alternative to the alienation they feel in classrooms where they are perceived as failures. Other Type IV students cling to the hope that they will, by chance, graduate from high school. Some develop elaborate and unrealistic plans ("I will stay here seven years if I have to to graduate") to protect themselves from the hopelessness they feel. However, such plans do not eliminate fear and uncertainty.

Many Type IV youth appear to be paralyzed with respect to future planning and express feelings of impotence about what they should do. While they believe that school success is necessary for future opportunities, their continued failure serves as a reminder that they are somehow inadequate. Many appear to "drift" away—a pattern described by LeCompte and Dworkin (1991).

For the most part, we find that Type IV youth have internalized messages from teachers and other students in their school environments that they are uncooperative, unmotivated, and responsible for their dismal records. While some blame themselves for their lack of success, others alternate between self-blame and criticism of both the dominant cultural ideology that "anyone can make it" and a system generally unresponsive to their needs. This "contradictory consciousness" is similar to that voiced by the dropout youth described by Fine (1991).

Another common theme among Type IV youth is their description of less than positive interactions with people in the school environment. Many perceive callousness and hostility from teachers and peers that threaten their personal integrity or leave them feeling devalued because of their ethnicity, culture, and/or language. From their perspective, they are singled out and "picked on" for reasons of ethnicity, gender, values and beliefs, and/or personal attributes. For these students in particular, feelings of social marginalization appear to affect their ability to profit from educational settings. As the case of Sonia illustrates, for minority students in this category such interactions may also send negative messages about the relationship between ethnicity and schooling. (See Davidson, 1996, for further discussion.) The voices of Type IV students mirror those of other at-risk and dropout youth who describe their reactions to teachers whose actions the students interpret as uncaring or insensitive (cf., Deyhle, 1995; LeCompte & Dworkin, 1991; Stevenson & Ellsworth, 1993; Wehlage & Rutter, 1986).

Finally, our observations and interviews suggest that Type IV students often do not have access to information relevant to their lives, nor do they know how to obtain such information. In some schools, programs and services are simply unavailable. In other cases students are unaware of programs and services that are actually in place in the school environment (e.g., tutoring, work/study, training opportunities, physical and mental health services, etc.). In other words, for many of these youths there are no bridges to opportunities that do in fact exist. And in some cases, even though students are aware of programs, they feel that adults dismiss their interests, concerns, or questions. These students' high absenteeism and frequent invisibility make them particularly vulnerable to not obtaining the assistance they need. Further, teachers and other adults who adopt a triage mentality often give up on Type IV youths, thus making them especially at-risk for not receiving information that could positively affect their school and future circumstances. This is particularly unfortunate since the inability of these students to cross borders successfully does not necessarily imply that they are completely opposed to school. In fact, many Type IV youths voice a desire to obtain the skills necessary to succeed.

Overall, the resounding theme of Type IV youths is that classroom and school climate features do not support their needs. For these students, in particular, structural borders appear to be paramount.

Type V: Congruent Worlds/Border Crossings Resisted

We describe Type V youths as those who find it impossible to navigate transitions even though the values, beliefs, and expectations across their worlds are very much the same. While our description is limited by our experience with only one Type V youth, we believe that the themes that emerge from Robert's case are not unique. Over 150 teachers with whom we have worked resoundingly state that the patterns illuminated by this particular case study are reminiscent of students they have known. Teachers' comments also attest to the fact that students like Robert provide a special challenge to educators.

There are no apparent reasons why Type V youths do not do well in school. In fact, common beliefs about why children fail—uncaring families; parents' lack of school involvement; undeveloped academic skills; lack of interest in academic subject matter; involvement in drugs, gangs, and alcohol; or preoccupation with peer activity that is anti–school success—often do not apply. Many teachers are baffled about these youths' lack of success and are frequently frustrated in their attempts to understand and impact their academic performance. Other teachers attribute these students' school failure to personal characteristics (i.e., lack of motivation, defiance of authority, self-destructive tendencies, etc.). In Robert's case, teachers' efforts were almost entirely oriented toward obtaining his compliance rather than modulating to characteristics and differences not usually accommodated within the school environment. We suspect that students like Robert, whose worlds are the same but who nevertheless fail to succeed, may well require special efforts both with respect to understanding the origin of their resistance and in creating alternative approaches to engage their interest and cooperation (in Robert's case, linking academic credit to his work with a professional artist). Such creative approaches require institutional flexibility—that is, the willingness and orientation of teachers and others not only to consider but also to promote alternative classroom and school-level practices. As Robert's case vividly illustrates, explanations for student failure that fail to take into account the match between school structures and services and students' needs serve only to solidify the borders that students encounter.

Type VI: Different Worlds/Smooth Transitions

In the Students' Multiple Worlds Study, four students describe Type VI patterns—that is, exceptionally smooth transitions between home, school, and peer worlds that are culturally different. While only a small number of youths describe these patterns, we do comment on similarities we find.

For these students, border-crossing strategies were developed early and continue to be practiced often. Interestingly, all four of these youths grew up in environments where adults modeled border-crossing skills. For example, two young women (one Filipina and one Chinese-American) were from professional families headed by well-educated and culturally sophisticated parents—they had lived and worked in countries around the world. Further, these two students had both attended international schools in a variety of countries where diversity was seen as a strength, teachers worked successfully with students from a variety of backgrounds, and expectations that people will interact and learn from each other were the norm. While now settled permanently in the United States, these young women and their families continue to travel extensively and often. A third male student grew up in a third-generation Italian-American family in which Italian continued to be spoken, Italian connections were maintained, and old-world Italian celebrations and rituals were practiced. The fourth student, a European American female, lived in a biracial household as a result of her mother's remarriage. This family's close friends included people from two different cultural groups. In all of these families, parents not only valued but also modeled connections and interactions with people of diverse backgrounds. Further, they expected their children to develop border-crossing skills and they provided support for them to do so.

Second, these students describe their families as confident in their ability to maintain their own cultural integrity. For example, they are not worried that their children will become so assimilated or confused about their identity that they will lose connection with their own cultural heritage. As a result, the parents promote and encourage their children to affiliate with people from diverse cultural groups, believing that in so doing their lives will be enhanced.

Third, these students say that peers and adults generally react positively to their sociocultural differences—in other words, they do not feel that their ethnic and cultural backgrounds are disparaged. In fact, three of the four students implied that their differences functioned as a form of social capital—for example, some peers were interested in and intrigued by the cultural aspects of their backgrounds. Others expressed interest and even jealousy that others have "culture" or the opportunity to learn a second language at home. In other words, sociocultural differences for these students functioned as boundaries rather than borders in that differences were not devalued.

Teachers' perceptions and behaviors with respect to these students were similar to those of their peers. For example, three of the students described teachers who showed a genuine interest in their cultural heritage, encouraged them to share their cross-cultural experiences in the classroom, and spoke openly and positively (in front of other youths) about their unique backgrounds. We suspect that teachers' identification of these students as having experiences worth sharing in part stems from the fact that they are academically strong. Therefore, their contributions were valued and esteemed. Teachers' interest in and incorporation of these youths' background experiences into the classroom is a major theme that emerges from interviews with teachers and students. It is possible that Type VI students thus believe that they have little to lose and indeed may have something to gain by displaying aspects of their ethnicity.

Unfortunately, other students in our study also have unique and varied cross-cultural experiences but are not identified as valuable class contributors or are not viewed positively by their peers. While these students may or may not stand out academically, their families are often not as well educated and their parents' careers are less visibly distinguished. When teachers take an interest in and value the unique background experiences that students bring to school, cultural borders can be transformed into boundaries. We include Type VI youth in our typology as an illustration of what is possible even when the sociocultural components of students' worlds are different. When students have opportunities to acquire border-crossing strategies—that is, to interact positively with people from different cultural and socioeconomic groups, when their own personal experiences are held in high esteem and perceived as valuable and worthwhile, and when they are encouraged to share their experiences with their teachers and other students, the likelihood of smooth transitions is increased.

TRANSFORMING BORDERS INTO BOUNDARIES

Our emphasis thus far has been on identifying the unique characteristics of youths who exhibit specific transition and adaptation patterns. In this section we turn our attention to the importance of transforming borders into boundaries (Erickson, 1993). We begin with a consideration of borders between students and adults as we reflect on students' relationships with teachers and pedagogical methods that impact students' lives in school. We also review the ways in which we have used the Students' Multiple Worlds Model to sensitize teachers to the borders and difficulties that students face.

Second, we consider borders between students and their peers, pointing out the need for educators to give serious time and attention to the quality of peer relationships in school. We believe that enabling students to develop respectful and connecting relationships with those who are different from themselves is particularly critical in a society where issues of diversity are paramount. We also describe our own work with high school youths using the Students' Multiple Worlds Model as the core curriculum.

Third, we discuss the importance of reducing borders between students' home and school worlds. Drawing on data from the Students' Multiple Worlds Study as well as the extensive literature on the importance of home/ school connections, we address the critical need to promote positive inter-actions and meaningful collaborative arrangements between parents and edu-cators.

In our final section, "Creating Border Transformative Classrooms," we argue for the need not only to assist students in their efforts to navigate dif-ferent worlds but also to examine and critique the borders that exist in their school environment as well as in the broader society. Here we describe our collaborative work with a high school English teacher to develop curricu-lum and pedagogical practices based directly the Students' Multiple Worlds Model and Typology.

Addressing Borders Between Students and Adults

Students across category types raise a number of common themes with respect to their relationships with teachers. Teachers' attitudes, the way in which teachers structure classroom environments, the types of relationships they cultivate with students, and the pedagogical methods they use all im-pact students' ability to connect meaningfully with adults in school settings (Phelan et al., 1992).

Teachers' Relationships with Students. A recurring and frequent theme in students' comments is the tremendous value they place on teachers they perceive as interested in them as students and as people. While this may appear to be an obvious and necessary element of the teacher/student rela-tionship, it is surprising how frequently students identify teachers as dis-respectful and detached. Interestingly, students' and teachers' perceptions are frequently at odds. Many teachers with whom we spoke would be deeply troubled to know that students see them as uncaring adults.

A related theme across student types is the tremendous value that ado-lescents place on having teachers who care. For many students, caring is the attribute most necessary to the establishment of a meaningful student/teacher relationship. Teachers who demonstrate explicitly that they care about students are in a much better position to win their cooperation in academic endeavors. The students in our study confirm what other researchers report— that caring teachers are critical to creating bridges between students and adults (Le Compte & Dworkin, 1991; Noddings, 1984, 1992; Prilliman, Eaker, & Kendrich, 1994; Eaker-Rich & Van Galen, 1996). At the classroom level, teachers' attitudes as well as pedagogical practices can mitigate, to some extent, students' feelings of isolation (Phelan et al., 1992). For example, teachers whom students perceive as caring, considerate, and open often create classroom environments that foster the free exchange of ideas.

Students do, however, define caring in a variety of ways. For example, some students (often those who are academically high achieving) associate assistance with schoolwork as indicative of teachers who care. For these youths, caring can be expressed by teachers who take the time to carefully read and critique papers and write comments. For such students, academic assistance demonstrates that teachers are aware of and concerned about helping them meet long-term educational goals. For other students (particularly those having trouble with academic work), teachers' attitudes and personality characteristics (e.g., patience, humor, tolerance, ability to listen) and person-to-person assistance with schoolwork constitute caring. Many of these youths express a preference for direct, personal interaction. For them, caring means the expression of interest and concern that goes beyond assistance with schoolwork. Explicit statements affirming their value and worth as individuals and demonstrating that teachers like them personally are critical to building bridges between students and adults.

Whether teachers are perceived as caring appears to have direct consequences for the teacher/student relationship. If a teacher is viewed as *not* caring, students report a lack of incentive to do schoolwork or participate in class. Caring teachers reduce the possibility that borders between teachers and students will develop. Further, caring teachers ease students' transitions between home and school, helping them to transform varieties of other kinds of borders into manageable boundaries.

Borders between adults and students are also avoided when teachers exhibit humor, openness, and consideration, all of which serve to bridge age and status barriers and connect students with adults in school environments. The implicit message from students across types is that they want to feel connected personally to their teachers. They also say they like teachers who are open—that is, who engage in communication that lets students know that teachers have thoughts, feelings, and experiences that both enliven and go beyond the academic content of the classroom. For example, students respond positively to teachers who share their ideas and draw on their own experiences to supplement course material. When teachers communicate excitement and enthusiasm and students see that the teacher is engaged actively (rather than merely attempting to transmit content), they are more likely to become involved themselves.

Further, students across types talk about the importance of having teachers who are considerate—who treat them with respect and are attuned to their needs. For example, one student described a favorite teacher as trying to coordinate her tests so students didn't have four other tests on the same day. Alternatively, students express frustration that teachers frequently do not understand the pressures they feel or the stress that results from trying to juggle the competing demands in their lives. This is especially true for minority youth across category types who frequently report distant and depersonalized relationships with adults and differential treatment from teachers, which they feel is related directly to their ethnic backgrounds (Davidson, 1996).

In general, students characterize teachers as those who like students and like to teach and those who don't. They know that some teachers would rather not be teaching and they describe others who act as if they don't like adolescents generally. Over and over again we hear the comment, "The teacher can really make a difference." There is no question that teachers' attitudes are critical to building bridges between adults and students.

Pedagogy as a Bridge Between Students and Adults. While teacher attitudes are critical to relationships with youth, pedagogy also plays an important role in student/teacher relationships. Here again, students across category types raise a number of common themes.

Almost all of the students in our study say they prefer active rather than passive learning—that is, transaction rather than transmission. There is no question that students want to learn from teachers, rather than simply read textbooks. Students unanimously talk about their dislike of reading textbook chapters and answering end-of-chapter questions. They invariably describe these classes as boring and compare them unfavorably with those in which pedagogical methods encourage active participation. Students agree that textbook teaching alone is a sure way to dull their interest in subject matter knowledge. Further, when students face psychosocial, sociocultural, linguistic, or other borders, these kinds of classrooms serve only to exacerbate problems that already exist.

Teachers who depend on lecturing as a primary pedagogical method also risk alienating students, who are quick to distinguish between teachers who talk *with* them and those who talk *at* them. Students across types speak negatively of teachers who "preach," or try to coerce them to a particular point of view. They prefer instead teachers who draw them into the learning process by facilitating class discussions where ideas are explored, and thoughts, feelings, and opinions are shared. This kind of pedagogy provides a critical bridge for all students, making them feel validated as thinking, feeling individuals whose ideas are important. Students praise teachers who demonstrate respect for all class participants, utilize pedagogical methods that create a safe environment, and encourage students to take an active role.

In addition to students' preference for dynamic pedagogy, almost all say they favor teachers who are willing and able to assist them in understanding the material, who take the time to explain concepts and ideas carefully and thoroughly, and who demonstrate a commitment to help them learn. Even though this seems an obvious definition of a successful teacher, it is surprising the number of times students describe teachers whom they perceive as impatient and irritable when they attempt to obtain help. Time and again students describe their frustration in trying to master course material and the failure of teachers to assist them. In contrast, students talk with animation about teachers who leave room in the schedule for guided practice, questioning, and the exploration of ideas. When describing "good" teachers, students invariably mention those who are able to make course content comprehensible.

When students do not understand the material and find the teacher unapproachable, borders are created or reinforced and students feel frustrated and discouraged. Some are brave enough to persist in asking questions. Others are fearful of revealing their inability to comprehend. The consequences are profound. While some students turn to their friends and parents for assistance, other students withdraw or allow priorities other than schoolwork to take precedence. As a consequence they fall further and further behind. In schools where alternative resources are available (for example, peer tutoring programs), some students reach out for help. However, for many, continued frustration and failure make structural borders insurmountable.

Students across types say that teachers who are sensitive and empathetic to their problems in mastering subject matter knowledge make a big difference in their feelings about school and their ability to achieve academically. When teachers are inflexible and unable to discuss alternative points of view, when they depend solely on textbooks or are unable to engage with students over course content, students suspect that they are deficient in subject matter knowledge. Even more important, when teachers are not forthright about their own level of understanding, students not only lose respect for teachers as individuals, but their confidence in schools and learning is undermined as well. In order to build bridges that enable students to participate fully and without fear, it is crucial that teachers model and promote norms of interaction that ensure consideration and respect for all individuals. When classroom activities are varied, when students participate actively, and when a variety of pedagogical methods are utilized, students across types report a high level of interest and engagement regardless of the subject.

Sensitizing Teachers to Borders Between Adults and Youth. Over the past 4 years we have adapted short abbreviated versions of the case studies in this book as the basis for in-service programs for teachers. Similarly, we have used full-length versions of these cases as part of the core curriculum for a master's degree course in education. In this section we describe these efforts as a part of a larger agenda to develop ways of reducing and/or eliminating borders between teachers and students—particularly the socioeconomic and sociocultural borders that frequently separate white mainstream teachers from the poor, working-class, and minority youth with whom they work. In particular, we emphasize the use of case studies as a means of portraying students' lives and involving teachers in discussions and analysis of educational contexts, curriculum, and pedagogy. For example, we find that the questions and issues raised by teachers as they analyze the types of borders that students face and the transition patterns they employ can be translated into curriculum content and policies. It has been our experience that the presentation of student cases draws educators in and engages them in independent, constructive analysis about the types of classroom and school contexts that promote meaningful student-teacher relationships. Further, case studies allow teachers to examine their own attitudes and beliefs. We have aimed these efforts at sensitizing teachers to the borders that students face as well as assisting them in building bridges between themselves and the youths they teach.

In-service Programs for Teachers. In the summer of 1993 Hanh Cao Yu, in collaboration with Don Hill, director of the Professional Development Center of the Stanford School Collaborative, designed and implemented a series of one-day staff-development workshops that involved teachers in a critical analysis and discussion of the Students' Multiple Worlds Model and Typology. Using abbreviated versions of the case studies in this book, teachers discussed the types of borders and boundaries that diverse students encounter and the ways in which classroom and school structures impact students' ability to navigate their worlds successfully. While the teachers in these in-service workshops all remarked about the similarity of the cases to students in their classes, none had thought specifically about the energy and effort students' daily transitions require. According to these teachers, the Students' Multiple Worlds framework allowed them to not only think about students in a more holistic way but also to consider transition and adaptation patterns as critical factors in students' ability to connect with schools and learning. Consideration of this framework and the discussion of individual youths portrayed in the case studies led teachers to consider how the model, typology, and case materials could be integrated into their own curriculum. As one teacher said, "This is a good way to unpack kids' problems and see the dimensions of students' lives."

Perhaps one of the most important outcomes of these in-service workshops was the way in which the case studies provided a springboard for teachers to examine and discuss their own educational practices in direct relationship to students' needs. For example, in considering borders between student groups, teachers began to generate ideas for the ways in which they could play a more active role in promoting interaction and collaboration among diverse youths. Likewise, they began to consider specific classroom strategies (curricular and pedagogical) that would reduce the possibility of structural borders. What was apparent was that teachers were very interested in reflecting on their own roles with respect to reducing borders between adults and students.

Master's Degree Students in Education

For most of the years that I have spent in school my time has been consumed with reading what someone else thought kids were thinking and feeling. Having an opportunity to read case studies as a part of this course has brought to life, for the first time, the actual feelings and experiences that make or break the success of a student from their perspective. I found as I read their comments that what was once just a nameless, faceless "problem" from the teacher's or administrator's perspective was actually a student who had real feelings and experiences. The "problem" was actually not in the child/student, it was the borders that separated them. .

Diane, Master's Degree Student
University of Washington, 1995

During the past 5 years, Phelan has used the case studies in this book as part of the core curriculum for an education course at the University of Washington, Bothell, Social Contexts of Youth: Perspectives on Culturally Diverse Students. Many of the participants in this graduate course are experienced teachers and others work with young people in a variety of educational settings. These professionals read one or two cases a week and analyze themes, ideas, and issues raised by the case-study materials in weekly class discussions. The case studies dramatize students' lives and allow teachers to think about situations with which they are familiar. At the same time, themes embedded in the cases raise issues that engage class participants in independent, constructive thinking as they consider responses to the challenges that diverse youths face.

A major assignment for this course requires teachers to complete a case study of one student, conducting formal and informal interviews and observations over a 10-week period. During class discussions teachers identify and discuss issues and themes embedded in the cases and relate them to the case studies they and their classmates are completing as well as their own work in schools. The approach is inductive—in other words, students move from specific cases to broader generalizations and theoretical issues. Supplemental readings such as Nel Noddings's (1992) *The Challenge to Care in Schools,* David Schoem's (1991) *Inside Separate Worlds: Life Stories of Young Blacks, Jews, and Latinos,* Penny Eckert's (1989) *Jocks and Burnouts,* and Mike Rose's (1990) *Lives on the Boundary,* as well as numerous journal articles reinforce themes and ideas found in the case studies and challenge students to reflect on important contemporary educational issues. Students' responses to reading and conducting case study research are extremely positive. Perhaps most important, using case studies to illuminate the Students' Multiple Worlds Model and Typology provides a means to assist teachers in reducing borders between themselves and their students. As one teacher said, "The most significant part of reading the case studies was getting to know kids I'm afraid I may not have taken the time to or had the opportunity to if I were teaching at their school."

Addressing Borders Between Students and Peer Groups

Students across category types talk about the quality of peer relationships at school as extremely important. Particularly significant are students' perceptions of boundaries and borders between student groups and the ease with which they can be traversed. In some cases, boundaries are fluid and students move among diverse peer groups with ease. For example, an African-American student is easily approached by a white friend as he mixes with other black students at lunch time. In this type of environment, students describe everybody as getting along (for the most part), and they see few differences between students who live in diverse parts of the city or in different locations in the suburbs. Interaction between groups is experienced as easy and unproblematic. Although students hang out with their friends generally, tension and fear do not prevent associating freely with others.

In other schools, borders between groups are rigid and students distance themselves from others. In these situations, students are more likely to attribute negative stereotypes to students different from themselves and view themselves (or others) as outsiders. Intergroup relationships and border-crossing behaviors have other schoolwide consequences as well. For example, students' self-perceptions can be affected by outside definitions of their group. Negative as well as positive attributes can be internalized. Further, pejorative stereotypes from others can push students toward peer-group norms—even when the norms are anti–school success. And finally, tension between groups diverts energy from academic goals.

The quality of intergroup relationships also affects students' interactions in classrooms. In schools where boundaries are fluid and other students are viewed as benign, students can more easily make new friends in classes. In these circumstances, students are able to participate fully and work easily with others—they are not restrained by group stereotypes or fear. In contrast, in schools where borders between groups are rigid and crossings are infrequent, students are less inclined to work cooperatively with those different from themselves. They are also less likely to support detracking efforts, which frequently separate them from their friends.

The conundrum is that academic tracking is a practice that appears to contribute to distant and at times hostile relationships between student groups. Tracking often separates youths by ethnicity and social class (Oakes, 1985), a pattern that held true for students in our study as well. Thus tracking helped contribute to social categories, as the divisions emanating from tracking produced meanings about the relative intelligence and competence of individuals from different groups as well as their behavioral tendencies and interests. Tracking also contributed to a sense of social isolation and cultural estrangement among youths in our sample, thereby contributing to the development of antagonistic relationships (Davidson, 1996).

Several scholars have promoted detracking and cooperative groups as ways to address issues such as those described above (Cohen & Lotan, 1995; Miller & Harrington, 1992; Oakes, 1985). They describe particular strategies that not only promote positive student/student interaction in detracked classrooms, but also prevent replication of unequal status relationships in cooperative groups. (See Davidson, 1996, for a summary of this literature and further discussion.) As part of the Students' Multiple Worlds Study, we engaged in a different type of effort, which also appears to hold promise for addressing borders between student groups. We believe that interventions to positively impact students' relationships with each other are important at all levels within school environments. Particularly necessary are strategies that enable students to articulate and examine their own presuppositions about other social and cultural groups in a context that makes explicit unequal power relationships in the classroom, school, and larger society. An effort of this type is described below.

Reducing Borders Between Students: Working with High School Youths. In spring 1992, in collaboration with a high school social studies teacher and a school counselor, we developed a group investigation project that involved high school youths in an examination of abbreviated versions of the case studies found in this book. (See Phelan & Davidson, 1994, for an extended discussion of this project.) Our purpose was to elicit students' understanding of the circumstances portrayed, their thoughts about the accuracy and fit of the cases to the typology we had developed, and their view of the overall significance of the findings. The 12 high school juniors who participated in this project were diverse with respect to cultural background, gender, ethnicity, social class, and academic achievement. Some of the students were in advanced-level classes while others were in regular and lower-track classes. None were failing or appeared to be in imminent risk of dropping out of high school.

The one-hour group investigation sessions were conducted once a week over a period of 7 weeks. Students read and discussed eight case vignettes selected to illustrate the first four types described in the Students' Multiple Worlds Typology. As the students read and discussed the cases (which included descriptions of cultural factors affecting adolescents' relationships with peers and school), they began to relate the ideas and themes to their own lives, reflecting on the ways in which they personally respond to pressures emanating from their own cultural backgrounds. Further, they began to articulate and examine their own presuppositions about other social and cultural groups. Finally, they began to notice and talk about social stratification within their school setting.

We found the experience of using case studies particularly conducive to assisting adolescents in understanding their own situations with respect to their lives and experiences. Because these cases contained a great deal of variety, students found themselves sometimes quite familiar with the circumstances in one case and quite unfamiliar with those in another. Their ability to analyze the thoughts and actions of a particular student depended, to some extent, on the congruence of the case with their own life experience. When students were more familiar with a particular case, they frequently assisted other participants by communicating their understanding of the situation. Exposure to same-age peers' explanations and points of view enabled students to begin to understand and empathize with the feelings and perspectives of others.

Students' written comments following the sessions confirmed our perception that the participants very much liked reading and talking about youths their own age. The content had indeed engaged their interest and stimulated thoughtful and prolonged discussions. The quote below illustrates the feelings expressed by most of these youths:

[*European-American male*] I found the experience very enlightening. It was a good way for me to "break out" of my usual group of friends and talk openly about issues that are important to me. The cases were a good spark for discussion of ourselves. Each of us had a first impression, which then changed as the discussion went on. It was a good experience for me to keep on shattering my preconceptions about people. (Written response)

Students say that using case studies as a stimulus for discussion is helpful in making them more aware of their own assumptions, goals, values, and beliefs. Over time, they also began to perceive these as potential biases in their social interactions with others. Further, students began to take important first steps in examining unequal power relationships in their classrooms, school, and the larger society.

Addressing Borders Between Students' Home and School Worlds

There is little debate in the literature or among practitioners about the importance of fostering family/school relationships. Evidence continues to accumulate documenting a positive relationship between parent involvement and students' school-related behaviors, including academic performance, attitudes, and motivation (cf. Chavkin, 1993; Comer, 1980; Comer & Haynes, 1991; Delgado-Gaitan, 1990, 1993; Epstein, 1995; Henderson, 1987; Ryan, Adams, Gullotta, Weissberg, & Hampton, 1995; Sanders, 1996b). At the same time, there continues to be a widely held view that many parents, particularly those of low-income and minority youth, are either uninterested or incapable of assisting in their children's education. In fact, recent national surveys cite parents' lack of interest and support as the most significant educational problem (Carnegie Foundation for the Advancement of Teaching, 1988; Elam & Gallup, 1989, cited in Moles, 1993). Stemming from a deficit perception of children and families, the assumption is made that students' family and home culture are lacking and parents do not know how to appropriately interact with, motivate, or teach their children (Bereiter & Engelmann, 1966; Deutsch, 1967; Hess & Shipman, 1965).

Contrary to these beliefs, there is a massive amount of evidence documenting the fact that almost all parents are intensely interested in their children's education and further that they very much want to be involved in meaningful and productive home/school relationships (cf. Chavkin, 1989; Dauber & Epstein, 1993; Henderson, Marburger, & Ooms, 1986; Lareau, 1987; Lueder, 1989; Rich, 1988). Information from the Students' Multiple Worlds Study supports these findings. For example, almost all students say that their parents are very much concerned about their academic performance and, in fact, they see school success as directly linked to future opportunities. It is clear that these families, regardless of ethnicity or socioeconomic status, have internalized cultural messages about the relationship between education and upward mobility. Further, 80% of the students in our study say that their parents not only encourage them to succeed but also that they consistently pressure them to do so. In other words, students perceive their parents to be actively involved. There are, however, differences among parents with respect to how they relate to their children over school-related matters. For example, some students (particularly Type I and Type VI youth) say that their parents help them with homework, call the school when they have questions, intervene when there are problems, and generally serve as advocates in a system with which they are familiar. Other students, particularly immigrant and minority youth and those whose parents are themselves not well educated, say that though their parents encourage them to do well they are unable to provide specific assistance, either with school work or as advocates in the educational system (Phelan et al., 1994).

While we know that parents want to help their children and say that they would welcome specific support from schools in order to do so, there continue to be lower rates of family/school involvement for low-income and minority families. Numerous scholars and educators have discussed reasons for this and have identified barriers to optimal home/school relationships (Leitch & Tangri, 1988). Foremost in their concerns are limited skills and knowledge on the part of both teachers and parents, restricted opportunities for interaction, and psychological and cultural factors (see Moles, 1993, for an extended discussion of these barriers).

We believe that it is imperative for educators to move away from deficit views of children and families and to focus instead on ways to eliminate borders between students' home and school worlds. A great deal of evidence suggests that meaningful, collaborative relationships are possible when problems of misperception, mistrust, and differences in values and beliefs about education are acknowledged and addressed (cf. Connors & Epstein, 1994; Delgado-Gaitan, 1993, 1994; Epstein, 1986; Sanders & Epstein, in press). Further, there is increasing documentation of successful programs in schools and districts throughout the country—that is, programs that involve not only mainstream parents but also those that have traditionally been disenfranchised with respect to home/school collaboration (cf. Burch, Palanki, & Davies, 1995; Calabrese, 1990; Chavkin, 1993; Cochran & Woolever, 1983; Collins, Moles, & Cross, 1982; Comer, 1980, 1989; Delgado-Gaitan, 1991; Epstein, Coates, Salinas, Sanders, & Simon, 1996; Moles, 1993; Rich, 1988; Sanders, 1996 a,b; Stenmark, Thompson, & Cossey, 1986; Wynn, Merry, & Berg, 1995). These programs, which differ greatly with respect to emphasis, goals, and strategies, provide important models for how families and schools can work together productively. There are also a number of common premises that undergird many of these efforts. Foremost, parents are viewed as valuable contributors and important resources in their children's education. Program development begins with the identification of family and community strengths and the assumption is made that parents are not only capable but that they very much want to be involved in their children's education. Beliefs and assumptions about parent's inadequacies, disinterest, and inabilities are explicitly rejected. Second, there is an emphasis on empowerment—that is, an explicit effort is made to involve parents as collaborators and decision makers in their children's education. The goal is to enhance and support the strengths that parents already bring. Third, there is recognition that traditional parent-involvement strategies are not adequate to meet the needs of diverse families. Thus, educators and parents together focus their efforts on developing new, nontraditional methods of family/school collaboration (cf. Cochran & Dean, 1991).

While programs to date provide important examples of successful and innovative home/school partnerships, a great deal of work remains. The fact that many teachers and educators continue to resist involving parents collaboratively because of misperceptions about parents' interests and abilities speaks to the critical importance of focusing energy and attention on addressing borders between home and school.

Creating Border Transformative Classrooms

In a previous section, we described the positive outcomes that emerged as high school students worked with case-study data from the Students' Multiple Worlds Study. However, one difficulty we encountered when doing this work was that students lacked the background necessary to formulate, without assistance, questions about social and structural factors that limit access and perpetuate inequalities in their school and in the broader society. This first effort led us to believe that a more in-depth and complex consideration of such issues and problems might well be possible if curriculum were developed to include historical and literary materials highlighting peoples' encounters with borders and boundaries across time and context.

In an effort to adapt our model in such a way, we are currently working with Penny Bullock, a talented high school English teacher in Bellevue, Washington. In developing curriculum for an American literature class, Mrs. Bullock is utilizing the framework and typology generated from the Students' Multiple Worlds Study to support her ongoing efforts to create a border-transformative classroom (Davidson, 1992). In her upper level (junior/senior) literature classes, Mrs. Bullock asks students to consider and analyze the ways in which characters in works of literature have dealt with borders, boundaries, transitions, and adaptation strategies. For example, *The House on Mango Street* by Sandra Cisneros (1991) and *The Dollmaker* by Harriette Arnow (1954) illustrate vividly the characters' encounters with socioeconomic, sociocultural, and gender borders. As high school students read and consider these particular pieces, Mrs. Bullock not only asks them to identify borders that people face but also guides them in discussions about adaptation strategies that people use. Likewise, poems such as *Refugee Ship* by Lorna Dee Cervantes (1981) and *I Am Joaquin* by Rudolfo "Corky" Gonzales (1972), and Amy Tan's (1987) short story *Fish Cheeks*, illuminate difficulties of living between two worlds and people's attempts to navigate the borders that separate their lives. Finally, F. Scott Fitzgerald's (1953) *The Great Gatsby* illustrates a different and dysfunctional adaptation strategy as Jay Gatsby attempts to deal with the socioeconomic borders he encounters as a young man.

Intertwined with this literature, students read and discuss abbreviated versions of the case studies in this book. Moving between specific pieces of literature and contemporary cases studies of their peers, students reflect on borders, boundaries, and adaptation strategies across time and place. The multicultural literature that Mrs. Bullock has selected as her core curriculum allows her to incorporate issues of race, class, and gender into class discussions as students analyze social and structural factors in the larger society that create borders and perpetuate inequalities and unequal access to opportunities. Finally, as students reflect on the literature they read as well as the case studies, they quite naturally begin to consider the borders they face and adaptation patterns they have adopted. By using historical and literary materials, we find that students gain more sophisticated and complex understandings of the social and structural origins of borders and boundaries and are thus able to reflect more thoughtfully not only on their own lives but on the lives of diverse peers as well. Finally, involving students in a consideration of varieties of adaptation strategies allows them to reflect on the patterns and strategies in their own lives, possible alternatives, and the positive and negative consequences that can emanate therefrom.

FINAL THOUGHTS

From the beginning of this study, students were our guides as we attempted to uncover those things that affected their lives in schools. Rather than assuming that minority status, linguistic differences, part-time employment, peers, and/or poverty necessarily create problems for young adults, we asked students to tell us what affects their lives and their ability to connect with and engage in educational settings. Throughout this project we listened to what adolescents had to say and we involved them in critiquing and evaluating our work. The lessons they have taught us have been invaluable. Not only have their ideas allowed us to expand our original conceptualizations but they have also provided us with a broader understanding of the patterns that diverse youths adapt as they negotiate their various worlds.

Emerging directly from students' descriptions of their lives, the Students' Multiple Worlds Model and Typology provide teachers and others a holistic way of thinking about their students. By considering the various contexts that students encounter and the ways in which they make transitions between their worlds, we bring a different dimension of the complexities of adolescence into view. Further, our emphasis on the borders that students face directs attention away from individual and family characteristics as the cause for at-risk youth. Our conceptualization and the cases we present allows an "at-promise," rather than an "at-risk," view (Swadener & Lubeck, 1995). Rather than looking for "youth with problems," the emphasis is on uncovering borders that prevent youth from optimal social, emotional, and academic growth. Thus the Students' Multiple Worlds Model becomes an important tool for identifying and addressing problems that *all* youths face.

The examples in this chapter also point to other implications of this work for practice—the training of counselors, parent education, school climate, and most obviously teacher education and curriculum. In order to create environments where students are able to work together in classrooms, to solve problems jointly, and to have an equal investment in schools and learning, we need to identify institutional structures that eliminate borders without requiring young people to give up or hide important features of their lives. This requires more than simply understanding other cultures. It means that students must acquire skills and strategies to work comfortably and successfully in divergent social settings and with people different from themselves.

REFERENCES

Abi-Nader, J. (1990). A house for my mother. *Anthropology and Education Quarterly, 21*(1), 41–58.

Alpert, B. (1991). Students' resistance in the classroom. *Anthropology and Education Quarterly, 22*(4), 350–366.

Arnow, H. (1954). *The dollmaker.* New York: Macmillan.

Au, K. H. (1980). Participant structures in a reading lesson with Hawaiian children: Analysis of a culturally appropriate instructional event. *Anthropology and Education Quarterly, 11*(2), 91–115.

Au, K. H., & Mason, J. (1981). Social organizational factors in learning to read: The balance of rights hypothesis. *Reading Research Quarterly, 17*(1), 115–152.

Barth, F. (1969). *Ethnic groups and boundaries: The social organization of culture difference.* Boston: Little, Brown.

Benedict, R. (1938). Continuities and discontinuities in cultural conditioning. *Psychiatry, 1,* 161–167.

Bereiter, C., & Engelmann, S. (1966). *Teaching disadvantaged children in the preschool.* Englewood Cliffs, NJ: Prentice-Hall.

Bloch, M., & Swadener, B. B. (1992). Relationships among home, community and school: Multicultural considerations and research issues in early childhood. In C. Grant (Ed.), *Research and multicultural education: From margins to the mainstream* (pp. 165–183). Philadelphia: Falmer.

Bourdieu, P., & Passeron, J. C. (1977). *Reproduction in education, society, and culture.* Beverly Hills, CA: Sage.

Bullough, R. V. (1989). *First-year teacher: A case study.* New York: Teachers College Press.

Burch, P., Palanki, A., & Davies, D. (1995). *From clients to partners: Four case studies of collaboration and family involvement in the development of school-linked services* (Report 29). Baltimore: Center on Family, Communities, Schools and Children's Learning, Johns Hopkins University.

Burnett, A. (1990–1991). *Youth survey: An analysis.* Palo Alto, CA: Palo Alto Youth Council.

Calabrese, R. L. (1990). The public school: A source of alienation for minority parents. *The Journal of Negro Education, 59*(2), 148–154.

Carnegie Foundation for the Advancement of Teaching. (1988). *Report card on school reform: The teachers speak.* Princeton, NJ: Author.

Casey, K. (1993). *I answer with my life: Life histories of women teachers working for social change.* New York: Routledge.

Cazden, C. B. (1990). Differential treatment in New Zealand: Reflections on research in minority education. *Teaching and Teacher Education, 6*(4), 291–303.

Cazden, C. B., & John, V. P. (1971). Learning in American Indian children. In M. L. Wax, S. Diamond, & F. O. Gearing (Eds.), *Anthropological perspectives on education* (pp. 252–271). New York: Basic Books.

Cervantes, L. D. (1981). Refugee ship. In *Emplumada*, p. 41. Pittsburgh: University of Pittsburgh Press.

Chandler, M. (1978). Adolescence, egocentrism, and epistemological loneliness. In B. Presseisen, D. Goldstein, & M. Appel (Eds.), *Topics in cognitive development: Language and operational thought* (Vol. 2). New York: Plenum.

Chavkin, N. F. (1989). Debunking the myth about minority parents and the school. *Educational Horizons, 67*, 119–123.

Chavkin, N. F. (1993). *Families and schools in a pluralistic society.* Albany: State University of New York Press.

Chun, K. (1995). The myth of Asian American success and its educational ramifications. In D. T. Nakanishi & T. Y. Nishida (Eds.), *The Asian American educational experience: A source book for teachers and students* (pp. 95–112). New York: Routledge.

Cisneros, S. (1991). *The house on Mango Street.* New York: Vintage Books.

Clark, R. M. (1983). *Family life and school achievement: Why poor black children succeed or fail.* Chicago: University of Chicago Press.

Clasen, D. R., & Brown, B. B. (1985). The multidimensionality of peer pressure in adolescence. *Journal of Youth and Adolescence, 14*(6), 451–468.

Clement, D., & Harding, J. (1978). Social distinctions and emergent student groups in a desegregated school. *Anthropology and Education Quarterly, 9*(4), 272–283.

Cochran, M., & Dean, C. (1991). Home-school relations and the empowerment process. *Elementary School Journal, 91*(3), 261–269.

Cochran, M., & Woolever, F. (1983). Beyond the deficit model: The empowerment of parents with information and informal supports. In I. E. Sigel & L. Laosa (Eds.), *Changing families* (pp. 225–247). New York: Plenum.

Cohen, D. K. (1991). Revolution in one classroom (or, then again, was it?). *American Educator: The Professional Journal of the American Federation of Teachers, 15*(2), 16–23, 44–48.

Cohen, E. G. (1986). *Designing groupwork: Strategies for the heterogeneous classroom.* New York: Teachers College Press.

Cohen, E. G., & Lotan, R. A. (1995). Predicting equal-status interaction in the heterogenous classroom. *American Educational Research Journal, 32*(1), 99–120.

Coleman, J. S. (1963). *The adolescent society: The social life of the teenager and its impact on education.* New York: Free Press.

Collins, C. H., Moles, O., & Cross, J. (1982). *The home-school connection: Selected partnership programs in large cities.* Boston: Institute for Responsive Education.

Comer, J. P. (1980). *School power.* New York: Macmillan.

Comer, J. P. (1989). Parent participation in schools: The School Development Program. *Family Resource Coalition Report, 8*(2), 4–6.

Comer, J. P., & Haynes, N. (1991). Parent involvement in schools: An ecological approach. *Elementary School Journal, 91*(3), 271–277.

Connors, L. J., & Epstein, J. L. (1994). *Taking stock: The views of teachers, parents, and students on school, family, and community relationships* (Report No. 49). Baltimore: Center for Research on Effective Schooling for Disadvantaged Students, Johns Hopkins University.

Dauber, S. L., & Epstein, J. L. (1993). Parents' attitudes and practices of involvement in inner-city elementary and middle schools. In N. F. Chavkin (Ed.), *Families and schools in a pluralistic society* (pp. 21–49). Albany: State University of New York Press.

Davidson, A. L. (1992). *The politics and aesthetics of ethnicity: Making and molding identity in varied curricular settings.* Ph.D. Dissertation, Stanford University.

Davidson, A. L. (1996). *Making and molding identity in schools: Student narratives on race, gender, and academic engagement.* Albany: State University of New York Press.

Delgado-Gaitan, C. (1987). Traditions and transitions in the learning process of Mexican children: An ethnographic view. In G. Spindler & L. Spindler (Eds.), *Interpretive ethnography of education: At home and abroad* (pp. 333–359). Hillsdale, NJ: Lawrence Erlbaum Associates.

Delgado-Gaitan, C. (1990). *Literacy for empowerment: The role of parents in children's education.* London: Falmer.

Delgado-Gaitan, C. (1991). Linkages between home and school: A process of change for involving parents. *American Educational Journal, 100*(1), 20–46.

Delgado-Gaitan, C. (1993). Research and policy in reconceptualizing family-school relationships. In P. Phelan & A. L. Davidson (Eds.), *Renegotiating cultural diversity in American schools* (pp. 139–158). New York: Teachers College Press.

Delgado-Gaitan, C. (1994). Socializing young children in Mexican-American families: An intergenerational perspective. In P. Graeenfield & R. Cocking (Eds.), *Cross-cultural roots of minority child development* (pp. 55–86). Hillsdale, NJ: Lawrence Erlbaum Associates.

Delgado-Gaitan, C., & Trueba, H. (1991). *Crossing cultural borders: Education for immigrant families in America.* New York: Falmer.

Deutsch, M. (1967). The disadvantaged child and the learning process. In M. Deutsch (Ed.), *The disadvantaged child.* New York: Basic Books.

Deyhle, D. (1995). Navajo youth and Anglo racism: Cultural integrity and resistance. *Harvard Educational Review, 65*(3), 403–444.

Dornbusch, S. M., Ritter, P. L., Leiderman, H. P., Roberts, D. F., & Fraleigh, M. J. (1987). The relation of parenting style to adolescent school performance. *Child Development, 58,* 1244–1257.

Eaker-Rich, D., & Van Galen, J. A. (1996). *Caring in an unjust world: Negotiating borders and barriers in schools.* Albany: State University of New York Press.

Earle, R. S. (1992). Homework as an instructional event. *Educational Technology, 32*(4), 36–41.

Eckert, P. (1989). *Jocks and burnouts: Social categories and identity in the high school.* New York: Teachers College Press.

Edmonds, R. (1979). Some schools work and more can. *Social Policy, 9*(5), 28–32.

Eisner, E. W. (1985). *The educational imagination: On the design and evaluation of educational programs.* New York: Macmillan.

Elam, S. M., & Gallup, A. M. (1989). The 21st annual Gallup poll of the public's attitudes toward the public schools. *Phi Delta Kappan, 71*(1), 41–54.

Entwisle, D. R., & Alexander, K. L. (1995). A parent's economic shadow: Family structure versus family resources as influences on early school achievement. *Journal of Marriage and the Family, 57,* 399–409.

Epstein, J. L. (1986). Parents' reactions to teacher practices of parent involvement. *The Elementary School Journal, 86*(3), 277–294.

Epstein, J. L. (1995). School/family/community partnerships: Caring for the children we share. *Phi Delta Kappan, 76*(9), 701–712.

Epstein, J. L., Coates, L., Salinas, K. C., Sanders, M. G., & Simon, B. (1996). *Partnership-2000 schools manual: Improving school-family-community connections.* Baltimore: Center for Research on the Education of Students Placed at Risk, Johns Hopkins University.

Erickson, F. D. (1993). Transformation and school success: The politics and culture of educational achievement. In E. Jacob & C. Jordan (Eds.), *Minority education: Anthropological perspectives* (pp. 27–52). Norwood, NJ: Ablex.

Erickson, F. D., & Bekker, G. J. (1986). On anthropology. In J. Hannaway & M. E. Lockheed (Eds.), *The contributions of the social sciences to educational policy and practice: 1965–1985* (pp. 163–182). Berkeley, CA: McCutchan.

Erickson, F. D., & Mohatt, G. (1982). Cultural organization in two classrooms of Indian students. In G. D. Spindler (Ed.), *Doing the ethnography of schooling: Educational anthropology in action* (pp. 132–175). New York: Holt, Rinehart & Winston.

Featherstone, D. R., Cundick, B. P., & Jensen, L. C. (1992). Differences in school behavior and achievement between children from intact, reconstituted, and single-parent families. *Adolescence, 27*(105), 1–12.

Fine, M. (1991). *Framing dropouts: Notes on the politics of an urban public high school.* Albany: State University of New York Press.

Fiske, S. T., & Taylor, S. E. (1978). Salience, attention, and attribution: Top of the head phenomena. In L. Berkowitz, (Ed.), *Advances in experimental social psychology: Volume II* (pp. 249–288). New York: Academic.

Fitzgerald, F. S. (1953). *The great Gatsby.* New York: Scribner.

Fordham, S. (1988). Racelessness as a factor in black students' school success: Pragmatic strategy or pyrrhic victory? *Harvard Educational Review, 58*(1), 54–83.

Furstenberg, F. F. (1990). Coming of age in a changing family system. In S. S. Feldman & G. R. Elliott (Eds.), *At the threshold: The developing adolescent* (pp. 147–170). Cambridge, MA: Harvard University Press.

Gallimore, R., Boggs, J., & Jordan, C. (1974). *Culture, behavior and education: A study of Hawaiian Americans.* Beverly Hills, CA: Sage.

Gaventa, J. (1980). *Power and powerlessness: Quiescence and rebellion in an Appalachian valley.* Urbana: University of Illinois Press.

Gibson, M. A. (1993). The school performance of immigrant minorities: A comparative view. In E. Jacob & C. Jordan (Eds.), *Minority education: Anthropological perspectives* (pp. 113–128). Norwood, NJ: Ablex.

Gilligan, C. (1982). *In a different voice: Psychological theory & women's development.* Cambridge, MA: Harvard University Press.

Goetz, J. P., & LeCompte, M. D. (1984). *Ethnography and qualitative design in educational research.* San Diego: Academic.

Gonzales, R. (Corky). (1972). *I am Joaquin.* New York: Bantam Books.

Gray, J. (1985, March 17). A black American princess: New game, new rules. *The Washington Post*, pp. E1, E5.

Hakuta, K. (1986). *Mirror of language: The debate on bilingualism.* New York: Basic Books.

Heath, S. B. (1982). Questioning at school and at home: A comparative study. In G. D. Spindler (Ed.), *Doing the ethnography of schooling: Educational anthropology in action* (pp. 102–131). New York: Holt, Rinehart & Winston.

Henderson, A. (1987). *The evidence continues to grow: Parent involvement improves student achievement.* Columbia, MD: National Committee for Citizens in Education.

Henderson, A., Marburger, C. L., & Ooms, T. (1986). *Beyond the bake sale: An educator's guide to working with parents.* Columbia, MD: National Committee for Citizens in Education.

Hess, R. D., & Shipman, V. (1965). Maternal influences upon early learning: The cognitive environment of urban pre-school children. In R. D. Hess & R. M. Bear (Eds.), *Early education: Current theory, research, and action* (pp. 869–885). Chicago: Aldine.

Hiltz, S. R., & Turroff, M. (1993). *The network nation: Human communication via computers.* Cambridge, MA: MIT Press.

Hoffman, D. M. (1988). Cross-cultural adaptation and learning: Iranians and Americans at school. In H. T. Trueba & C. Delgado-Gaitan (Eds.), *School and society: Learning content through culture* (pp. 163–180). New York: Praeger.

Huynh, D. T. (1989). *Introduction to Vietnamese culture* (2nd Ed.). San Diego: San Diego, State University, Multifunctional Service Center.

Jencks, C., Smith, M., Acland, H., Bane, M., Cohen, D., Gintis, H., Heyns, B., & Micelson, S. (1972). *Inequality: A reassessment of the effects of family and schooling in America.* New York: Basic Books.

John, V. P. (1972). Styles of learning—styles of teaching: Reflections on the education of Navajo children. In C. B. Cazden, V. P. John, & D. Hymes (Eds.), *Functions of language in the classroom* (pp. 331–343). New York: Teachers College Press.

Johnson, D. W., & Johnson, R. (1981). Effects of cooperative and individualistic learning experiences on interethnic interaction. *Journal of Educational Psychology, 23*(3), 454–459.

Johnson, D. W., & Johnson, R. (1989). *Cooperation and competition: Theory and research.* Edina, MN: Interaction Book Company.

Johnson, D. W., & Johnson, R. (1991). Cooperative learning and classroom and school climate. In B. Fraser & H. Walberg (Eds.), *Educational environments: Evaluation, antecedents and consequences* (pp. 55–74). New York: Pergamon.

Kanter, R. M. (1977). Some effects of proportions on group life: Skewed sex ratios and responses to token women. *American Journal of Sociology, 82*(5), 965–990.

Kinney, D. A. (1993). From nerds to normals: The recovery of identity among adolescents from middle school to high school. *Sociology of Education, 66*, 21–40.

Lareau, A. (1987). Social class differences in family-school relationships: The importance of cultural capital. *Sociology of Education, 60*, 73–85.

Larkin, R. W. (1979). *Suburban youth in cultural crisis.* New York: Oxford University Press.

LeCompte, M. D., & Dworkin, A. G. (1991). *Giving up on school: Student dropouts and teacher burnout.* Newbury Park, CA: Corwin.

Lee, S. (1996). *Unraveling the "model minority stereotype": Listening to Asian American youth*. New York: Teachers College Press.

Leitch, M. L., & Tangri, S. S. (1988). Barriers to home-school collaboration. *Educational Horizons, 66,* 70–74.

Losey, K. M. (1995). Mexican American students and classroom interaction: An overview and critique. *Review of Educational Research, 65*(3), 283–328.

Lueder, D.C. (1989). What do parents want from principals and teachers? *Educational Leadership, 47*(2), 15–17.

Matute-Bianchi, M. E. (1986). Ethnic identities and patterns of school success and failure among Mexican-descent and Japanese-American students in a California high school: An ethnographic analysis. *American Journal of Education, 95*(1), 233–255.

McDermott, R. P. (1987). The exploration of minority school failure, again. *Anthropology and Education Quarterly, 18*(4), 361–364.

McDermott, R. P., & Gospodinoff, K. (1979). Social contexts for ethnic and school failure. In A. Wolfgang (Ed.), *Nonverbal behavior: Applications and cultural implications* (pp. 175–196). New York: Academic.

McLaughlin, M. W. (1993). What matters most in teachers' workplace context? In J. W. Little & M. W. McLaughlin (Eds.), *Teachers' work: Individuals, colleagues, and contexts* (pp. 79–103). New York: Teachers College Press.

McLaughlin, M. W., & Talbert, J. E. (1990). The contexts in question: The secondary school workplace. In M. W. McLaughlin, J. E. Talbert, & N. Bascia (Eds.), *The contexts of secondary school teaching: Teachers' realities* (pp. 1–16). New York: Teachers College Press.

McLaughlin, M. W., & Talbert, J. E. (1993). *Contexts that matter for teaching and learning: Strategic opportunities for meeting the nation's educational goals*. Stanford: Center for Research on the Context of Secondary School Teaching.

Mehan, H. (1979). *Learning lessons*. Cambridge: Cambridge University Press.

Meisner, D. (1995). *Self-reflective essay on high school years*. Unpublished manuscript. University of Washington, Bothell.

Mirande, A., & Enriquez, E. (1979). *La Chicana: The Mexican-American woman*. Chicago: University of Chicago Press.

Miller, N. H., & Harrington, H. J. (1992). Social categorization and inter-group acceptance: Principles for the design and development of cooperative learning teams. In R. Hertz-Lazarowitz & N. Miller (Eds.), *Interaction in cooperative groups* (pp. 203–227). New York: Cambridge University Press.

Moles, O. C. (1993). Collaboration between schools and disadvantaged parents: Obstacles and openings. In N. F. Chavkin (Ed.), *Families and schools in a pluralistic society* (pp. 21–49). Albany: State University of New York Press.

Moll, L. C., & Diaz, S. (1993). Change as the goal of educational research. In E. Jacob & C. Jordan (Eds.), *Minority education: Anthropological perspectives* (pp. 67–82). Norwood, NJ: Ablex.

Neira, C. (1988). Building 860. *Harvard Education Review, 58*(2), 337–342.

Noddings, N. (1984). *Caring: A feminine approach to ethics & moral education*. Berkeley: University of California Press.

Noddings, N. (1992). *The challenge to care in schools: An alternative approach to education.* New York: Teachers College Press.

Oakes, J. (1985). *Keeping track: How schools structure inequality.* New Haven, CT: Yale University Press.

Ogbu, J. (1983). Minority status and schooling in plural societies. *Comparative Education Review, 27*(22), 168–190.

Ogbu, J. (1993). Variability in minority school performance: A problem in search of an explanation. In E. Jacob & C. Jordan (Eds.), *Minority education: Anthropological perspectives* (pp. 83–111). Norwood, NJ: Ablex.

Olympia, D. E., Sheridan, S. M., & Jensen, W. (1994). Homework: A natural means of home-school collaboration. *School Psychology Quarterly, 9*(1), 60–80.

Phelan, P., & Davidson, A. L. (1994). Looking across borders: Students' investigations of family, peer, and school worlds as cultural therapy. In G. D. Spindler & L. Spindler (Eds.), *Pathways to cultural awareness: Cultural therapy with teachers and students* (pp. 35–60). Thousand Oaks, CA: Corwin.

Phelan, P., Davidson, A. L., & Cao, H. T. (1991). Students' multiple worlds: Negotiating the boundaries of family, peer and school cultures. *Anthropology and Education Quarterly, 22*(3), 224–250.

Phelan, P., Davidson, A. L., & Cao, H. T. (1992). Speaking up: Student's perspectives on school. *Phi Delta Kappan, 73*(9), 695–704.

Phelan, P., Davidson, A. L., & Yu, H. C. (1993). Students' multiple worlds: Navigating the borders of family, peer and school cultures. In P. Phelan & A. L. Davidson (Eds.), *Renegotiating cultural diversity in American schools* (pp. 52–88). New York: Teachers College Press.

Phelan, P., Yu, H. C., & Davidson, A. L. (1994). Navigating the psychosocial pressures of adolescence: The voices and experiences of high school youth. *American Educational Research Journal, 31*(2), 415–447.

Philips, S. U. (1972). Participant structures and communicative competence: Warm Springs children in community and classroom. In C. B. Cazden, V. P. John, & D. Hymes (Eds.), *Functions of language in the classroom* (pp. 370–394). New York: Teachers College Press.

Philips, S. U. (1983). *The invisible culture: Communication in classroom and community on the Warm Springs Indian Reservation.* New York: Longman.

Prilliman, R., Eaker, D., & Kendrich, D. M. (Eds.). (1994). *The tapestry of caring: Education as nurturance.* Norwood, NJ: Ablex.

Rich, D. (1988). Bridging the parent gap in education reform. *Educational Horizons, 66*(2), 90–92.

Rodriguez, R. (1982). *Hunger of memory: The education of Richard Rodriguez.* New York: Bantam Books.

Rosaldo, R. (1989). *Culture and truth: The remaking of social analysis.* Boston: Beacon.

Rose, M. (1990). *Lives on the boundary.* New York: Penguin Books.

Rumbaut, R. G., & Ima, K. (1988). *The adaptation of Southeast Asian refugee youth: A comparative study.* Washington, DC: U.S. Department of Health and Human Services, Family Support Administration, Office of Refugee Resettlement.

Rutter, M., Maughan, B., Mortimore, P., & Ouston, J. (1979). *Fifteen thousand hours: Sec-*

ondary schools and their effects on children. Cambridge, MA: Harvard University Press.

Ryan, B. A., Adams, G. R., Gullotta, T. P., Weissberg, R. P., & Hampton, R. L. (Eds.). (1995). *The family-school connection: Theory, research and practice*. Thousand Oaks, CA. Sage.

Sanders, M. G. (1996a). Action teams in action: Interviews and observation in three schools in the Baltimore school-family-community partnership program. *Journal of Education for Students Placed At Risk, 1*(3), 249–262.

Sanders, M. G. (1996b). *School-family-community partnerships and the academic achievement of African-American urban adolescents* (Report No. 7). Baltimore: Center for Research on Education of Students Placed At Risk, Johns Hopkins University.

Sanders, M. G., & Epstein, J. L. (in press). School-family-community partnerships and educational change: International perspectives. In A. Hargreaves, A. Lieberman, M. Fullan, & D. Hopkins (Eds.), *International handbook of educational change*. Hingham, MA: Kluwer Academic Publishers.

Schoem, D. (1991). *Inside separate worlds: Life stories of young blacks, Jews, and Latinos*. Ann Arbor: University of Michigan Press.

Sharan, S. (1980). Cooperative learning in small groups: Recent methods and effects on achievement, attitudes, and ethnic relations. *Review of Educational Research, 50*(2), 241–271.

Sharan, S., & Shachar, H. (1988). *Language and learning in the cooperative classroom*. New York: Springer.

Shulman, J. H., & Mesa-Bains, A. (Eds.). (1993). *Diversity in the classroom: A casebook for teachers and teacher educators*. Hillsdale, NJ: Research for Better Schools and Lawrence Erlbaum Associates.

Slavin, R. E. (1988). Cooperative learning and student achievement. In R. E. Slavin (Ed.), *School and classroom organization* (pp. 129–158). Hillsdale, NJ: Lawrence Erlbaum Associates.

Slavin, R. E., & Madden, N. A. (1989, February). What works for students at risk: A research synthesis. *Educational Leadership*, pp. 12–14.

Spindler, G. D. (1982). General introduction. In G. D. Spindler (Ed.), *Doing the ethnography of schooling: Educational anthropology in action* (pp. 1–13). New York: Holt, Rinehart & Winston.

Spindler, G. D. (Ed.). (1987). *Education and cultural process: Anthropological approaches*. Prospect Heights, IL: Waveland.

Spindler, G. D., & Spindler, L. (1992). Cultural process and ethnography: An anthropological perspective. In M. D. LeCompte, W. L. Millroy, & J. Preissle (Eds.), *Handbook of qualitative research in education* (pp. 53–92). San Diego: Academic.

Spindler, G. D., & Spindler, L. (Eds.). (1994). *Pathways to cultural awareness: Cultural therapy with teachers and students*. Thousand Oaks, CA: Corwin.

Spindler, G. D., Spindler, L., Trueba, H., & Williams, M. (1990). *The American cultural dialogue and its transmission*. New York: Falmer.

Spradley, J. P., & McCurdy, D. W. (1972). *The cultural experience: Ethnography in complex society*. Chicago: Science Research Association.

Steinberg, L., Lamborn, S. D., Darling, N., Mounts, N. S., & Dornbusch, S. M. (1994). Over-time changes in adjustment and competence among adolescents from authoritative, authoritarian, indulgent, and neglectful families. *Child Development, 65*, 754–770.

Steinberg, L., Lamborn, S. D., Dornbusch, S. M., & Darling, N. (1992). Impact of parenting practices on adolescent achievement: Authoritative parenting, school involvement, and encouragement to succeed. *Child Development, 63*, 1266–1281.

Stenmark, J. K., Thompson, V., & Cossey, R. (1986). *Family math.* Berkeley, CA: Lawrence Hall of Science, University of California.

Stevenson, R. B., & Ellsworth, J. (1993). Dropouts and the silencing of critical voices. In L. Weis & M. Fine, (Eds.), *Beyond silenced voices: Class, race, and gender in United States schools* (pp. 259–271). Albany: State University of New York Press.

Suarez-Orozco, C. E., & Suarez-Orozco, M. M. (1995). *Transformations: Immigration, family life, and achievement motivation among Latino adolescents.* Stanford, CA: Stanford University Press.

Suarez-Orozco, M. (1993). "Becoming somebody": Central American immigrants in U.S. inner-city schools. In E. Jacob & C. Jordan (Eds.), *Minority education: Anthropological perspectives* (pp. 129–143). Norwood, NJ: Ablex.

Suarez-Orozco, M. M., & Suarez-Orozco, C. E. (1993). Hispanic cultural psychology: Implications for education theory and research. In P. Phelan & A. L. Davidson (Eds.), *Renegotiating cultural diversity in American schools* (pp. 108–138). New York: Teachers College Press.

Suzuki, B. H. (1995). Education and the socialization of Asian Americans: A revisionist analysis of the "model minority" thesis. In D. T. Nakanishi & T. Y. Nishida (Eds.), *The Asian American educational experience: A source book for teachers and students* (pp. 113–132). New York: Routledge.

Swadener, B. B., & Lubeck, S. (1995). The social construction of children and families "at risk": An introduction. In B. B. Swadener & S. Lubeck (Eds.), *Children and families "at promise": Deconstructing the discourse of risk* (pp. 1–14). Albany: State University of New York Press.

Tabachnick, B. R., & Bloch, M. N. (1995). Learning in and out of school: Critical perspectives on the theory of cultural compatibility. In B. B. Swadener & S. Lubeck (Eds.), *Children and families "at promise": Deconstructing the discourse of risk* (pp. 187–209). Albany: State University of New York Press.

Tan, A. (1987). Fish cheeks. *Seventeen, 46*, 99.

Taylor, S. E., Fiske, S. T., Etcoff, N. L., & Ruderman, A. J. (1978). Categorical and contextual bases of person memory and stereotyping. *Journal of Personality and Social Psychology, 36*(7), 778–793.

Thomas, J. W. (1993). Promoting independent learning in the middle grades: The role of instructional support practices. *Elementary School Journal, 93*(5), 575–591.

Thuy, V. G. (1976). *Getting to know the Vietnamese and their culture.* New York: Frederick Ungar.

Trueba, H. T. (1988a). Culturally based explanations of minority students' academic achievement. *Anthropology and Education Quarterly, 19*(3), 270–287.

Trueba, H. T. (1988b). Peer socialization among minority high school students: A high school dropout prevention program. In H. T. Trueba & C. Delgado-Gaitan (Eds.), *School and society: Learning content through culture* (pp. 201–217). New York: Praeger.

Trueba, H. T., Moll, L. C., Diaz, S., & Diaz, R. (1982). *Improving the functional writing of bilingual secondary students* (Contract No. 400–81-0023). Washington, DC: National Institute of Education.

Ueda, R. (1987). *Avenues to adulthood: The origins of the high school and social mobility in an American suburb.* New York: Cambridge University Press.

Varenne, H. S. (1982). Jocks and freaks: The symbolic structure of the expression of social interaction among American senior high school students. In G. D. Spindler (Ed.), *Doing the ethnography of schooling: Educational anthropology in action* (pp. 211–239). New York: Holt, Rinehart & Winston.

Vigil, J. D. (1988). Group process and street identity: Chicano gangs. *Ethos, 16*(4), 421–445.

Vigil, J. D. (1993). Gangs, social control and ethnicity: Ways to redirect. In S. B. Heath & M. W. McLaughlin (Eds.), *Identity and inner-city youth: Beyond ethnicity and gender* (pp. 94–119). New York: Teachers College Press.

Vogt, L. A., Jordan, C., & Tharp, R. G. (1993). Explaining school failure, producing school success: Two cases. In E. Jacob & C. Jordan (Eds.), *Minority education: Anthropological perspectives* (pp. 53–66). Norwood, NJ: Ablex.

Walberg, H. (1986). What works in a nation still at risk. *Educational Leadership, 44*(1), 7–11.

Wehlage, G. G., & Rutter, R. A. (1986). Dropping out: How much do schools contribute to the problem? *Teachers College Record, 87,* 374–392.

Wetzel, J. R. (1989). *American youth: A statistical snapshot.* Washington, DC: Youth and America's future: The William T. Grant Commission on Work, Family, & Citizenship.

Wynn, J., Merry, S., & Berg, P. (1995). *Children, families, and communities. Early lessons from a new approach to social services.* Washington, DC: American Youth Policy Forum.

INDEX

ABOUT THE AUTHORS

Patricia Phelan is Associate Professor of Education at the University of Washington, Bothell. Dr. Phelan received her B.S. in Education from Oregon State University (1967), her M.A. in Anthropology (1978), and her Ph.D. in Anthropology of Education from Stanford University in 1981. Since that time she has been a faculty member in the Medical Anthropology Program at the University of California at San Francisco and at Stanford University. This book, as well as *Renegotiating Cultural Diversity in American Schools* (1993), co-authored with Ann Locke Davidson, and a number of articles co-authored with Ann Locke Davidson and Hanh Cao Yu, results from Dr. Phelan's work as a Senior Research Scholar at the Center for Research on the Context of Secondary School Teaching at Stanford University from 1989 to 1992. Dr. Phelan's research interests include the relationship between students' contexts and experiences and their engagement in educational settings, school and classroom features that impact culturally diverse student populations, and mental health issues of children and youth.

Ann Locke Davidson is currently Research Associate at the Learning Research and Development Center at the University of Pittsburgh. After first teaching in the People's Republic of China, she went on to receive her M.A. in Anthropology and Ph.D. in Curriculum and Teacher Education from Stanford University in 1992. Her research focuses generally on the relationships between school and classroom processes, the construction of identity in relation to schooling, and academic engagement, particularly among youths from historically disenfranchised groups. She has considered the relationships between alternative approaches to assessment and the construction of academic identity in working-class youths, virtual reality technological environments and the construction of technological identity in young girls, and the relationship between culturally mainstream approaches to education and the construction of alienated and engaged identities in ethnically diverse students. The latter investigation is the focus of her book *Making and Molding Identity in Schools: Student Narratives on Race, Gender and Academic Engagement.* Davidson is also, with Patricia Phelan, co-editor of *Renegotiating Cultural Diversity in American Schools.* Currently, Davidson is part of a diverse team investigating the social and educational impacts and processes of implementing the Internet in the Pittsburgh Public Schools.

Hanh Cao Yu is an educational researcher and social scientist at Social Policy Research Associates in Menlo Park, CA. Dr. Yu received her B.S. in Business Administration at the University of Southern California in 1989 and her doctorate in Administration and Policy Analysis from Stanford University School of Education in 1995. Her current research interests focus on immigrant education, the intersection of citizenship education and multicultural education, intergroup relationships among ethnically and culturally diverse students, and school-to-work reforms. She has co-authored a number of articles with Patricia Phelan and Ann Locke Davidson and has contributed to such journals as *Phi Delta Kappan, American Educational Research Journal,* and *Anthropology and Education Quarterly.* She has recently conducted a one-year study, The Complexity of Diversity: Understanding the Multiple Worlds of Vietnamese High School Students.